SOUTHBOROUGH WAR MEMORIAL

SOUTHBOROUGH WAR MEMORIAL

The stories of those commemorated

Researched and compiled by
Judith Johnson

First published in 2009
This edition published in 2018 by
Odd Dog Press
Copyright © Judith Johnson, 2018

Judith Johnson has asserted her right under the Copyright, Designs and Patents Act 1988 to be identified as the author of this work. All rights reserved. No part of this publication may be reproduced, stored in a retrieval system or transmitted in any form, or by any means (electronic, mechanical or otherwise) without the prior written permission of both the copyright owner and the publisher.

A CIP catalogue record for this book is available from the British Library.

ISBN 978-0-9562873-6-6

The text is set in Garamond.

Cover photograph and design by Martin Johnson

www.odddogpress.com

Foreword

My grandfather served in Mesopotamia and on the Western Front, and in his last days relived his time as a medical orderly and stretcher-bearer there. My husband's grandfather, while driving a lorry near Arras, had, on two separate occasions, the back of his truck blown away by a shell. A great number of us have family stories from both of the two World Wars of the twentieth century.

I read that many soldiers in the Great War paid to have metal identity discs made up; their pressed cardboard ones were found to be perishable, and they had a deep fear, which was to become realised for so many, that they would die and their bodies would be buried anonymously, their graves never to be visited by their loved ones.

I set out in 2002 to find out as much as possible about each person named on the Southborough War Memorial, in an attempt to record their stories. I hoped that, as a result, they would not merely be a list of names engraved on stone at the top of the Common, but remembered as individual souls, whose loss to the community must have had profound and far-reaching consequences.

The process of gathering names for war memorials included asking for submissions from local people, and was not entirely systematic. There were many whose names were not for one reason or another included, and this is the case for Southborough and High Brooms, whose other memorials include those at St Matthew's Church and St Matthew's Primary School in High Brooms. The Southborough War Memorial was dedicated on 13 February 1921.

In 2005, Lt Col A M Macfarlane, then President of the Southborough Society and local historian, wrote to the Town Clerk suggesting that William Roy McMillan's name be added to the War Memorial. After appropriate investigation, Private McMillan's name was subsequently added. Mrs Tracey Hook, a relative of Charles William Barton, took similar action, as did the families of Gordon Harvey Clarke and Dennis Livingstone McPhee.

For this project, I focused on the names lettered on the Southborough War Memorial; however, I am aware that there are many more, who through their association with Southborough, might very well be eligible for future commemoration. I will continue to list any names or details that come to my attention on my website in the section for those not commemorated. I have also added a section for the war-injured who survived the conflict.

A few words as to layout: the reproduction of photographs in this volume varies greatly – many are scanned-in photocopies of newspaper pages loaded on to microfilm – but I felt that any image I could find, however poor, was worth including. The text in bold at the beginning of each entry is as listed on the Commonwealth War Graves Commission (CWGC) website – with the exception of the words "in the Hythe disaster" in the case of those who died on 28 October 1915. Spellings and reported facts are reproduced from the source materials (eg Serjeant, from the CWGC site), even where there are discrepancies. First World War newspaper reports, for example, sometimes include various spellings of names, ages taken down differently etc – eg WH Godsmark's age is given as 30 by the CWGC, and 35 in the Tunbridge Wells Advertiser. Information was gathered by the CWGC some time after the conflicts, and readers will note that many women re-married after the deaths of their husbands, and were living at different addresses by the time entries were compiled. Also it seems that people living in Southborough in past times, many of them in rented accommodation, moved addresses quite frequently. I have taken out most of the archaic punctuation, for ease of reading, but have left in the custom at the time of hyphenating road names eg Springfield-road. Abbreviations have been left in where found in original text eg Coy for Company, Bn for Battalion. The Kent and Sussex Courier is referred to throughout as The Courier. Where an entry includes a cross-reference to another of those named on the Southborough War Memorial, it is printed in bold.

Readers may wonder, as I did, why members of the Royal Naval Division died on the Western Front and Gallipoli rather than at sea. The Naval Division was formed in August 1914. The Admiralty (Winston Churchill was First Lord) realised that with the mobilization they would have well over 20,000 men of the Reserve, for whom there would not be room on any warship. This surplus would be sufficient to form two naval Brigades and a Brigade of Marines available for Home Defence or for any special purpose. From this they formed the "Naval" Division, which participated in the defence of Antwerp in late 1914, then was shipped to Egypt prior to serving at Gallipoli. By the end of the Dardanelles campaign, the division's casualties were such that it no longer contained a significant number of naval servicemen, and in July 1916 it was redesignated as the 63rd Division, when the original Territorial Force 63rd (2nd Northumbrian) Division was disbanded. The division moved to the Western Front in France for the remainder of the war.

Lastly, the reader may be surprised to find how often it was reported that a man had been "killed instantly, and felt no pain". To those who had responsibility for writing letters home to families who had lost sons, husbands, fathers and brothers, it is understandable that they felt compelled to offer this comforting picture, rather than lay out what they may have felt was the often all too shocking truth of the real circumstances of their deaths. There is of course a massive body of work, both fictional and non-fictional, on the two World Wars. For those who wish to learn more about the Hythe disaster, so significant a tragedy for Southborough and High Brooms, Frank Stevens' book *Southborough Sappers of the Kent (Fortress) Royal Engineers* is highly recommended.

A digital edition of this book was published in 2012, and since then, the hard copy version has gone out of print. With the availability of print on demand, I am pleased to take this opportunity to make a hard copy edition available again, and to include some new information that has come to my attention since the first edition was published.

Judith Johnson
Southborough, February 2018
www.judithjohnson.co.uk

Those commemorated on the Southborough War Memorial

Henry Alcorn

Private G/6358, 8th Battalion, The Queen's (Royal West Surrey Regiment). Died 19 August 1917, age 31. Buried Grave II.E.15, Brandhoek New Military Cemetery No 3, Ypres, Belgium.

Henry Alcorn was born in Southwark, and enlisted at Woolwich. He was the brother of Fanny Waters, 3 Bedford Road, Southborough. William and Fanny Waters had a grocery business in Bedford Road.

From The Courier, 31 August 1917: ... *joined up at the outbreak of war, and had been in France 19 months. In January 1916, he was a victim to trench feet. Before enlisting he was employed by Mr W Waters, brother of Mrs Waters, 11a Forge-road. He has two brothers serving, one on a Red Cross boat and the other in the Machine Gun Section.*

Frederick Anderson

Private 51133, 4th Battalion, Bedfordshire Regiment. Died 1 October 1918, age 19. Buried in Grave III F7 at Sunken Road Cemetery, Boisleux-St Marc, (8 km south of Arras) Pas de Calais, France.

Fred Anderson was born in Southborough and lived at 5 Forge Road with his parents Edith Alice Anderson and Edward Anderson and his three sisters Nell (later Mrs Gorringe), Norah (later Mrs Baker) and Ethel May (later Mrs Stronghill), who was known locally as Little Ginny or May. Colin Stronghill, Fred's nephew, recalls his mother saying that they were a very happy-go-lucky family, who enjoyed parties

and get-togethers. If you lived in Southborough then, anyone who lived in High Brooms was known as a "High Brooms treacle-miner".

Pictured, from left to right: Nell, Norah, May

Fred's father was in the Services, and died in his forties after losing a leg to gangrene, according to family memories, caused by a cut from a rusty implement left lying on Southborough Common. He is mentioned in Frank Stevens' book *Southborough Sappers of the Kent (Fortress) Royal Engineers* which includes details of the Hythe disaster on 28 October 1915: *Edward Anderson KF 2982 5341209. Although not physically fit he went with the unit to Lemnos but then had to report sick, he was found to have a double rupture. He never rejoined the unit and finally arrived home after 2½ years, his youngest girl met him but could not recognise him. At the time of his return he was about 42. Lived in Forge Rd, Southborough and worked for Strange Builders. He had a family of wife, three girls and a boy.*

Although the Commonwealth War Graves Commission site gives Fred's age at death as 19, his family today feel that he may have been a few years younger than this, as he must have been born 1902/3 by their reckoning. Fred had been greatly upset by being approached on more than one occasion by women who presented him with white feathers. He was a big lad for his age, and they must have assumed that he was of the age to be in the forces but hadn't signed up, hence their making the gesture reserved for so-called cowards. Under this pressure, he joined up young, and lied about his age.

His family received a plaque from the government after his death, which is still in their possession, and pictured here.

The website www.firstworldwar.com/onthisday gives the following campaign detail for 1 October 1918: *British progress and take ground south of Le Catelet; stiff fighting near Bony and south of Cambrai. French take part of St Quentin.*

From the Courier, 11 October 1918 : ... *died of wounds in the 30th Casualty Clearing Station, through wounds received in the chest. His father joined up in the Royal Engineers again after the outbreak of war, and is now in France.*

Alfred Assiter

Chief Yeoman of Signals 168358, HMS Aboukir, Royal Navy. Died 22 September 1914, age 37. Commemorated on Chatham Naval Memorial, England, Panel 3. Husband of Sarah E Assiter, of 30, Amity Grove, West Wimbledon, London. Long Service and Good Conduct Medal. Awarded East and West Africa Medal (Benin Expedition), and China Medal 1900.

Chief Yeoman of Signals Alfred Assiter died when the Aboukir was torpedoed and sunk by U-9. The ship was one of three elderly Cressy class cruisers (the others were Hogue and Cressy) sunk by U-9 inside an hour. The encounter took place in the Dogger area of the North Sea, and in all, more than 600 men were lost from the three vessels. The incident forms the subject of the book *Three Before Breakfast* by Alan Coles (Kenneth Mason, 1979). Less than a month later, U-9 would sink the Hawke, on which **Chief Petty Officer George Henry Penfold** and Marine Private George William Walton perished. (Walton was a Southborough resident not mentioned on the Southborough Memorial.)

The following information is reproduced by kind permission of Darren Milford from his website www.worldwar1.co.uk/cressy.htm:

During the early months of World War 1 the Royal Navy maintained a patrol of old Cressy class armoured cruisers, known as Cruiser Force C, in the area of the North Sea known as the Broad Fourteens. There was opposition to this patrol from many senior officers, including Admiral Jellicoe and Commodores Keyes and Tyrwhitt, on the grounds that the ships were very vulnerable to a raid by modern German surface ships and the patrol was nick-named the "live bait squadron". The Admiralty maintained the patrol on the grounds that destroyers were not able to maintain the patrol in the frequent bad weather and that there were insufficient modern light cruisers available.

In the early hours of September 20th 1914 the cruisers HMS Euryalus, HMS Aboukir, HMS Hogue and HMS Cressy were preparing to go on patrol under Rear Admiral Christian in Euryalus. Normally the patrol was under command of Rear Admiral Campbell in HMS Bacchantes but he was absent so Christian helped fill the gap although he had other duties. The weather was too bad for destroyers to be at sea and unfortunately Euryalus had to drop out due to lack of coal and weather damage to her wireless. Rear Admiral Christian had to remain with his ship rather than transfer to another ship as the weather was too bad to transfer. He delegated command to Captain Drummond in Aboukir although he did not make it clear that Drummond had the authority to order the destroyers to sea if the weather improved, which it did towards the end of September 21st.

Early on September 22nd 1914 the German submarine U9 under the command of Commander Otto Weddigen sighted the Cressy, Aboukir and Hogue steaming NNE at 10 knots without zigzagging. Although the patrols were supposed to maintain 12-13 knots and zigzag the old cruisers were unable to maintain that speed and the zigzagging order was widely ignored as there had been no submarines sighted in the area during the war. U9 manoeuvred to attack and at about 6.25 am fired a single torpedo at Aboukir, which struck her on her port side. Aboukir rapidly suffered heavy flooding and despite counter flooding developed a 20 degree list and lost engine power. It was soon clear that she was a lost cause and Captain Drummond ordered her to be abandoned, although only one boat had survived the attack so most crew had to jump into the sea. At first Drummond thought that Aboukir had been mined and signalled the other two cruisers to close and assist but he soon realised that it was a torpedo attack and ordered the other cruisers away, but too late.

As Aboukir rolled over and sank, half an hour after being attacked, U9 fired two torpedoes at HMS Hogue that hit her amidships and rapidly flooded her engine room. Captain Nicholson of Hogue had stopped the ship to lower boats to rescue the crew of Aboukir, thinking that as he was the other side of Aboukir from U9 he would be safe. Unfortunately U9 had manoeuvred around Aboukir and attacked Hogue from a range of only 300 yards. The firing of two torpedoes affected the trim of U9 which broke the surface briefly and was fired on by Hogue without effect.

It only took Hogue ten minutes to sink as U9 headed for HMS Cressy. Cressy, under Captain Johnson, had also stopped to lower boats but got underway on sighting a periscope. At about 7.20 am however U9 fired two torpedoes, one of which just missed but the other hit Cressy on her starboard side, Cressy briefly firing on U9's periscope with no effect. The damage to Cressy was not fatal but U9 turned round and fired her last torpedo which hit Cressy, sinking her within a quarter of an hour.

Survivors were picked up by several nearby merchant ships including the Dutch Flora and Titan and the British trawlers JGC and Coriander before the Harwich force of light cruisers and destroyers arrived. Flora returned to Holland with 286 rescued crew who were quickly returned to Britain even though the neutral Dutch should have interned them. In all 837 men were rescued but 1459 died, many of which were reservists or cadets. In the aftermath of the attack the patrol by armoured *cruisers was abandoned, the stopping of major ships in dangerous waters banned and the order to steam at 13 knots and zigzag re-emphasised.*

A court of inquiry was set up and found that some blame was attributable to all of the senior officers involved - Captain Drummond for not zigzagging and for not calling for destroyers, Rear Admiral Christian was criticised for not making it clear to Drummond that he could summon the destroyers and Rear Admiral Campbell for not being present and for a very poor performance at the inquiry at which he stated that he did not know what the purpose of his command was. The bulk of the blame was directed at the Admiralty for persisting with a patrol that was dangerous and of limited value against the advice of senior sea-going officers.

Herbert William Avard

Private TF/2463, A Coy. 1st/5th Bn, Royal Sussex Regiment. Died 9 May 1915, age 23. Commemorated on Panel 20 & 21, Le Touret Memorial, Pas de Calais, France. Died on the same day, with the same regiment, and commemorated in the same cemetery as **Robert Bassett**.

From the Courier, 29 May 1915: *Private Herbert Avard, 5th Battalion Royal Sussex, only son of Mr & Mrs JW Avard, of the Gardener's Cottage, Bounds Park, is now officially reported missing. Private Avard joined "A" Company of the 5th Royal Sussex in September last, and went to the Front three months ago. His regiment was in the fierce fighting on the 9th May. A letter from him to a friend, together with some photographs, was found in a dug-out by a man of a Rifle regiment, who was himself afterwards wounded, and he sent them on. His parents are, of course, greatly distressed by the terrible suspense, but have not given up hope.*

From the Courier, 26 May 1916: *Mr and Mrs Avard have this week received official notice from the War Office presuming the death of their son Private HW Avard, who has been missing since May 9th last year. Private Avard was previously a member of staff at the Tunbridge Wells Advertiser.*

From the website www.firstworldwar.com/onthisday for 9 May 1915: *Second Battle of Ypres: British retake Wieltje. They fail in an attack on Aubers Ridge (Neuve Chapelle).*

Aubers Ridge involved mainly Wadhurst/Ticehurst men of the 5th Battalion, and modern-day Wadhurst is twinned with Aubers.

Alfred T Avis

Private 33147, 10th Bn, Yorkshire Regiment. Died 22 October 1916, age 29. Buried in Grave V.F.13 in Vermelles British Cemetery, Pas de Calais, France. Listed on Southborough War Memorial with Norfolk Regiment, formerly 12402 Queen's Own (Royal West Kent Regiment).

From the Courier, 3 November 1916: *Mrs Johnson, 11 Taylor-street, has received a letter from Second Lieutenant E Pepper, Yorkshire Regiment, in which he says:"It is with great regret that I have to inform you of the death of your son, Private A Avis, Yorkshire Regiment, who was killed while on sentry in the trenches. He was a fine soldier, and there is this consolation, that he did not suffer as he was killed instantly, being shot right through the heart." Private A Avis joined the Royal West Kent Regiment in March of this year, and transferred to the Yorks and sent to France in August. He had not been in France many weeks before he met his death. Before enlisting he was in the employ of Mr Sibthorpe for some years. This is the second son Mrs Johnson has lost; Private A Johnson was killed in August.* (See **Arthur Charles Johnson**.)

Charles Thomas Bailey

Gunner 300796, 2nd Div Ammunition Col, Canadian Field Artillery. Died 31 October 1918, age 22. Buried in Grave Plot 4. Row 301, Southborough Cemetery, England. Husband of Kathleen Lydia Bailey, of 61, Great Brooms Road, High Brooms.

Charles Bailey was born at Mayfield, Sussex on 8 October 1896. He was employed in farming. He enlisted at Sherbrooke, Quebec on 23 August 1915 and was unmarried at that time. His attestation paper lists his next-of-kin as Mrs GA Avis of 9 Providence Cottage, Cousley Road, Groombridge, Sussex. He died of influenza. From the Courier, 13 November 1918: *Mrs Bailey, of 36, High Brooms-road, has received news of her husband's death, which occurred at Alexandra Military Hospital, Cosham, Hants, on October 31st. Private CT Bailey was a member of the Canadian Forestry Corps, Broadwater Down Camp. He was buried with full military honours at Southborough Cemetery on November 7th.*

George Henry Bailey

Private 202347, 6th Bn, King's Own Scottish Borderers. Died 26 July 1918, age 19. Buried in Grave III.B.3. in La Kreule Military Cemetery, Hazebrouck, Nord, France. Son of George and Mary Bailey, of Southborough. Formerly 2129 Kent Cycle Corps.

Harry Ball

Private 35937, 8th Bn, Gloucestershire Regiment. Died 14 April 1918, age 18. Commemorated on Panel 72-75 of Tyne Cot Memorial, Zonnebeke, Belgium. Son of Henry Ball, 80 High Brooms Road, High Brooms; born in Shepherds Bush, London.

From the Tunbridge Wells Advertiser 30 May 1918: ...*His numerous friends in High Brooms will regret to learn that Pte H Ball, of the Gloucester Regiment, the son of Mr and Mrs Ball, of High Brooms-road, has been unofficially reported killed in a letter from their son's Commanding Officer. "Pte H Ball was killed in action about the 9th ult ...during the time he was with this Battalion he performed his duty in the very best spirit". Private Ball, who was only 19 years of age, was educated at High Brooms School. Before joining up, he was employed at Messrs Frowde's local shop. He joined up in May, 1917, and went to France on the 2nd of April last.*

From a newspaper report later in 1918: *Mr and Mrs H Ball of 80, High Brooms-road, have received a letter from their son, Pte AW Ball, who was posted as missing early in March, saying he is a prisoner of war in Germany, and up to the time of writing is well. Pte Ball joined the West Kent Regiment in February, 1916, and went to France in June the same year. He is an old High Brooms School boy, Mr and Mrs Ball had a son killed in action on the Western Front last April.*

Stephen Frederick Barden

Sergeant 723, 3rd Kent Fortress Coy, Royal Engineers. Died on 24 September 1915, age 31. Buried in Southborough Cemetery, England, Grave 6.254. Son of Stephen Barden; husband of Mrs E Marshall (formerly Barden) of 54 Meadow Road, Southborough. Born at Speldhurst.

From newspaper accounts of Sgt Barden's funeral dated 1 Oct 1915: *The death of Sgt Stephen Frederick Barden, 2-6th Company of the Kent (Fortress) Royal Engineers, son of Mr (the late) and Mrs Barden, of Holden Place, took place suddenly at Borden Camp, Sittingbourne, on Friday evening from heart failure, after a very short illness of about 2½ hours duration, at the age of 31 years. Much sympathy will be expressed with Mrs Barden, of 15 Charles-street, Southborough. They were married some two years and ten or eleven months ago, and have one little boy.*

Before the war, Sgt Barden was employed for some years as a gardener at Sir David Salomons', Broomhill. He joined the Engineers at the formation of the Company at Southborough, and was called to active service when it was mobilised. He was home for the week-end previous to his death, returning to camp on Monday morning. He was brought home on Monday evening, and was laid to rest in the Cemetery on Wednesday afternoon with full military honours. The cortege was headed by a firing party, and the band of the K(F)RE. The coffin was wrapped in the Union Jack, on which his cap and equipment was placed. Six sergeants of the Company acted as bearers, and about 50 of his comrades were present.

The Rev BC Mowll officiated at the service in the Cemetery Chapel and also at the graveside. After the service the firing party fired three volleys over the grave, and the buglers sounded the Last Post. Mr T Potter of Edward-street Southborough carried out the funeral arrangements, and floral tributes and messages of affection and sympathy were recorded from the following:

His sorrowing wife and Freddy; his sorrowing mother, brothers and sisters; in loving memory of our dear brother – from George, May and Maisie; in loving memory of our poor Fred – from George, Alice and family; to our dear brother Fred – from John and Edith; brother Bill and Julia; Agnes and Will; Arthur, May and Edwin; Harry and Nellie; Tom and Nellie; Edwin and Mabel; Herbert and Mabel; Captain DR Salomons; Mrs Batchelor; Mrs Knowles and daughter; Mr and Mrs A Barnes; from the Officers, NCOs and Men of the 1/7th Company Kent (Fortress) Royal Engineers; Captain Lefeaux and Officers, Borden Detachment, K(F)RE; MA Reeves; Mr and Mrs Pelling and family; from NCOs and men, 1/3rd Kent Field Company RE; Brethren of the RAOB, "Imperial" Lodge; 2/5th Kent (Fortress) Royal Engineers, Sergeants, Stockbury Camp; Officers of the 5th RW Kents and 6th Middlesex, Stockbury Camp; Mr & Mrs C Dowling; Miss Blackburn-Maze; Mr & Mrs Jeffery; Members of the NCOs Mess, Headquarters, Pier-Road, Gillingham; in loving memory of our dear old chum and comrade – from the Officers, NCOs and men of his own Company; Mr and Mrs A Jones; the Sappers of the 1/6th Company, RE; Mr and Mrs Chandler; the Gardeners at Broomhill; CH and Jack Tracey; the mounted section 1/3rd Kent Field Company, RE; AS and Mrs Lee; Mr WA Burfield.

How ironic that less than one month after his funeral, so many of Fred's comrades would themselves be lost on the Hythe.

HV Barnett

Sapper 1860 Kent Fortress Coy, Royal Engineers. Died 22 March 1915. Buried Southborough Cemetery, England, Grave 5.181.

From a local newspaper, 2 April 1915: *Pte Barnett of 4 North Farm-road, High Brooms, died last week at the Fort Pitt Hospital, Chatham. He joined the Kent (Fortress) Royal Engineers only two months ago. He was of a very studious turn of mind, and after leaving the Southborough Council School, continued his education at the Technical Institute, Tunbridge Wells, for engineering, gaining several certificates. He was, previous to joining the Engineers, employed by the High Brooms Brick Company as engineer. Pte Barnett was so enthusiastic to join the Army that he went under an operation in the Hospital in order to pass the medical test.*

The body was conveyed from Chatham by train on Friday, the band of his regiment and a number of his comrades also making the journey. The first part of the service was held in St Matthew's Church, and the interment took place at the Southborough Cemetery, the officiating clergyman being the Rev P. Orme, Vicar of St Matthew's. The mourners were: Mr and Mrs HV Barnett (Pte Barnett's parents), Master F Barnett, Miss E Farmer, Mrs Farmer, Mrs L Fenner, Mr HR Fenner, Mr and Mrs E Wells, Mr and Mrs J F Thomas, Miss D Fenner, Mr LW Andrews, and the Office Staff and Workmen of the High Brooms Brick Company, also No 7 Co of the Kent (Fortress) Royal Engineers. Mr CM Malpass was the organist during the service in the Church, and Mr H Ranger rendered a solo.

Henry Frederick Bartholomew

Sergeant G/1532 7th Bn, Queen's Own (Royal West Kent Regiment). Died 13 July 1916, aged 25. Commemorated on Pier and Face 11C of the Thiepval Memorial, Somme, France.

From the Courier, 11 August 1916: *Many people in Tunbridge Wells and Tonbridge, especially those associated with athletics, will deeply regret to hear of the death of Sergt H Bartholomew, son of Mr and Mrs H*

Bartholomew, of 47, Nursery-road, High Brooms. He was killed in action in France on July 14th, but intimation has only just been received from the War Office. He leaves a widow, and much sympathy will be extended to her and his parents. He joined the Army in September, the month after the outbreak of war, and went to France on July 25th last year, so that he had been nearly a year at the Front. Before joining the Colours he worked as a compositor at the Whitefriars Press, Tonbridge, and he gained a high reputation as an athlete in the town. He was goalkeeper for the Whitefriars' team, and held six medals, while he was also an excellent cricketer and quoits player. He was an old St John's School boy. In a letter to the widow, one of his officers, Second-Lieutenant TW Wills, writes on August 4th: "It grieves me greatly to have to tell you that your husband fell in action in Trones Wood in the early morning of July 14th. I know that such grief as this must cause you cannot be soothed by words, but I can assure you that at a time when others were inclined to lose their heads he behaved with magnificent courage and bravery, and set a splendid example to those around him. He was my Platoon Sergeant, and I valued him very highly. His influence with the men was great, and I could always rely upon him, even when the path of duty was roughest."

Henry Frederick Bartholomew pictured left, back row, 4th from left.

Henry Frederick Bartholomew on his wedding day.

From the Courier, 25 October 1918, a reference to Frederick's brother: *Private E Bartholomew, of the East Yorks Regiment, aged 19, son of Mr and Mrs Bartholomew, of 18, Hectorage-road, Tonbridge, was wounded on the 28th September, and is in Hospital at Bradford, progressing favourably. He joined the Colours in May, 1917, and went to France last April. Previous to enlisting he was employed at Adams' Dairies, Tunbridge Wells. His eldest brother was reported killed at Trones Wood in July, 1916.*

Charles William Barton

Private 6345615, 4th Bn, Queen's Own (Royal West Kent Regiment). Died 28 May 1940, age 21. Buried at Le Grand Hasard Military Cemetery, Morbecque, Nord, France, grave reference 5.C.3.

Charles William Barton, known as Bill to family and friends, was born on 21 May 1919. His mother Elizabeth (née Card) was to marry three times, Bill being the only son born to her with her first husband (Barton). Her second marriage was to a Mr Clarke, a Southborough man whose family lived in Springfield Road, who she met in St Dunstan's Hospital. The family recalls that he had been blinded in the First World War. Together, they had a daughter, Bill's half-sister Doris Clarke. Bill was known by the name of Clarke at school. When Mr Clarke died, Elizabeth re-married, this time to John Hook, himself a widower with three children, Ruby, Edith, and George (their mother was née Everest). John Hook, known as Jack, and his brother **George Hook** had served in the Forces in India for twelve years. John Hook and Elizabeth went on to have a son together, Eric, born December 1925. They all lived at 42, Springfield Road, Southborough. When he was called up in 1939, Bill was required to enlist under his birth-registered name of Barton. Eric Hook recalls that up to this point, the younger children had had no idea that this was Bill's real surname.

Bill was educated at St Peter's School, Southborough. He was a member of the Boys' Brigade, and used to take his brother Eric camping. Bill worked for John Spicer, butcher, in his St John's Road shop from the age of 14, learning the trade of slaughtering and butchering. Mr Spicer bought a new shop, next to the Kelsey Arms, and installed a manager, promising that when Bill was 21, he would take over the role. Sadly, this was not to be. Bill died on the same day, and is commemorated in the same cemetery, as **Frank Hemsley** and **Frank Sutcliffe**.

Eric Hook was 14 when Bill died. He volunteered at age 17 for the Royal Navy, on 23 March 1943, joining HMS Ashanti (see **William Winter**) when she was re-commissioned at London Graving Dock, Poplar, until December 1944, transferring to HMS Savage until December 1946. Eric served on the Russian convoys to Murmansk and Archangel, and recalls that sailors were not allowed on-shore by the Russians.

Frederick William Basnett

Trumpeter 4405, Dragoon Guards. Died 30 March 1918. Commemorated on Panel 1 of the Pozieres Memorial, Somme, France. Born in Wandsworth, London, enlisted Hounslow, resident in Southborough.

From the local press, 19 April 1918: *Official news has been received that Trumpeter F Basnett, Dragoon Guards (The Queen's Bays), only son of Mrs Lane and stepson of Mr Lane, "Flying Dutchman", was killed on March 30th. He joined as a trumpeter at the age of 14 years, his father being an old soldier, and had been in France since June, 1916. He was home on leave in October last. He was well-known in Southborough, having spent part of his childhood with his aunt, Mrs Gurr.*

The Pozieres Memorial relates to the period of crisis in March and April 1918 when the Allied Fifth Army was driven back by overwhelming numbers across the former Somme battlefields, and the months that followed.

Information from the website www.firstworldwar.com/onthisday gives the following campaign detail for the Western Front for 30 March 1918: *North of Somme in Boivy and Boyelles region (Cojeul River) heavy German attacks break down. South of Somme in Luce Valley, Demuin is lost and retaken by British.*

There is a further association with The Flying Dutchman, the former Public House on London Road. Private CT Eade is one of the numerous War Casualties connected to Southborough, but not listed on its War Memorial. The following was included in the Courier, 27 April 1917: *Private CT Eade, although working at the Arsenal, felt he ought to go to the Front, and he enlisted in the Essex Regiment, and last week was officially reported as having died of wounds received in action. Private Eade was the second son of Mr F Eade, late of the Flying Dutchman, and was at one time a prominent member of the Football Club, where his quiet manner and clean play made him respected by opponents as well as his Club mates.*

Southborough War Memorial

Robert Bassett

Private L/8557 2nd Bn, Royal Sussex Regiment. Died 9 May 1915, age 27. Commemorated on Panel 20 & 21 of Le Touret Memorial, Pas de Calais, France. Son of William Bassett; husband of Mary T McDowell (formerly Bassett) of 1, Elm Street, Belfast.

From the Courier, 9 July 1915 :*Pte R Bassett, Royal Sussex Regiment, son of Mr and Mrs W Bassett, of Charles-street, Southborough, was killed in action in France on May 9th whilst storming a German trench. Deceased leaves a wife and one child, who are in Ireland. He joined the Army at the age of 18, and had been two years with the Reserve when called up at the outbreak of war. Another brother served in the West Kent Regiment in the South African War.*

James George Bateman

Serjeant 43306, 36th Battery, Royal Field Artillery. Died 16 July 1916, age 28. Buried in Grave II.C.3 in Laventie Military Cemetery, La Gorgue, Nord, France. Born Dartford, enlisted at Woolwich.

From the Courier, 17 September 1915: *Sergt JG Bateman of 12 Holden Park-road, Southborough, came home on leave from the Front on Monday, after ten months' service in the field. Sergt Bateman was a Reservist, having served six years in the Artillery. He was called up at the declaration of war, and sailed for the Front on November 6th last year. His Battery dropped into action on the 12th, and they have been engaged in heavy fighting many times since, particularly at the memorable battle of Neuve Chapelle, in which his officer received the DSO. He has been in "warm quarters" on many occasions, and has had the good fortune to escape without a scratch. Sergt Bateman played through two seasons with Southborough Football Club.*

And on 28 July 1916: *...has been killed in action in the recent fighting. He died a soldier's death, doing his duty. He went through most of the early battles. On one occasion he had a narrow escape, a bullet striking the corner of a book in his pocket and glancing off sideway went through his clothing and slightly grazed his* skin... *before joining the Army he was in the employ of Messrs Cundell and Dungey, and leaves a widow and two children.*

His wife Emma Bateman lived in Charles Street at the time of his death, but thereafter moved into 12 Holden Park Road, Southborough with her mother, Mrs Coe, taking the front room (Mr Coe was a Chelsea pensioner). After his death Emma became a registered foster mother and brought up her family single-handedly. Her own children William James Bateman (known as Bill) and Dorothy (Mrs Fuller, who lived in Tonbridge after her marriage) were joined by several foster children.

C E Baxter

Private 34907 1st/4th Bn, The Loyal North Lancashire Regiment. Died 20 November 1917. Buried in Villers-Faucon Communal Cemetery Extension, Somme, France, Grave reference I.D.13.

The website www.firstworldwar.com/onthisday gives the following campaign detail for 20 November 1917: *Western Front: Surprise British advance at Cambrai. Third Army under Lt Gen Byng attacks on ten mile front, between St Quentin and River Scarpe. "Hindenburg Line" broken, numerous villages captured, over 8,000 prisoners taken.*

From the Tunbridge Wells Advertiser, 7 December 1917: *We regret to record the death in action of Pte C Baxter, of the Loyal North Lancashire Regiment, of 51, High Brooms-road, by shrapnel. Pte Baxter joined the Colours in June, 1916, and went to France in June, 1917. He was employed with the firm of Messrs Boots at their Pantiles branch for over eight years, and is an old Grosvenor School boy.*

Denis Walter Bean

Midshipman, HMS Rawalpindi, Royal Naval Reserve. Died Thursday 23 November 1939, age 18. Commemorated on the Plymouth Naval Memorial, Devon, England: Panel 35, Column 3. Son of Walter Whittaker Bean and Mary Florence Bean, of 5, Crendon Park, Southborough.

Fred Ongley recalls that Denis's father was the Woodwork Master at Judd's School in Tonbridge, and leader of the Allegro Dance Band.

Southborough War Memorial

The following edited extract is taken from *Against All Odds – HMS Rawalpindi* by Stephen Cashmore and David Bews: HMS *Rawalpindi* was launched in 1925 at the Harland & Wolf shipbuilding yard in Belfast, one of four 16,000 ton passenger ships built for the Peninsular and Orient Steam Navigation Company. Under the famous P&O flag the Rawalpindi (pictured below) settled down to a mundane career on the company's Britain to India route, via the Mediterranean and the Suez Canal.

On August 24th 1939, the Admiralty requisitioned Rawalpindi and began fitting her with eight 6-inch guns of World War 1 vintage. A week later, as the Wehrmacht's Panzers beat a swift and violent path into Poland, Britain declared war on Germany.

On the morning of November 23rd, His Majesty's Armed Merchant Cruiser Rawalpindi was patrolling the endless grey ocean wastes to the north of Faeroe. Most of her 276 crew were members of the Royal Naval Reserve. The day's routine had been enlivened by the commandeering of a Swedish freighter that had crossed the Rawalpindi's path earlier that morning. Leaving a boarding party in charge of the Swedish vessel, the Armed Merchant Cruiser resumed her patrol. Intelligence had been received that the German pocket battleship Deutschland was at large somewhere in the North Atlantic, and indeed the German warship's seizure of the neutral American merchantman City of Flint had caused a temporary diplomatic crisis in relations between Germany and the US. Be as this may, Rawalpindi's orders were to avoid combat with the Deutschland should she happen to come across her - such a course of action would clearly be suicidal. Instead, she was to radio the German ship's position back to Home Fleet HQ so that a battle squadron could be despatched to intercept her.

At 1530 hrs, with the winter sun about to sink below the horizon, Rawalpindi was steering an eastward course mid-way between Iceland and the Faeroes. It was a cold, calm afternoon. To port a fog bank was beginning to form; now and then the ship passed a solitary iceberg, white and eerie in the northern twilight. On the bridge stood Rawalpindi's Captain, Edward Coverley Kennedy, father of future media figure Ludovic Kennedy. A veteran Royal Navy officer, recently recalled to duty, 60-year-old Captain Kennedy's vast experience of sea life made him an ideal candidate for a command like Rawalpindi. A message from the crow's nest indicated that a ship had been sighted on the starboard horizon. The Captain ordered "Action Stations!" followed swiftly by a command to change course to port. The duty Radio Operator was told to send an enemy sighting report without delay. Next moment, her alarm bells going like the hammers of Hell, Rawalpindi steered full speed towards the fog bank's enveloping shelter. Smoke floats were lit and flung into the water. They failed to ignite. In an instant, Captain Kennedy ordered a course change to starboard where a large iceberg, about 4 miles away, held out a better promise of protection. But it was too late. The German warship was fast approaching, cutting off Rawalpindi's escape route. From her bridge the enemy flashed a signal 'Heave to!' backed up with a warning shell that sent up a fountain of spray some two hundred yards in front of Rawalpindi's bows. The Captain scorned these hostile gestures. A man cast in the mould of Nelson and Richard Grenville, Edward Kennedy had an inflexible sense of duty.

(Pictured below: The Scharnhorst, as seen from the Gneisenau heading for the North Atlantic November 1939:)

As the German warship drew closer, Kennedy took another look at her. This time he felt certain she was indeed the Deutschland. Accordingly, he ordered an amended message be sent at once to the Home Fleet HQ. Again the German bridge flashed 'Heave to!' and again the message was ignored, not least because at that very moment a second ship had been sighted to starboard. At first Captain Kennedy thought this must be a fellow member of the Northern Patrol, a British heavy cruiser, perhaps. But he was very much mistaken: the Rawalpindi, a hastily converted passenger liner with outdated guns and eggshell armour, was about to take on one of the mightiest warships in the Kriegsmarine.

Caught between two superior enemies Kennedy realised that his last hour was at hand. While the Rawalpindi's Signal Officer was correctly identifying the newcomer as a German battle-cruiser, the Chief Engineer appeared on the bridge to hear the Captain declare; "We'll fight them both, they'll sink us - and that will be that. Goodbye". He shook the Chief's hand, turned on his heel and cleared the decks for action.

From his vantage point on the Scharnhorst's foretop, Captain Hoffmann ordered the signal 'Abandon your ship!' to be sent. To his astonishment, the Rawalpindi failed to respond to this message. Was the captain mad? Surely no sane person would pit eight obsolete 6-inch guns against the combined weight of eighteen modern 11-inch monsters, firing at a point-blank range of only 4 miles? Filled with a mixture of bewilderment and silent admiration, Hoffmann commanded the 'Abandon ship!' signal be repeated. It was - twice, and twice it went unheeded. With a heavy heart, Hoffmann prepared to give the signal for the Scharnhorst to open fire. He was a moment too late: a salvo of 6-inch shells from Rawalpindi's four port guns burst harmlessly against the second German battle-cruiser, Gneisenau, commanded by Admiral Marshall and twin sister of the Scharnhorst. At the same moment a similar salvo was on its way to Hoffmann's ship. It was 1545. Barely a quarter of an hour had gone by since Rawalpindi's first sight of the hostile vessels. Another 15 minutes and it would all be over.

The first salvo from Scharnhorst slammed into the Boat Deck, directly under the Rawalpindi's bridge, killing almost everyone on it and demolishing the radio room; from now on Rawalpindi was unable to transmit any further radio messages. She didn't have to. At his base on the Clyde, the Home Fleet's Commander-in-Chief was actioning Rawalpindi's first signal. A veritable armada of British warships had been ordered to intercept the German battle-cruisers, among them HMS Newcastle, HMS Delhi; and the heavy cruisers Norfolk and Suffolk, were hurrying full steam ahead to the scene of action. Would they arrive too late? It seemed so. A cluster of 11-inch shells from Gneisenau struck Rawalpindi's main gun control station, killing everyone there and immobilising one of her starboard guns. Caught in a murderous crossfire, Rawalpindi had no hope of survival.

By some miracle, Captain Kennedy had lived through the direct hit on Rawalpindi's bridge. Undaunted he sent for Chief Petty Officer Humphries. As he did so a shell burst in the ship's engine room, knocking out the dynamos that supplied vital electric power to the shell hoists in the magazines. Kennedy ordered Humphries to go round all seven surviving gun turrets and tell their commanders to continue firing independently now that the central control system was out of action. Chief PO Humphries was also to enlist all spare hands in the thankless task of manhandling 6-inch shells from magazine to gun turrets. And still the storm of German shells continued to burst against the gallant little ship.

It was hopeless. Ablaze from stem to stern, her guns being picked off one by one, Rawalpindi was doomed. A badly wounded loader crawling on his hands and knees, a 6-inch projectile clasped to his weary body, recalled an episode from his training time at shore-based HMS Ganges when, for the crime of 'producing unsuitable noises during a gunnery class,' he was sentenced to carry similar shells up and down Laundry Hill. Meanwhile, beside another 6-inch gun, its firing mechanism jammed solid, a man gone out of his mind with shock and terror, was roaring at his companions to help him get it freed oblivious to the fact that the he was shouting at dead men. Below decks, in the ship's magazine the lights had gone out. A sailor groped his way above to find the Rawalpindi on fire. At once he shouted to his companions to flood the magazine and join him immediately on the upper deck. Arriving there they found things were perilous indeed. Cordite sticks and live shells were rolling about, surrounded by flames. The newcomers lost no time in throwing these dangerous munitions overboard.

In desperation, Captain Kennedy went aft with two ratings to try and lay a covering smoke-screen, while up on deck Chief Petty Officer Humphries was struggling to get wounded men into lifeboats. Suddenly, out of the smoke and flames a rating appeared. "The Captain's been killed, Chief," the smoke-blackened rating announced. By now fires were blazing everywhere, the ship's water supply had failed and its steering gear was out of action. There was nothing for it but to abandon ship. A lifeboat filled with some forty wounded men was prepared for lowering into the sea, but it turned turtle and hit the water upside down, leaving the men to flounder helplessly in the freezing waves. Others were more successful, and for a moment it seemed as though a good number of the *Rawalpindi's* crew would escape their ship's doom. It was not to be. At 1600 hours a tremendous explosion broke the gallant merchant cruiser in two. A shell from one of *Scharnhorst's* 11-inch guns had found *Rawalpindi's* forward magazine. Her spine broken in half, the stricken vessel began to sink, one of its guns still firing crazily into the air. Tragically for those trying to get clear of the sinking ship, the *Scharnhorst* having closed in for the kill, swung hard about, swamping the *Rawalpindi's* lifeboats. Then, in keeping with naval chivalry, the German battle-cruiser reduced speed and returned to rescue the survivors struggling in the freezing sea.

Darkness was fast falling on this melancholy drama when the last survivors were plucked from a watery grave. They totalled 38. Their companions, all 238 of them, had gone down with the *Rawalpindi*. The whole action was over and done in barely quarter of an hour.

By now the first of the British warships had arrived on the scene. HMS *Newcastle* and HMS *Delhi*, wary of drifting into range of the superior firepower of the German ships, began shadowing the battle-cruisers as they headed west, all the while sending back messages to the Home Fleet. Alerted by this intelligence a posse of cruisers and destroyers, soon to be joined by the battleship *Warspite* and the great battle-cruisers *Hood* and *Repulse* began converging on the forward track of the fugitive Germans. It looked as though the game was up for *Scharnhorst* and her sister ship, that *Rawalpindi's* sacrifice might not be in vain after all. But the northern climate owes no favours to anyone, no matter how mighty they may consider themselves to be. A squall arose; the German ships escaped. Had the British possessed radar at this early stage of the War, it is doubtful whether *Scharnhorst* and *Gneisenau* would have made it back to port. As it was, they lived on, a constant threat to British merchant shipping in the North Atlantic.

On Boxing Day 1943, in the icy seas off the North Cape of Norway, the *Scharnhorst* met her doom. As she prepared to intercept the Arctic convoy JW55B on her way from Loch Ewe to Russia, *Scharnhorst* encountered a superior British force. Pulverised by the 15-inch guns of the battleship *Duke of York*, her steering shattered, her superstructure on fire from end to end, the proud *Scharnhorst* finally succumbed to a 21-inch torpedo fired by the cruiser HMS *Belfast*. The German battle-cruiser's *magazines blew up and she rolled over and sank, taking with her 1,968 men. A mere 36 survived.*

(Pictured left: After returning from the Northern Patrol attack the Scharnhorst moves slowly through the opened Kaiser Wilhelm Bridge in Wilhelmshaven with a tug alongside).

Thomas Peter Bellingham

Private 4432, 6th Battalion Australian Infantry, D Company. Commemorated on the Villers-Bretonneux Memorial, Somme, France. Died 26 July 1916, age 24. Son of Daniel Bellingham, of 2 South View Road, High Brooms.

Thomas Peter Bellingham (SP on Southborough War Memorial) emigrated to Australia at the age of 19. He was a farm labourer at Boort, Victoria, and had been a member of the Territorials in England. He embarked at Melbourne on 28 January 1916, on HMAT A32 Themistocles.

From the Courier, 18 August 1916: ... *eldest son of Mr and Mrs D Bellingham, of 51, South View-road, was instantly killed by shrapnel ... he was unmarried and an old St Barnabas School boy ... was employed by Messrs Parker and Hammick, of Mount Ephraim, for four years ... he joined up in September 1915, in the 2nd Infantry Brigade Expeditionary Force, sailing from Australia in January 1916 to Egypt. From there he went over to France, reaching there in early April. His parents regret they have not seen him since he left England on April 8th, 1911. Private CH Lulham, his step-brother, of the ASC (MT) has been in France about four months, and been ill in Hospital about eleven weeks, but is now quite well and fit, and back at his post.*

Sergeant RC Parker (3893) stated *"I had Bellingham with me at Pozieres. On 25 July 1916 we were in the village making an advance when his head was blown off. I saw it happen. Previously we had been in the same dugout. The padre Major Miles took the man's papers and I believe buried him at the spot but his friend Private W Crust knows all about it."*

Later on, in March 1917, Lance Corporal Crust confirmed that Bellingham had been killed instantly by a piece of shell while going up the front line. *"He was buried by some Pioneers. The place he was killed in is called Pozieres. Regarding his description, he was about 5ft 8ins and thick set. Fair hair and complexion with blue eyes."*

Sydney Wyborn Betts

Sapper KF743, 1st/3rd Kent Field Coy Royal Engineers. Died 28 October 1915. One of many men from High Brooms and Southborough who perished when the Hythe went down off Gallipoli. He is commemorated on the Helles Memorial, which stands on the tip of the Gallipoli Peninsula in Turkey. Panel 23 to 25 or 325 to 328. Dee's Directory for 1915 gives Sydney's address as 11, Meadow Road, Southborough.

From Frank Stevens' book *Southborough Sappers of the Kent (Fortress) Royal Engineers*: *Sydney was the adopted son of Mr & Mrs Groombridge of 10 Albion Square, Tunbridge Wells. His home was 81 Silverdale Road, High Brooms where his wife and two children lived. He is reported to have been in the Territorial Force for four years but this may have been another unit of the TF. He received a prize for musketry in 1913, was an employee of the Cadena Café on the Pantiles and attended St Johns School.*

The Courier, 21 July 1916 reports: *Mr Groombridge, of 10 Albion Square, has truly contributed his share in the great struggle, for three sons have already given their lives for King and Country, and a fourth is now lying seriously wounded at Endell-street Military Hospital, London, Lance-Corporal Frederick Charles Groombridge ... Private H Groombridge, Royal West Kents, was killed in action on the 18th April, 1915; Private J Groombridge, Royal Sussex Regiment, died of wounds on the 10th May 1915, and Driver S Betts, an adopted son, was drowned in the Hythe disaster.*

Southborough War Memorial

Henry Bird

Private H Bird, Buffs (East Kent). Henry Bird was born in Hadlow in about August 1877. He joined The Buffs in 1896 and served with the 2nd Battalion until 1903 when he was discharged. During this period the Battalion fought in the Boer War but Private Bird is not listed in the rolls of men who served there. He married Fanny Bishop on 28 October 1911 and they had two boys; Henry, born in July 1911 (his surname was Bishop so he may have been from a previous marriage) and James, born in December 1913. He was a farm labourer when he rejoined The Buffs on 12 November 1914. He stood 5'7" and weighed 161 lbs. He went overseas on 20 October 1915 to join the 6th Battalion but was back home at the depot on 30 November. The reason is not known. He was back in France with the 8th Battalion on 27 January 1916 and home again on 7 July. He was discharged from the army on 16 August 1917 suffering from severe bronchitis. He was awarded a weekly pension of 8s 3d. By now his father was dead and his mother was living at an unknown address in Canada.

His address on discharge is given alternatively as 29 Great Brooms Road, 19 High Brooms Road and 90 High Brooms Road. He died in the third quarter of 1919. His wife was awarded a pension of 26s 8d and 23s 6d for the children. Michael Mills, Buffs Regiment historian writes: *His date of death puts him within the eligibility of a CWGC headstone but because he died after discharge he is not eligible. This is a very grey area because if it can be proven that his death was attributable to war service he could be accepted for the register. It could be argued that the army had accepted some responsibility by paying his widow a pension on his death.*

Cecil John Bone

Sapper KF 854, 1st/3rd Kent Field Coy, Royal Engineers. Died 25 October 1915, age 18. Commemorated on the Helles Memorial, Turkey, Panel 23 to 25 or 325 to 328. CWGC gives death date as 25 October 1915, but according to Frank Stevens he drowned on 28 October 1915 on the Hythe.

Frank Stevens writes: *Born in Tonbridge, Cecil Bone moved to Southborough (1911) and then to High Brooms where he lived with his parents John and Elizabeth Bone at 1 Wolseley Road,*

High Brooms. Bone joined the Kent (Fortress) Royal Engineers Cadets in 1912. Employed by Mr Churcher, fruiterer of Tunbridge Wells. He drowned on 28 October 1915. Commemorated also on Slade School and St Matthew's Memorials.

The Courier, 19 November 1915, states that he was the only son of Mr & Mrs J Bone of 29A Gordon Road, High Brooms. Dee's Directory for 1915 gives the address as 31 Forge Road, Southborough.

Henry William Bonwick

Private PS/3513 12th Bn, Middlesex Regiment. Died 22 October 1917. Commemorated on Panel 113 to 115 of the Tyne Cot Memorial, Zonnebeke, West-Vlaanderen, Belgium. Born Southborough, enlisted East Grinstead, resided Colemans Hatch, Sussex. Third son of Mrs Bonwick, Castle-street, Southborough.

Private Bonwick was a Derby recruit in 1915 and went to France in 1916. An old boy of St Peter's School, aged 33, he left a widow and child.

Albert Boorman

Private G/13153, 7th Bn, Royal Sussex Regiment. Died 18 September 1918, age 42. Buried in Epehy Wood Cemetery, Epehy, Somme, France. Grave II.B.23. Son of Hannah Boorman, Pembury; husband of the late Annie Rose Boorman.

www.firstworldwar.com/onthisday includes the following for 18 September 1918: *Great British advance on 16 mile front north-west of St Quentin, extending from Holnon Wood to Gouzeaucourt; over 6,000 prisoners and a number of guns captured; outer defences of Hindenburg Line stormed in many places. French, in liaison with British, capture Savy Wood and Fontaine-les-Cleres. End of Battle of Epehy.*

From the Courier, 18 October 1918: *Much sympathy is felt in the neighbourhood of High Brooms for Mrs A Boorman, of 5, Gordon-road, who has received official news that her husband, Pte A Boorman, of the Royal Sussex Regiment, was killed in action on the Western Front on the 18th of September. Pte Boorman, who was 37 years of age, joined the Royal Sussex Regiment in June, 1915, and went to France in the same year. He leaves a widow and six children, the youngest being five years old, and has had only one leave since he has been in France. Previous to joining up he had been employed, since a lad, by the High Brooms Brick Company, and was an old High Brooms School boy. Mrs Boorman has two brothers and four brothers-in-law with the colours.*

Brian Anthony Botten

Private 6355621, 1st Bn, Queen's Own (Royal West Kent Regiment). Died on Saturday 12 August 1944, age 20. Son of Thomas Hartridge Botten and Miriam Botten, 67 Edward Street, Southborough. Buried in Caserta War Cemetery, Italy: Grave ref. I.C.20.

From the Courier, 28 July 1944: *Private BA Botten, son of Mr and Mrs TH Botten of 67 Edward-street, Southboro', has been severely wounded by shrapnel in the stomach and back in the fighting in the Central Mediterranean seat of war. He has written home very cheerfully to his parents and says he is going on well. His brother, Sergeant DT Botten, RE, is in the same area and is hoping to be able to visit his brother in hospital.* And from the Courier, 25 August 1944: *Mr and Mrs TH Botten have just received the sad news that their son Private BA (Tony) Botten died in hospital on August 12. He has borne his sufferings bravely and has written cheerful letters from hospital to his parents, who have also received a very nice, sympathetic letter from the Assistant Matron of the hospital, written earlier on the same day that he died, in which she stated he was not so well.*

George Botten

Private 5064, 48th Bn, Australian Infantry, AIF. Died 3 May 1918, age 32. Buried at Crucifix Corner Cemetery, Villers-Bretonneux, Somme, France. Grave III.C.10. Son of John and Mary Ann Botten. Brother of Mrs Annie M Friend of 7 Taylor Street, Southborough.

From the CWGC site: *The Cemetery site became famous in 1918, when the German advance on Amiens ended (on 23 April) in the capture of Villers-Bretonneux by German tanks and infantry. On the following day the 4th Australian and 5th Australian Divisions, with units of the 8th and 18th Divisions, carried out "an enterprise of great daring"(Sir Douglas Haig's Despatch of 20 July 1918), and recaptured the whole of the village.*

Clive Maier writes: *George Botten emigrated to Australia at the age of 24. A blacksmith at Woodanilling, Western Australia, he embarked from Freemantle on HMAT A9 Shropshire on 31 March 1916. Posted to Egypt, he had only been in France about six weeks when he was wounded.*

From the Courier, 18 August 1916:*The sisters of Private G Botten, 48th Battalion 12th Brigade Australians, have received a letter from the sister of the General Hospital in France saying that Private Botten had been seriously wounded in the back and wrist. Private Botten is the youngest son of the late Mr and Mrs Botten of The Forge, Speldhurst Road, where he worked before going to Australia six years ago. He was familiarly known amongst his friends as "Boxer". In a letter to his sister, Mrs Tolhurst, Edward-street, received last Friday, Private Botten said he was well, but the shells were flying in all directions, and they could guess there was "something" doing there.*

Enquiries were made in 1918 by his sister Annie Botten and Mrs E Metcalf of Trotting Hill, Southborough. Private HJ Beard 3622 stated on 23 July from No 16 General Hospital: *We were in D Company, XIV Platoon; he came from West Australia. We went over together in the same Lewis gun team in an attack on Monument Wood, Villers Bretonneux. It was about 3am when we went over. After getting over about 200 to 300 yards he fell beside me. I asked him if he was hit and he said "Yes". It was dark and I could not see how he was wounded. I had to go on. He did not get back nor was his body brought in and up to a short time ago there was no news of him. My impression is that he is dead."* Later on Private DL Sexton 6888 testified, *"I saw him lying dead on the field."*

Victor Bowden

Private 22005 6th Bn, The Buffs (East Kent Regiment). Died 16 May 1918. Buried in Mailly Wood Cemetery, Somme, France: Grave II.K.14. The initials VJ are given on the Southborough War Memorial; VG on the CWGC register. Born in Cambridge, and enlisted at Stratford, Essex, Victor Bowden had an address in Cromer at the time of his death.

Michael Mills, Buffs historian, writes: *On 16th May 1915, four officers and ninety-six men from D Company carried out a successful trench raid on Hawthorn Ridge near Beaumont Hamel in order to identify the enemy and inflict* casualties. Heavy casualties were inflicted on the enemy (thirty were known to have been killed) and there was considerable damage to enemy trenches by British artillery. Three unwounded prisoners were captured for the loss of six Buffs killed and twelve wounded. The men killed were Charles Masters, George Butterfield, Leonard Bubb, Jack Instein, Percy Hickman and Victor Bowden.

Bernard John Richard Brady

Flying Officer 90403, 615 Squadron, Royal Air Force (Auxiliary Air Force). Died Wednesday 14 August 1940, age 20. Buried in Southborough Cemetery, England: Grave ref. Sec 11, Grave 383. Son of Bernard and Daisy Brady, of Southborough.

In May 1940 the Squadron was based at RAF Kenley, which that year became Sector Station HQ for B Sector, 11 Group, Fighter Command. It was severely attacked on 18 August 1940, and many times during the Battle of Britain.

Chris McCooey's book *Voices of Southborough and High Brooms* records the following memory: *Mrs Jill Wickens (née Grove) lives in Chestnut Avenue now but during the war she lived at the bottom of Edward Street, in a stone cottage that had been built for one of Sir David Salomon's workers.*

"As a child we used to play outdoors all the time. Sometimes we used to take food to a man living in the old quarry opposite Kibbles Lane. We thought he was a spy, most likely a double agent. Next door to us at 99 Edward Street lived Bernard and Daisy Brady and their family. Their son Bernard John Richard, who we called John, went to the Skinners' School from 1930 to 1936. He was in Knott House. Even at school he was mad keen to join the RAF but, of course, he was too young. Once he borrowed an umbrella from my sister and jumped out of his first floor window using the umbrella as a parachute! He broke his leg. When he was old enough he joined up and became a pilot officer in 615 Squadron which was part of the BEF and took part in defending the retreat of the soldiers as they were evacuated from Dunkirk. The squadron lost twenty-five Hurricanes in France. John was shot down and injured in June 1940 and he died two months later in England."

Lewis Walter Bridger

Farrier TS/394 5th Reserve Park, Army Service Corps. Died 25 December 1914, age 37. Buried in the south-east corner of Wavrans-sur-L'Aa Churchyard, Pas de Calais, France. Husband of EO Bridger, of 8 Castle Street, Southborough.

From the Courier, 1 January 1915: *Farrier Bridger died suddenly at the Front on Christmas Day. He was a blacksmith by trade, well-known in Southborough, and a prominent member of the Salvation Army.* Listed with Royal West Kent on Memorial and in Dees's Directory, 1915.

Jabez Bridgland

Private 24611 9th Bn, Essex Regiment. Died on Friday 30 November 1917, age 23. Commemorated on the Cambrai Memorial, Louverval, Nord, France: Panel 7 and 8. Born Southborough, enlisted Ilford, Essex, resided Seven Kings, Ilford. Son of William Edwin Bridgland, 61 Edward Street, Southborough.

From the CWGC website: *The Cambrai Memorial commemorates more than 7,000 servicemen of the United Kingdom and South Africa who died in the Battle of Cambrai in November and December 1917 and whose graves are not known. Sir Douglas Haig described the object of the Cambrai operations as the gaining of a 'local success by a sudden attack at a point where the enemy did not expect it' and to some extent they succeeded. The proposed method of assault was new, with no preliminary artillery bombardment. Instead, tanks would be used to break through the German wire, with the infantry following under the cover of smoke barrages. The attack began early in the morning of 20 November 1917 and initial advances were remarkable. However, by 22 November, a halt was called for rest and reorganisation, allowing the Germans to reinforce. From 23 to 28 November, the fighting was concentrated almost entirely around Bourlon Wood and by 29 November, it was clear that the Germans were* ready for a major counter attack. During the fierce fighting of the next five days, much of the ground gained in the initial days of the attack was lost. For the Allies, the results of the battle were ultimately disappointing but valuable lessons were learnt about new strategies and tactical approaches to fighting.

From the Courier of 14 December 1917: *Great sympathy will be felt for Mr Bridgland, 61 Edward-street, in the death of their son, Drummer J Bridgland, Essex Regiment, who was killed in France on November 30th. He joined the Army two years ago, and was drafted to France after nine weeks' training. Before enlisting he was employed by the United Kingdom Tea Company.*

Jabez died on the same day as **William Young.** Dee's Directory 1915 listed S Bridgland (KFRE) and J Bridgland (HMS Teal), both resident at 61 Edward-street; the author considers the following refers to the brother of Jabez, notwithstanding the different initial.

From the Courier, 28 May 1915: *Two Southborough men, Seaman-Gunner J Bridgland (son of Mr and Mrs WE Bridgland) and Able Seaman Arthur Stringer (son of Mr & Mrs C Stringer) were on HMS Triumph, which was torpedoed in the Dardanelles in Tuesday. It is hoped they are among the saved.*

And on 18 June 1915, a photograph (left) and text appeared: *The two Southborough survivors of HMS Triumph, Seaman-Gunner J Bridgland & Able Seaman A Stringer, returned home unexpectedly last Sunday evening, to the great relief and joy of their parents and friends. Both are reticent with regard to their individual experiences and modestly disclaim any personal credit. They were many times under the hottest fire. Everything possible had been done by closing the water-tight doors, and the torpedo nets were out as a safeguard, though the torpedo cut through them. When it struck the ship both of them were below, but managed to struggle up through water and coal dust on to the sloping deck, and muster with the ship's company, who showed that steadiness in danger which is the proud heritage of the British Navy. Discipline reigned supreme, and not until the order was given did the men leap into the water, Bridgland being picked up by a trawler, and Stringer by a merchantman. The boats effecting the rescue were under shrapnel fire the whole time. The men have been granted a well-earned fourteen days' leave. The men lost the greater part of their personal belongings, and Seaman-Gunner Bridgland had collected a number of beautiful silk articles and other curios from China during his three years at the China Station, all of which went to the bottom.*

Southborough War Memorial

Richard John Bristow

Sapper 1568 1st/3rd Kent Field Coy Royal Engineers. Died 28 October 1915, age 26, in the Hythe disaster. Commemorated on the Helles Memorial, Turkey, Panel 23 to 25 or 325 to 328. Son of Mr & Mrs H Bristow. Born Sevenoaks.

The family moved to Southborough about 1906, and lived at 10 Meadow Road. Richard Bristow enlisted on November 9th, 1914 and was unmarried at the time of his death. Dee's Directory 1915 lists him as Bristowe.

Leonard C Brooman

Private Leonard C Brooman 5256. Leicestershire Regiment. Not listed on the CWGC website as one of the thirteen men named Brooman who died in the First World War.

From the Courier, 27 October 1916: *Miss Brooman, Bedford-road, has received information that her brother, Pte LC Brooman, of the Leicesters, who carried on business as a builder in Bedford-road, has been seriously wounded, and that he is in the Casualty Clearing Hospital. Miss Brooman received a postcard from him on Tuesday, saying that he had been admitted to the Hospital, and from the fact that he is able to write himself, it is hoped that he is going on well. Private Brooman joined the 6th Leicesters in March, and went to France in June.*

A cross with the inscription "Leonard Brooman, Died of Wounds 1921" was left at the Southborough War Memorial on Remembrance Sunday 2006, and presumably before that date.

Arthur Archie Brotherhood

Private 232 1st Coy, Australian Machine Gun Corps. Died 4 October 1917, age 25. Commemorated on the Ypres (Menin Gate) Memorial, West-Vlaanderen, Belgium: Panel 31. Son of Mrs A

Brotherhood of 10 Great Brooms Road, High Brooms. Husband of Mrs Sarah Brotherhood of 27 Sturt Street, Darlinghurst, New South Wales, Australia. Brother of Ernest Brotherhood.

The website www.firstworldwar.com/onthisday gives the following for 4 October 1917: *Western Front: British advance on eight mile front, anticipating by a few minutes a German attack east of Ypres; 3,000 prisoners. In counter-atttack Germans regain some ground south-east of Polygon Wood.*

From the Tunbridge Wells Advertiser, 19 October 1917: *Mrs Brotherhood received a letter from another son, Frank who is a lance-corporal in the Queen's Regiment in France, saying he had met his brother Archie, and they had spent a jolly day together, and another letter on Wednesday telling his mother that his brother was wounded by a sniper on the 3rd inst and died before he got to the dressing station.*

Pte Brotherhood, who lost the sight of his right eye after the battle of Bullecourt, was 25 years of age, and went to Australia with a party of lads from High Brooms, sent out by the Kent Colonising Association about 4½ years ago. He has been in the Australian Army over two years, and after some time in Egypt went to France, where he has been for eleven months. He was an old High Brooms School boy. Mrs Brotherhood has lost another son in the war, he being killed at the battle of the Somme.

Clive Maier's research shows: *Arthur Archie Brotherhood was a labourer at Sydney, New South Wales. He enlisted on 4 January 1916 and embarked from Sydney on HMAT A40 Ceramic on 14 April 1916. He joined the Machine Gun Corps on 17 December 1916. He was known to his pals as Archie.*

Accounts of his death vary. Captain JW Richards said that he was wounded at Broodeseendi but was able to walk to the dressing station where he was hit by a shell and killed, probably instantly. He was buried at the dressing station. Corporal R Telford 3143 said he was hit in the spine by a shell fragment, died shortly after and was buried at the back of the trench. Private A Ayre 1312 said he was killed instantly by a shell while at his gun, and was buried where he fell. Private A Mellor 340 said Brotherhood was hit in the back by a machine gun bullet, and that he was conscious and "pretty cheerful" after bandaging. Featherstone W414 said he was hit through the hip by a bullet and died two hours later.

From the Courier, 2 February 1945, mention of Brotherhoods serving in the Second World War: *Mr J Brotherhood, 82, of 10, Great Brooms-road, has four grandchildren serving: Ethel, employed by the Air Ministry, Basil, a Corporal in the RAF, Leslie, a member of the REME recently home from Burma, and Lionel, a telegraphist in the RN.*

Ernest Brotherhood

Private G/15440 11th Bn, Queen's Own (Royal West Kent Regiment). Died 7 October 1916. Commemorated on the Thiepval Memorial, Somme, France: Pier and Face 11 C.

www.firstworldwar.com/onthisday 7 October 1916: *Western Front: British and French advance on Albert-Bapaume Road. British advance 1,000 yards and capture Le Sars.*

From the Tunbridge Wells Advertiser, 18 May 1917: *Mr and Mrs Brotherhood, of 10, Great Brooms-road, High Brooms, have received news that their son, Pte Ernest Brotherhood, who has been missing since October 7th, is now reported killed in action. Pte Brotherhood, who was 29 years of age, joined the Royal West Kent Regiment on the 29th of May, 1916, and went to France the following September. He was an old High Brooms School boy, and formerly worked for Mr Wilson, butcher, of Calverley-road, Tunbridge Wells. He was married, with one child. He has two brothers with the colours in France, one in the Australian Gun Section, and the other in the Queen's Royal West Surreys.*

And from the Courier, 18 May 1917: *A chum of Private Brotherhood writes that they went into a trench on October 7th, and a bomb burst which buried twelve of them, but he was dug out uninjured. Afterwards they looked round, but could not find Brotherhood, and it is thought that he must have been blown up by another shell.*

F Brown

Private 12432 9th Bn, Royal Sussex Regiment. Died Sunday 23 June 1918. Age 32. Buried in Southborough Cemetery, England, Grave ref: 4.135. Husband of Florence V Brown, of 46 Nursery Road, High Brooms.

Frank Brown, writes his grandson Roger Brown, was born in Pembury on 20 July 1885. He was the youngest of eight children born to Irad Arthur Brown and Miriam Brown (nee Mewett). Miriam died in November 1885 of typhoid fever, leaving Irad with four children under 10, and Frank just four months old. Not surprisingly, he very quickly found a housekeeper and married her in 1889.

The family had moved to High Brooms by 1891, where Irad and his sons were all builders, bricklayers or brickmakers (pictured here with his brothers and father, Frank on far right aged approx thirteen). They lived variously in High Brooms Rd, Nursery Rd and Silverdale Rd. Frank was placed as a bricklaying apprentice in due course with John Jarvis & Co.

He was among the men who built the Opera House in Tunbridge Wells (see photo - Frank in 2nd row from front, 5th from the left). The family story is that whilst working on the dome inside the building, he fell off the scaffolding and into a pile of sand on the floor. Amazingly, he was not badly injured, but was sacked on the spot for being careless. Frank married Florence Victoria Camfield at St John's Church on 16 May 1909, and they had four children: Grace Emily (b.1909), Doris Violet (b.1912), Frank William (b.1916) and Ronald (died at 10 days old).

From the Courier. 4 May 1917: *Mrs F Brown, of 46, Nursery-road, High Brooms, has been officially notified that her husband, Private F Brown, Royal Sussex Regiment, was wounded on the 11th April. It appears that himself and several comrades were in a shell-hole, when a shell alighted close by, exploded, and buried some of the men, Private Brown being hit in the back. He is now at a Base Hospital in France. This is the third time Brown has been among the casualties. On December 28th last he was wounded in the face, and having spent a month in Hospital returned to the firing line. A fortnight previous to his recent misfortune Brown was in a trench which was blown up, but escaped with a grazed arm. He is the youngest son of Mr JA*

Brown, of 55, South View Road, High Brooms. In a cheery letter to his wife, Private Brown says he "hopes soon to be again with the 'Boys'."

From the Tunbridge Wells Advertiser, 2 November 1917: *Pte F Brown is suffering from trench fever, and is in hospital in Oxford. He joined up in May, 1916 ... Mrs Brown has had a cheerful letter from her husband, saying that he is progressing very favourably. Previous to joining up he worked for Mr Bates as a bricklayer. He is an old St Augustine's School boy and has two brothers with the colours.*

After a month at base hospital in France, by October 1917 Frank had been transferred to Oxford, and then eventually to Tickford Abbey Military Hospital in Newport Pagnell, Bucks. A letter from a nursing sister there warned Florence that *he is daily losing strength, but is comfortable and has everything he needs*, and then there was a last letter from his doctor: *Dear Mrs Brown, I cannot tell you how much I feel for you. We had learnt to be so fond of your husband that we can sympathise very fully. I know something of what your loss must be. He bore his illness which I feel sure he knew must be the end of his life, with the courage of a true gentleman which he was in every sense. It must be harder to die lonely of an illness in hospital than in the field of battle. But he never showed the slightest sign of discontent or fear. I do hope the dear children will some day understand what a splendid father they had. May God grant you strength to bear the loss and loneliness. We can sympathise but can help you so little.*

Frank had been an old and much respected member of the High Brooms Club and Institute, having served on the committee for a number of years, and was an old St Augustine's School boy. His funeral service was held at St Matthew's Church and he was buried at Southborough Cemetery with full military honours. His son Ronald was born on 21 December 1918, but died ten days later and was buried in his father's grave on 4 January 1919, as was Florence when she died in 1968. Because it is a Commonwealth War Grave with a military headstone, the family were not able to add details of the later burials.

George James Brown

Private S/1325 1st Bn, Queen's Own (Royal West Kent Regiment). Died 1 January 1915, age 37. Commemorated on the Ypres (Menin Gate) Memorial, Ypres, West-Vlaanderen, Belgium: Panel 45 and 47. Son of Louisa Mapson (formerly Brown), of 41 Bedford Road, Southborough and the late George Brown.

Dee's Directory 1915 lists L Brown, of above address, serving with the 4th Royal Sussex. Also, George's brother was killed in 1917, though he is not for some reason commemorated on the Southborough War Memorial. The Tunbridge Wells Advertiser of 30 November 1917 records the death (note that it refers to Mrs Clapson, whereas the CWGC record refers to Mrs Mapson): *Mrs Clapson, of 41 Bedford Road, has received news that her second son, Pte H Brown, Royal West Kent Regiment, was killed in action on October 4th. Joining the colours at the outbreak of the war, he went to France two years ago, and during that time he has been twice wounded. Pte Brown leaves a wife and four children, who are now residing at Plaxtol.*

Henry Brown

Private 266228 1st/12th Bn, The Loyal North Lancashire Regiment. Died 23 July 1919, age 37. Buried in Southborough Cemetery, England, Grave ref: 4.143. Husband of LV Rowswell (formerly Brown), of 73 Springfield Road, Southborough.

From the Courier, 25 July 1919: *We regret to record the death of Mr Henry Brown, of 73, Springfield-road, who died at the General Hospital on Wednesday, at the age of 36 years, from illness due to the effects of exposure while in the Army. He leaves a widow and two children, with whom the greatest sympathy is felt.*

Leonard Francis Bryant

Gunner 2042403, 314 Bty, 29 Searchlight Regt, Royal Artillery. Died Tuesday 10 December 1940, age 20. Son of Albert Edward and Agnes Ethel Bryant. Buried in Southborough Cemetery, England: Grave ref. Sec, 11 Grave 382.

From the Courier, 20 December 1940: *Much sympathy is felt for Mr and Mrs A Bryant, of 25, Manor-road, Southborough, whose son, Gunner Leonard Bryant, of a Searchlight Company, was killed recently on active service. The funeral took place at Southborough Cemetery on Monday with military honours, four of the late Gunner Bryant's comrades acting as bearers, officers of his unit also being present.*

Albert Reginald Bullen

Aircraftman 2nd Class 1628933. Died Saturday 24 October 1942, age 18. Buried in Southborough Cemetery: Grave ref. Sec. 11 Grave 386. Son of William John and Sarah Matilda Bullen, 52 Yew Tree Road.

Jerry Jones of High Brooms recalls the following details: Born in High Brooms, parents William and Matilda Bullen, with brothers Bill, Bob and Bernard, and sister Nellie, Bert attended High Brooms Boys' School and Tunbridge Wells Technical School. He then worked for Fremlins in their Monson Road office. He joined the Royal Air Force at age 18 and was killed when the hotel in Skegness in which he and many other 18 year olds were staying during their initial six weeks' training period was destroyed by a German bomb.

The Courier of 30 October 1942 reported that Albert had been a member of St John's Football Club, and was a sound inside-left.

Garnett Henry Butler

Private 12149 2nd Bn, Grenadier Guards. Died 20 September 1914. Buried in Guards Grave, Villers Cotterets Forest, Aisne, France: Grave ref: 15. Husband of AA Butler, of 114 London Road, Southborough. Although the CWGC record gives the initials GH, the Southborough War Memorial gives them as GJ. Dee's Directory for 1915 gives the address as Broomhill Lodge.

The CWGC information on the Cemetery includes the following: *To the north and north-east of Villers-Cotterets is the great forest through which the I Corps marched on 1 September 1914, and it was on that day the three Rearguard Actions of Villers-Cotterets were fought. In one of these actions the 4th (Guards) Brigade, covered the rear of the 2nd Division and the Irish Guards, the 2nd Grenadiers and the 3rd Coldstreams fought their way to Villers-Cotterets with some loss. The main action began about the "Rond de la Reine", a clearing on the main road now marked by the Guards' Memorial; the Guards' Grave is just south-west of the memorial on the south-east side of the main road. The Guards' Grave was made originally by the people of Villers-Cotterets and was put nearly into its present form by the Irish Guards in November 1914. The graves of four officers and one man of the Guards were moved here from Villers-Cotterets Communal Cemetery after the Armistice.*

V Carter

Private S/290549 60th Field Bakery, Army Service Corps. Died Friday 1 November 1918, age 33. Husband of Lily M Carter, of 30 Cambridge Rd, Bexhill-on-Sea, Sussex. Buried in Tunbridge Wells Cemetery, England: Grave Ref. C.14.280.

Southborough War Memorial gives Regimental details: RASC (MT). Kelly's Directory for 1917 lists only one Carter – Albert Carter, of 12 Edward Street, who may be a relative of V Carter. The Courier of 8 November 1918, which reports a number of deaths and the subsiding of the influenza epidemic at High Brooms, mentions that Pte V Carter was one of the victims buried that week, was brought home from Hastings, and given a military funeral.

William Edward Cass

Second Lieutenant Royal Flying Corps and General List. Died 4 June 1917, age 21. Buried in Southborough Cemetery, England: Grave Ref: 6.262. Son of John William and Elizabeth Jane Cass.

William's brother RH Cass enlisted in the Royal Navy in July 1915 and the Courier of 9 June 1916 reported: *Assistant Clerk RH Cass, RN of HMS Warrior was on board the Warrior in the Jutland naval battle last week, and arrived home last Monday, looking none the worse for his experiences. It will be recalled that the Warrior had to be abandoned during the fight, and Mr Cass was safely transferred to another ship, though his personal belongings were lost. Mr Cass, who is only 17 years of age, joined the Navy last July.*

The Courier, 8 June 1917, reports the death of William Edward Cass (named Albert Edward in error): *A most promising Army career was on Monday nipped in the bud by an accident of a distressing character, in which a youthful airman, Albert Edward Cass, whose home is at 60, Prospect-road, Southborough, met his end at the early age of 21 years under tragic circumstances. Described as a most capable aeronaut, and having secured his pilot's certificate on the previous Friday only, he flew on the day in question from his base to Southborough, and here, within a very short distance of his home, gave an exhibition which was witnessed by many hundreds. He "looped the loop" and performed other feats in clever fashion, and the spectators marvelled at his daring, which, however, was to have but a fatal ending, for he suddenly made a spiral dive and crashed to earth, nose-diving into the trunk of an apple-tree in the garden of Oakdale. He was found strapped to his machine in an unconscious condition, having sustained injuries which resulted in his death in Crowther's Hospital forty-five minutes later.*

That he was "swanking" because he was within reasonable distance of his home was the belief of many who witnessed the occurrence, but of this they may quickly disabuse themselves, for as it was elicited at the Coroner's enquiry, it was absolutely essential for airmen to accustom themselves to these feats; in fact, they have to perfect themselves in this direction before they become qualified to receive their pilot's certificate, and so be competent to compete with the enemy. The tragic end of this young and useful life will prove a great loss both to the Army and the country at large. He was the eldest son of the late Mr JW and Mrs Cass, and a younger son is a 2nd-Lieutenant in the Royal Navy. He was educated at Tonbridge School, and went to Canada in 1913. He joined up at the declaration of war, and came over with the first contingent of the RCHA as a Gunner. He was wounded in France in 1915, while a bombardier. He obtained a Commission in the Royal Flying Corps in August, 1916, and acted as an observer in France for some months. He returned to England to qualify as a pilot, and was gazetted about a week ago, after training in various parts of the Kingdom.

Leonard Cheesman

Private 6353968, Queen's Own (Royal West Kent Regiment). Died Thursday 12 August 1943, age 20. Buried in Syracuse War Cemetery, Sicily, Italy: Grave ref. I.E.5. Son of John and Ethel Cheesman, of Hastings, Sussex. Brother of J Cheesman of 12 Broomhill Park Road, Southborough.

From the Courier, 27 August 1943: *News has been received by Mr and Mrs John Cheesman, of 34, Colebrook-road, High Brooms, that their second son, Leonard, has been killed whilst on active service. He was attached to the Army Pay Corps. In a letter from his Commanding Officer, it was stated that Pte Cheesman died as a result of an accident in Sicily. Educated at High Brooms School, Pte Cheesman was employed by the Home and Colonial Stores in Camden-road before he joined the Forces two years ago. He would have been 21 on September 4th. Before the outbreak of war he served as a messenger to the First-Aid Post at Southborough. He was also a Probationer at High Brooms Toc H Group, and an active member of the Lodge of Good Templars.*

Pete Simmonds of High Brooms recalls that Tom Cheesman (possibly a relative?) and Roy Edwards, both from High Brooms, were captured at Dunkirk, marched back to Germany and survived the War.

James Chilton

Rifleman 471882 12th Bn, London Regt (The Rangers). Died Sunday 8 September 1918, age 22. Buried in Southborough Cemetery, England: Grave Ref. 4.138. Son of Richard and Emma Chilton, 23 Bedford Road, Southborough.

From the Courier 6 September 1918: *Mr & Mrs Chilton have received news that their son Rifleman J Chilton, London Regiment, has been seriously wounded and has been transferred to Southwark Military Hospital, East Dulwich. He enlisted three years ago under the Derby Scheme, and has served 19 months in France. He is an old Grosvenor School boy.*

W Chuter

Private 21121 2nd Bn Hampshire Regiment. Died 9 August 1916 age 19. Buried in the Potijze Chateau Wood Cemetery, Ypres, West-Vlaanderen, Belgium: Grave ref. A.27.

CWGC gives Pte Chuter's parents as Henry Thomas and Eliza Chuter, of 25 Muchland Road, New Eltham, London. He was born in the parish of St Barnabas, Tunbridge Wells, and enlisted there while resident in Southborough. His number was formerly 5658, Royal Sussex Regiment, his regiment given on the Southborough Memorial. The 1914 Kelly's Directory lists a Mrs J Chuter, 29 Nelson Road, Tunbridge Wells.

The CWGC website includes the following information on the Potijze Chateau Wood Cemetery which may relate to the circumstances of his death: *Potijze was within the Allied lines during practically the whole of the First Word War and although subject to incessant shell fire, Potijze Chateau contained an advanced dressing station. Potijze Chateau Wood Cemetery was used from April 1915 to June 1917, and three times in 1918. Among those buried in the cemetery are 46 officers and men of the 2nd Hampshire Regiment (Row A) and 19 of the 1st Royal Inniskilling Fusiliers (Rows E and F) who died in a gas attack in August 1916.*

Gordon Harvey Clarke

Pilot Officer 139592, 620 Squadron Royal Air Force Volunteer Reserve. Died 12 August 1943, age 32. Buried St Desir War Cemetery, Calvados, France: Grave ref. Coll grave VIII, 1-8. Son of Arthur and Lily Sophia Clarke (nee Harvey) of Southborough, Kent. ACA Pilot Officer Clarke took off from Chedburgh at the controls of Stirling III bomber BK713 QS-E, bound for Turin. The aircraft crashed at Mittainvilliers (Eure-et-Loire), 14km WNW of Chartres. The crew of eight were all killed and are buried at St Desir. (Name added to Southborough War Memorial post 2013)

Gordon Harvey Clarke's daughter Susan Davies, an alumna of Tunbridge Wells Grammar School, writes: *My father was born in 1910. His father Arthur was from Matlock in Derbyshire and was one of the early apprentices at Rolls Royce in Derby. He worked all his life for a wealthy man called Arthur Gibbs, first in Bramley, Guildford, and then in Tunbridge Wells. He maintained and drove the Bentleys and Rolls Royce cars all over the world. Lily Sophia was a head gamekeeper's daughter from Dorset who became ladies' maid to Lady Strachey. My father had a younger brother, Richard Clarke. Both were brought up in Bramley and attended Guildford Grammar School. My father matriculated in 1927 with Maths, Physics, English, French and History. He became an articled clerk with a firm of chartered accountants in London and qualified in 1933 with a position of 17th in the Institute of Chartered Accountants results. He worked for the firm of Herbert Hill and Co and became a partner. By then he and his family had moved to Tunbridge Wells.*

In 1936 he married my mother, Phyllis Marjorie Clara Smith of Tunbridge Wells (known as Marjorie). I was born in 1941 and my brother Timothy in 1942.

My father was a keen cricketer and golfer and smoked a pipe. I'm not sure when he volunteered for the RAF but think it was 1942. At the time of his death we were living at 21 Yew Tree Road Southborough. My maternal grandmother always spoke very highly of him and said he was a lovely kind man. He trained as a pilot at Cranwell and was also at Banbury. He and the crew were originally buried near where they crashed at Chartres but their remains were later transferred.

Stephen William John Collins

Sergeant 6345628, 6th Bn, Queen's Own Royal West Kent Regiment. Died Tuesday 17 November 1942, age 23. Commemorated on Medjez-El-Bab Memorial, Tunisia: Face 26. Son of Richard and Mary Sophia Collins (Kelly's Directory 1940 gives residence as 15 Western Rd); **husband of Kathleen E. Collins, of Barry, Glamorgan.**

The CWGC site includes the following: *In May 1943, the war in North Africa came to an end in Tunisia with the defeat of the Axis powers by a combined Allied force. The campaign began on 8 November 1942, when Commonwealth and American troops made a series of landings in Algeria and Morocco. The Germans responded immediately by sending a force from Sicily to northern Tunisia, which checked the Allied advance east in early December. The Medjez-el-Bab Memorial commemorates almost 2,000 men of the First Army who died during the operations in Algeria and Tunisia between 8 November 1942 and 19 February 1943 and who have no known graves.*

Edward Albert Cooke

Sergeant L/11009 4th Bn, Royal Fusiliers. Died 22 July 1916, age 37. Commemorated on the Thiepval Memorial, Somme, France: Pier and Face 8C, 9A and 16A. Born Bury St Edmunds, enlisted Hounslow. Husband of Janet Cooke, of Northfield Road, Speldhurst, Kent.

The CWGC information on the Thiepval Memorial includes the following: *On 1 July 1916, supported by a French attack to the south, thirteen divisions of Commonwealth forces launched an offensive on a line from north of Gommecourt to Maricourt. Despite a preliminary bombardment lasting seven days, the German defences were barely touched and the attack met unexpectedly fierce resistance. Losses were catastrophic and with only minimal advances on the southern flank, the initial attack was a failure. In the following weeks, huge resources of manpower and* equipment were deployed in an attempt to exploit the modest successes of the first day. However, the German Army resisted tenaciously and repeated attacks and counter attacks meant a major battle for every village, copse and farmhouse gained. At the end of September, Thiepval was finally captured. The village had been an original objective of 1 July. Attacks north and east continued throughout October and into November in increasingly difficult weather conditions. The Battle of the Somme finally ended on 18 November with the onset of winter.

Edna Lily May Cooper

Leading Aircraftwoman 2011598, Women's Auxiliary Air Force. Died Tuesday 29 August 1944, age 24. Buried in Moascar War Cemetery, Egypt: Grave Ref. 4.E.6.

Edna Cooper is listed under RAF on the Southborough War Memorial. From the Courier, 8 September 1944: *Much sympathy will be extended to Mr and Mrs Cooper, of 26, Wolseley-road, High Brooms, in the bereavement they have sustained in the death of their only daughter, LAC Edna Lily May Cooper, who contracted fever and died in the General Hospital, Cairo. They received notification on Friday. Edna joined the WAAFS in 1941 at the age of 21. In the early part of this year she volunteered for service overseas, and went out to Egypt in May. She will be missed by many friends, especially those who were with her when she attended High Brooms Girls' School. On leaving school she was employed as an assistant in one of the business establishments in the town. It was only a month ago that Mr and Mrs Cooper were notified that their youngest son, Flight-Sergeant Engineer Eddie Cooper, must be presumed to have been killed while on operations over Berlin a year ago.*

Edwin George Cooper

Sergeant 1219550, Flight Engineer, 35 Sqdn, RAF Volunteer Reserve. Died Tuesday 24 August 1943, age 20. Commemorated in Charlottenburg 1939-1945 War Cemetery, Berlin, Germany: Joint Grave 4.B. 22-23.

Edwin Cooper is buried in the same cemetery as **Cyril Wickens**. His elder sister Edna is mentioned above. Their parents William Herbert and Tamar Lily Cooper lived at 26,

Wolseley Road, High Brooms. An undated newspaper cutting featuring the photograph reproduced here reads:...*have received official notification that their son must now be presumed to have lost his life. He was reported missing last August from an operational flight over Berlin. Educated at the High Brooms Council School, Sergt Cooper was formerly employed at the Royal Kent Laundry. He joined the RAF in January 1941 after serving in the ATC.*

Clive Maier's research shows that: *Flight Engineer Edwin George Cooper took off at 2020 hours from Graveley in Halifax II bomber JB786 TL-G. The objective was Berlin. The aircraft was shot down, probably by the combined action of flak and night fighters, and crashed in the target area. Three of the crew of seven were killed and the others taken prisoner. Edwin Cooper lost his life in a massive raid on Berlin involving 727 aircraft – 335 Lancasters, 251 Halifaxes, 124 Stirlings and 17 Mosquitos. The Mosquitos were used to mark various points on the route. The raid was only a partial success. The Pathfinders were unable to identify the centre of Berlin and much of the attack fell outside the city. Despite that, civilian casualties were very heavy. Bomber Command lost 56 aircraft – 23 Halifaxes, 17 Lancasters and 16 Stirlings - amounting to 7.9% of the heavy bombers in the attack. This was the greatest single night's loss in the war up to that point.*

Percy William Cox (P Coppins)

Rifleman R/22320 1st Bn, King's Royal Rifle Corps. Died 3 May 1917. Commemorated on the Arras Memorial, Somme, France: Bay 7.

The website www.firstworldwar.com/onthisday gives the following for 3 May 1917: British attack east of Arras on 12 mile front, taking Fresnoy and break through "Hindenburg" switch at Queant: progress also at Cherisy and Fontaine Wood.

Percy is recorded on the Southborough War Memorial as Private P Coppins, and this may be explained by the following from the Courier, 25 May 1917, which perhaps indicates he was Mrs Coppin's son from a former marriage: *Mr and Mrs Coppin, 4, The Retreat, London-road, have been informed that their eldest son, Private P Cox, King's Royal Rifles, was killed on May 3rd. He joined the Army 18 months ago, and had been in France for eight months. Pte Cox was well known and respected and was an old Southborough football player. Sympathy will be extended to his wife and parents in their sad loss.*

Southborough War Memorial

William Alfred Crockford

Private M2/103947, RASC (MT). Died 4 April 1919, age 33. Buried in Southborough Cemetery, England: Grave ref. 3.312. Son of James and Catherine Crockford, of Southborough; husband of Edith Lucy Ralph (formerly Crockford, nee Cuthbert), of 5 Meadow Road, Southborough.

From the Courier, 11 April 1919: *Mrs WA Crockford (widow), Mrs J Crockford (mother) and Brothers and Sisters of the late Mr WA Crockford, 5 Meadow-road, Southborough, desire to return heartfelt thanks for kindness shown during his illness, for letters and messages of sympathy and for the many beautiful floral tributes.*

Arthur George Damper

Private 77158, 1st/7th Bn, Durham Light Infantry, (formerly 540970 1st/7th Bn, DLI). Died Wednesday 27 March 1918. Commemorated on Pozieres Memorial, Somme, France: Panel 68 to 72.

Arthur Damper joined the Royal Engineers (Kent Fortress), No 3 Coy, in 1912, No 726. It is possible he migrated, as Arthur George Damper re-appears in February 1915 as No 1725. He lived at 63 London Road, Southborough, the third of four sons. Later on, along with hundreds of Royal Engineers from all over the country he was transferred into Pioneer Battalions of the infantry, his being 1/7 Durham LI. He went to France in September 1917 and was killed when the Germans launched the 'Spring Offensive'. In this action Pioneer Battalions, RE and all manner of rear area men were put into the line and suffered heavy casualties.

www.firstworldwar.com/onthisday for 27 March 1918: *Germans advance on both sides of Somme in night attack, reaching Sally le Sec (12 miles from Amiens), but lose ground in British counter-attacks. Germans afterwards fail in attacks from Bucquoy to Rosieres and are checked near Lassigny and Noyon, but take Montdidier after rapid advance.*

Southborough War Memorial

William Davies

Driver 2235, 1st/3rd Kent Field Coy, Royal Engineers. Died on 28 October 1915 in the Hythe disaster. Commemorated on the Helles Memorial, Turkey: Panel 23 to 25 or 325 to 328.

Southborough Sappers of the Kent (Fortress) Royal Engineers includes the following: Joined the KFRE in the early part of 1915, having previously been employed by the Iron Foundry. Unusually his father was serving in France and his brother at Gallipoli. The family home was at 96 Auckland-road, Tunbridge Wells, and prior to his death by drowning he had a good job in the galleys on board HMT Scotian which took them to Lemnos.

Joachim Charles Dean

Sergeant 812230, Wireless Operator/Air Gunner, 150 Squadron, Royal Air Force (Auxiliary). Died Sunday 31 May 1942, age 29. Buried in Southborough Cemetery, England: Grave ref. Sec 11. Grave 384.

John V Phillips, whose mother-in-law is Joachim Dean's niece, writes: *Joachim Charles Dean was born on 26 January 1913, the eldest son to Albert and Alice Dean and older brother to Frederick and Muriel. Albert Edward Dean was born in 1888 in Melbourne, Australia, moving to England in about 1901 with his parents, who had emigrated there about 15 years previously. Albert was a painter and decorator like his father, trading in and around Southborough. Joachim was always referred to by the family as Charlie, and before the war he worked in a furniture shop in Southborough (possibly called Jones). He married a local girl, Eileen Muriel Reeves, on 25 December 1934 at St Matthews, High Brooms. She was from 26 Nursery Road, High Brooms, daughter of Marshall Reeves, a railway inspector.*

Family lore has it that Joachim was killed in a plane accident when a bomb became stuck in the bomb bay on returning from a mission. His death certificate shows that he died at Mottrams Farm, Faldingworth, Lincolnshire. The area was just farmland at the time, but later that same year the Ministry of Defence bought land at Faldingworth and constructed an RAF airfield. At the time of Joachim's death 150

Squadron was stationed at Snaith in Yorkshire, also known as Pollington, and 150 was the first operational squadron to use it, from July 1941 to October 1942. WR Chorley's *Bomber Command Losses* states that the flight took off from Snaith at 23.15 hrs on 30 May, and crashed at Mottrams Farm, Faldingworth, 4 miles SW of Market Rasen. The aircraft's target that night had been Cologne, and was part of the famous Thousand Bomber Raid. As well as being the largest number of aircraft which had ever been sent on one raid, there was also a record number of casualties, with 41 aircraft being lost.

Thomas Joseph Dean

Private 5372, 6th Bn, Royal Irish Regiment. Died 5 August 1917. Buried in Tyne Cot Cemetery, Belgium: Grave ref. X.C.21. Born in Holloway, London.

From the Courier, 31 August 1917: *Very great sympathy will be felt for Mr and Mrs Goldthorpe, 55, Springfield-road, in the sad news received of the death of their nephew, Signaller Tom Dean, 6th Irish Regiment. Deceased had been brought up by them from the age of five years. He joined the Royal West Kents at the outbreak of war, and was afterwards transferred to the 6th Irish. He was sent to France in October 1916. He will be remembered as a keen footballer, being liked and respected by all his mates and fellow players. The following letter was received by Miss Jeffrey from a Lieutenant: "Dear Miss Jeffrey, I take this opportunity to write to you and try to express to you my sympathy in your sad loss. I found your address on the back of an envelope with the request that all this wallet contained was to be forwarded on to you. There was nothing else in the pockets except a few francs, and I have enclosed value with a P.O. Now in tendering my deep sympathy to you, I am sure you would like to know that Thomas felt no pain, and was killed instantly along with the Major commanding his Company and two of his comrades. His death was sudden, and he was attending to his signalling duties at the time. He was a very popular fellow, both with his officers and men, and we all mourn his loss. As far as I know, there are no other effects; but should any turn up they will be sent on to you or his uncle. Trusting that the Lord will assist you to bear this great loss and also all his relations is the devout wish of his Platoon Officer. I should have told you that he is buried on the battlefield a few yards from where he was killed."*

Charles Henry Delves

Private 35733 2nd/4th Bn, The Loyal North Lancashire Regiment. Died 8 June 1918, age 44. Buried in Couin New British Cemetery, Pas de Calais, France: Grave ref. G.13. Son of John Delves, of 13 Danvers Road, Tonbridge; husband of Annie Turner (formerly Delves) of 21 Stewart Rd, High Brooms.

Alfred John Diggens

Private G/21138, 8th Bn, Queen's Own (Royal West Kent Regiment). Died 24 June 1917, age 21. Commemorated on Ypres (Menin Gate) Memorial: Panel 45 and 47. Eldest son of Alfred J and MA Diggens, of 17 Norton Road, Southborough.

From the Courier, 13 July 1917: *Private Alfred Diggens, Machine Gunner, RWK Regiment ... "your son was killed instantly by a shell which burst close beside him early in the morning of the 24th June ..." Educated at King Charles' School, where his father was master, he joined the Army about a fortnight after the outbreak of war and went to France in July 1916. He was only 17½ years when he joined and was previously at Martin and Windsor's, learning the motor engineering. During the time he was in France, he had some narrow escapes, and only a few weeks before he was killed he was blown a distance of 15 yards, but was unhurt ... a Lewis Gunner ... "very cool in the Line"... "a good sportsman, always representing both the Battalion and the Company at football and running" ... "he was the leading Gunner of our Company and he has done some good work. We laid him to rest in a nice little spot and we also erected a cross over him and we have made him quite a nice grave."* Sadly, since Private Diggens is commemorated on the Menin Gate Memorial, this grave was later lost.

In 2009, Frank Chapman wrote of Alfred's father, in the Kent and Sussex Courier's Warwick Notebook: *HEADMASTER'S 35 YEARS IN CONTROL AT SCHOOL Boys who wrote left-handed had no problem at King Charles School, Tunbridge Wells, 100 years ago. The Headmaster, Mr W A Diggens, experimented with ambidextrous training in 1904, issuing copy books to all classes for practice in left-handed writing. Mr Diggens, who retired in 1914 after 35 years as head, has been described as "a born organiser and stickler for details ... a thorough scholar, and skilful imparter of knowledge, a firm disciplinarian* but a humane and humorous master". Diggens' scripture lessons were said to be "full of profit and delight". He was "a mighty host" in English grammar, but "the slacker's most pitiless foe". His experimental introduction of shorthand and book-keeping classes as additional skills for his boys upset a school inspector who regarded them as "of little educational value".

GH Diton

Corporal 50932, 19th Bn, Middlesex Regt. Died 11 August 1917. Buried in Klein Vierstraat British Cemetery, Heuvelland, West-Vlaanderen, Belgium: Grave ref. III.A.17. (Southborough War Memorial gives initials as CH).

The photograph on the left of Corporal GH Diton was published in the Tunbridge Wells Advertiser on 24 August 1917. An undated press-clipping, which must surely refer to this man, but where the name is perhaps misspelt, reads as follows: *Mrs Ditch, of High Brooms, has received intimation from the War Office to the effect that her husband, Corpl GH Ditch, of the Middlesex Regiment, who was previously reported wounded on the 21st of July, but remained on duty, is now stated to have been killed in action on August 11th. Corpl Ditch is a Hastings man, and much sympathy will be felt for his widow.*

Sydney George Dixon

Stoker 1st Class C/SKX1609, HMS Sherwood, Royal Navy. Died Saturday 12 December 1942, age 20. Buried at St John's (Mount Carmel) Roman Catholic Cemetery, Newfoundland, Canada. (Plot NNE Corner, Grave 2.)

Syd, as he was known to the family, was born on 21 December 1921, at 63 Great Brooms Road, High Brooms, and lived there with his parents William and Florence Annie Dixon and his grandparents, Mary and Charles Gorringe. The family moved from there to Manor Road, Southborough and then later back to High Brooms, to No 7 Stewart Road, when Syd was 16. He had two sisters, Doris (4 yrs younger) and Beryl (11 yrs younger).

Syd went to High Brooms' Boys School (pictured above, 3rd from left, 2nd row back).

Apart from liking fishing, (see left, standing) Syd loved music, and he had music lessons from the age of eight. When he started work, at WG Harris & Co in Grosvenor Road, he used to come home at lunchtime and play the piano, and in the evenings and weekends, friends used to come round and listen while he played for them.

Syd signed up for the Royal Navy in May 1941. The last time he went off to sea, all the family went to wave him off at the bridge by the High Brooms brick-yard. His ship, HMS Sherwood, was moored off St John's, Newfoundland on 12 December 1942, when a party came on board asking if there was anyone who could play the piano. There was to be a Forces' dance that evening in the Knights of Columbus Hostel in St John's, and the pianist couldn't make it. Syd willingly volunteered, and during the evening, tragically, a fire began in which 110 people died, including Syd. He was buried in a military funeral at the Mount Carmel Roman Catholic Cemetery in St John's, where the majority of over thirty 1939-1945 War graves contain victims of the fire, most of the casualties belonging to the Newfoundland Regiment.

The family still have a copy of the newspaper article about the fire, given to them by Newfoundland Regiment soldiers billeted nearby in Bidborough at that time, who sent home for an issue for them.

Syd's sister Beryl also has a model of HMS Sherwood which Syd had been making for her before his death, and which he had mentioned in a letter home, "for Buzz". Syd would have been 21 on the 21st December, nine days after he died, and his parents were planning for a 21st birthday party for him on his next leave home, which sadly never came. Syd's mother and father found it terribly hard to come to terms with his death, as sadly is so often the case in war, because they had not seen his body, and its emotional impact on the whole family was, as expected, devastating. Whenever someone knocked on the door, or in the children's case, if their mother was out of the house for too long, it caused the family great anxiety over the following years. Beryl and Jim Fulker visited St John's in the mid-1990s, and saw not only Syd's grave, but also a memorial which had been erected recently to those who died.

Harold Bernard Dowdell

Private 4296, 1st/15th Battalion, London Regiment (Prince of Wales' Own Civil Service Rifles). Died Friday 15 September 1916, age 23. Commemorated on Thiepval Memorial, Somme, France: Pier and Face 13C.

Information from the website www.firstworldwar.com/onthisday gives the following campaign detail for 15 September 1916: *Great British advance (third phase) on the Somme, a six-mile front to depth of 2 or 3,000 yards. Flers, Martinpuich, Courcelette and whole of High Wood taken. New heavy armoured cars (Tanks) used for first time, north of Pozieres to east of Guillemont.*

Southborough War Memorial

Harold (pictured left, between two pals) was born on 7 December 1892. His great-niece believes he was studying agriculture locally before going to France, which may explain why he is named on the Southborough War Memorial, though his family was living in South London.

Harold's brother 2nd Lieutenant Ernest George Dowdell (Border Regiment, Special Reserve, 3rd Battalion attached to 8th Battalion, pictured below right) also fought and died in the War. He was awarded the Military Cross in April 1917 "for conspicuous gallantry and devotion to duty. He twice passed through a very heavy hostile barrage and obtained the most valuable information. He was wounded." (London Gazette, 17 April 1917). Ernest died on 22 March 1918 and is commemorated on the Arras Memorial, Bay 6.

The following moving extracts are taken from the diaries of their father, which also mention their brothers Will, Rob and Reg:

1916

Saturday 1 January - *Letter from Hospital from Ern saying had arrived there from the Front with Trench feet. With good luck could drop into Steamer for England!!*

Tuesday 4 January - *Letter from Ern: from 1st Hospital Birmingham where arrived on Saturday evening.*

Wednesday 5 January - *I saw Ernie at Hospital. The dear boy little altered in the long 6 months since we said goodbye at W'loo (26 June 1915).*

Saturday 8 January - *Harold went to B'ham.*

Sunday 9 January - *Harold going Rainham this week for firing. A prelude I fear to early departure for – where? East – or West?*

Thursday 13 January - *Wire from Will saying he was coming home on short leave.*

Friday 14 January - *Very little altered in face and form my dear Will arrived from somewhere at 6.30pm – A joyful meeting. Thank God, that within 10 days I have seen the dear boys back.*

Saturday 15 January - Will and Maggie went to Eastbourne. Harold had arrived earlier so we spent some time together. I wonder when, if ever, and where he and Harold will meet again. In truth the joy of having Will home does not prevent my being most depressed – perhaps especially because of the probability of dear affectionate Reg having to join the Army and thus wrecking all his hopes of speedy home making.

Tuesday 18 January - Went to Red Cross Hospital to see Ernie (Chamberlains House, Moseley nr Birmingham). Seemed v. well – On my reaching home heard that Reg was rejected on medical grounds and has armlet so one big anxiety lifted! Thank God!

Saturday 22 January - Harold home this evening. Advised leaving for Winchester next week.

Friday 28 January - Fear now that men rejected as medically unfit will have to be re-examined –

Tuesday 15 February - At 2pm said 'Good-bye' to Ern, who left for Winchester to report himself. Oh, these 'Good-byes'!!

Friday 3 March - PC from my dear Harold, written on Thurs, saying "We are leaving tomorrow morning at 7.30, "Good-bye". My dear, dear boy! The youngest! This afternoon went to my darling's grave and thought how her gentle loving spirit may be near to him.

Saturday 4 March - At 9.45 had letter from Harold dated Southampton this morning saying he was leaving tonight for France.

Sunday 5 March - Ern arrived home on 4 days' leave. Glad to think that last night was calm for Harold's crossing.

Tuesday 7 March - Rec'd Harold's first card from France.

Thursday 9 March - Rec'd Harold's first letter from France.

Friday 24 March - Spoke with Rob of the feared calling up of his Group of married men.

Friday 7 April - Ern arrived from Winchester as Best Man for Reg's wedding.

Saturday 8 April - Red Letter day, Reg and Dorothy's wedding. The sun shone brightly and all went well. God bless them.

Monday 1 May - Rec'd letter dated last Wed: from Harold saying he had gone to Hospital with something like fever.

Wednesday 3 May - On this day Harold expected to return to Trenches.

Saturday 6 May - Letter from Harold dated Wed: saying had gone to Hospital nearer base and was better.

Sunday 7 May - Very, very anxious about Rob. Almost certain he will have to join the Colours. His Appeal next Tuesday. Am not free from anxiety about Reg. He has to be re-examined probably.

Friday 12 May - Package to H. Letter from H of Tuesday last. Went to Rob's – He is exempted conditionally for 6 months, which is better than I feared.

Monday 22 May - Harold under date Friday spoke of being v. tired, and wanting rest.

Tuesday 23 May - Harold under date Sat. said going into Hospital.

Wednesday 24 May - Wrote Harold – but have his saying no use writing more until he rejoins his Battn. He is now in Hospital with Influenza -

Monday 29 May - A day of grief for the sorrows of others – Under date last Friday Harold writing from Hospital spoke in guarded terms of what he might not explain fully. He was v anxious about his friends. Today with his letter came one from Ern asking whether Harold was in Hospital on Sunday the 21st inst and telling a sad story of terrible fighting and losses at Vimy Ridge of the 20H Lnd – mentioning names known to him and Reg. Many of his own pals killed or taken prisoners! Wrote the three boys.

Thursday 1 June - Recd letter written on Sunday and Monday from Harold, from Hospital in French School.

Friday 2 June - Recd letter from Maggie from Alness, written on Wed: saying "Ships had gone out" and that up to that time she had spent 6 hours daily with Will.

Saturday 3 June- Disastrous news – Gt naval fight in wk: our losses were 14/16 vessels incl 3 Battleships and thousands of lives – on Wed afternoon – Germans appear to have suffered heavily, but not equal to our losses. It took place in the N. Sea. Now know why Maggie heard of ships going out – My dear Will! Later at 3.30 wire from Maggie "Will safe".

Tuesday 6 June - Another disaster: Ld Kitchener and his staff drowned by sinking of HMS "Hampshire" off the Orkneys – "A prince and a great man has fallen".

Sunday 11 June - Absorbingly interesting letter from Will to Ern telling of the gt battle in N. Sea and in part of the Boadicus share in it.

Friday 16 June - Letter from Harold dated 12th saying he was going to the Trenches again "quite unexpectedly".

Saturday 17 June - Letter from Ern: hopeful of getting two stripes soon.

Tuesday 5 September - Card from Harold dated 1st inst, saying he feared post cards would be soon the chief means of communication.

Wednesday 6 September - Letter from Harold dated last Sunday. The dear boy had dreamed the night before that he was home on leave and saw me looking v well "Unfortunately it was too short"!!

Monday 11 September - Rec'd card from Harold dated 7th inst.

Wednesday 13 September - Rec'd letter from Harold dated 7th inst.

Friday 15 September - Rec'd letters from Harold dated 10th and 11th. News today of gt advance by English – 6 miles extent – in West.

Monday 18 September - Rec'd Card from Harold dated 14th. "All well".

Saturday 23 September - Becoming anxious at not hearing from Harold.

Monday 25 September - Foreboding of evil to my Harold.

Tuesday 26 September - A miserable day. Heard at Somerset House that the 1/15th Regt was in Action on 17th. Promised I shd have card when any news of Harold and full of anxiety.

Wednesday 27 September - At L'pool, and back today, over-burdened with anxiety abt Harold.

Thursday 28 September - At 7pm a letter from the Front saying that my dear Harold was killed last week – no date nor place given. Was going over trench when shell killed him instantly - his friend (Donald) adds. He was buried and record kept. So is fulfilled the dread presentiment ever with me since we parted at Winchester. My dear dear boy. He has joined his mother, and I - !! Ern came until tomorrow evening.

Saturday 30 September - Many letters of sympathy. Echoes and shadows in the home. I am not stunned but overwhelmed. My dear brave loving cheerful, thoughtful boy. The saddest week for two years.

Wednesday 4 October - A letter from Will which gives me most serious concern. The dear boy is heart-broken regarding himself as responsible for Harold's death because he urged me to let him join the army before he was obliged. I wrote in reply a long letter of loving remonstration and denial.

Saturday 7 October – "Blow golden trumpets mournfully for all golden youth that fled, for all shattered hopes that lie, Where God has laid quiet dead, under an alien sky. But blow triumphant music too, Across world from sea to sea, Because the heart of youth was true, Because England proved to be Even greater than we knew."

Wednesday 11 October - A letter from dear Will confessing that he was wild and overwrought with grief when he wrote before.

Thursday 12 October - Do not like a letter from Ernie telling of having already received a final paper for Exam – much earlier than expected. Does this portend a speedy departure, and more heart-wringing farewells.

Thursday 19 October -
A. J. Donald
No 6 Ward
Royal Victoria Infirmary
Newcastle-on-Tyne
17/10/16
"The part of the Line we were in was HIGH WOOD".
Poor fellow – he is badly wounded.

Monday 23 October - Ernie writes that being one of those declared eligible he sits for the final Exam tomorrow instead of a month later.

Saturday 28 October - Ern: arrived. Having passed Exam will be at home until gazetted.

Monday 30 October - "The Times" had notice of dear Harold's death.

Tuesday 31 October - *Rec'd my letters posted on 12th and 13th Sept – which he never saw! Don't think I will open them, I am sure I wrote nothing that I would regret.*

Friday 3 November - *"The Times" had notice of Ern's appointment as II Lt. Sad news thru one of Rob's friends that dear Harold may have been buried with others of his Coy in one grave.*

Saturday 4 November - *War Office notice to Ern to report at Barrow on 10th inst. Much depressed by the thought that I may never know the exact spot where my dear boy lies.*

Thursday 9 November - *My dear Ernie leaving Euston tonight for Barrow. He may get leave before going out, but quite uncertain.*

Saturday 11 November - *Rec'd first letter from "II Lieut: EGD"! I write it with passionate pride.*

Friday 24 November - *Letter from Director of Graves saying the resting place of dear Harold not yet ascertained.*

Tuesday 5 December - *Ern returned tonight on leave until Thursday then to report to Victoria Station and to report at 9am at Folkestone to join the British Armies in France.*

Thursday 7 December - *Harold's Birthday. My dear Harold's birthday, and at 7.15 this evening said 'Good-bye' to my dear Ernie. God only knows whether we shall ever meet again... Ern said "farewell" at home. Reg went with him to Brockley Lane Station.*

Monday 11 December - *Rec'd first letter from Ernie on active service for second time. Simply headed "8 December 1916 – on way to base"! Evidently he crossed over to Boulogne on Friday night.*

Sunday 31 December - *On the last day of 1915 I wrote full of anxiety & sad forebodings – now I look back upon the saddest of days. My brave loving Harold has joined my darling, and added to my memories of love and trust. Sad, yet proud I am. My dear Harold!! My darling Rosa!! Are they really far off? The vacant places and the silent voices are with me, and more than these! The future is dark, but I don't believe the War will last much longer. While it lasts my daily prayer is for the safety of my dear boys Will and Ernie – still I am not free from apprehension regarding Rob and Reg. God help them all and help me to be worthy of all their unvarying love and confidence.*

1918

Saturday 19 January - *Letter from Ernie replying to mine re Service at St Paul's, and saying that though not far from High Wood he had not yet been able to get there.*

Monday 4 February - *Ernie arrived at 6.30 having left Boulogne at 12 midday. 14 days' leave. Had no idea of the dear boy's leave coming yet!*

Sunday 17 February - Ernie's last evening. Hymns at his suggestion: "Lord and all mankind", "Eternal Father", "For all the saints", "Oh God Our Help in Ages Past". "Mobilise" at 10.00. All clear 12.45. Very bad. Ernie left at 6.15 for France.

Monday 18 March - Rec'd Ernie of 15th. It seems to me in a graver vein than usual and I am almost apprehensive.

Thursday 21 March - Tonight news of German gt offensive in the West over 50 mile front.

Friday 22 March - Letter from Ern dated 19th. Have replied. The news from West so far is good. But who can help being anxious and nervous now that the titanic struggle seems nearing the climax.

Saturday 23 March - News not good. Germans claim 16,000 prisoners and 200 guns at W up to yesterday. Sir D. Haig's report v cautiously worded. Went to hear "Crucifixion" at City Temple.

Sunday 24 March - Sad news – Germans now claim 30,000 prisoners and capture of (Peronne? Browne?)

Monday 25 March - Still graver news. 'The Times' seriously discussing possibility of Amiens falling. I am getting anxious about Ernie.

Tuesday 26 March - Graver still. Germans taken Bapaume. Evidently fierce fighting round (? Langient?). Tea at Charterhouse with Mr Miles. Said "Goodbye" to my dear Will at Cannon St station 1pm en route to Dover. Heavy heart.

Wednesday 27 March - "Times" says "more hopeful last night", but consider next few hours critical.

Thursday 28 March - Our position still critical but reports more favourable from Sir D Haig. We appear to have successfully counter-attacked. Arrived Brighton in miserable weather – fitting!

Friday 29 March - Advance on French front towards Amiens.

Saturday 30 March - News rather more favourable. Huns appear to be held. General Fochs made General in Chief Command of Allied Forces.

Sunday 31 March - Huns reported 12 miles from Amiens. We appear to be doing better. E – Beautiful Intercession Service at Wesleyan Church. Spoke to a lad who in figure and age reminded me touchingly of my dear Harold. V anxious about Ernie.

Monday 1 April - At 10 o'c Rob came with WO wire. My dear brave son Ernie was killed on Friday 22nd. No details. I am overwhelmed. So all my apprehensions were justified! The news reached home at 4.30 y'day afternoon.

Tuesday 2 April - News that up to y'day (the 12th day of gt battle) Huns had failed to cut their way thro' to Amiens. With aching heart I reached home in afternoon. My desolate home.

Wednesday 3 April - Letter from Lt. Col Best telling how my dear boy was always in front of band of officers and men who fought like lions until he was shot through the head and killed instantly at 9 o'clock in morning of 22nd March.

Thursday 4 April - Reg had most pathetic letter from Muriel Westerton. For the first time I realise somewhat of the inexpressible sorrow which young hearts suffer – I should have liked this girl I am sure.

Friday 5 April - Came to Beckenham until morning. News still v grave from the West. My dear Will's grief pitiful.

Saturday 6 April - God help my dear boys Rob and Reg, in view of all the probabilities of calling up now imminent. So ends this terrible week in utter personal sorrow and grave national danger.

From letter to Reg, dated 3 November 1918, from Muriel Westerton, West Leigh, Formby:

"*He went, disdaining to stay in a soft job behind the lines while his fellows were in the Mill, and asked me to forgive him and perhaps be prouder of him ... he went and God has taken him from me.*"

John Edgar Dunn

Lance Corporal 43159, 5th/6th Battalion Cameronians (Scottish Rifles). Formerly 22906 King's Own Scottish Borderers. Died 3 October 1918. Buried in Villers Hill British Cemetery, Villers-Guislain, Nord, France: Grave ref. V.B.2

John Edgar Dunn was known as Jack by his family when a small boy. His parents were John Dunn and Laura Dunn (formerly Avis). They had three other children: Florence Mary, Laura Julia and Emily Charlotte Victoria. The family lived at 8 Bedford Road at the time of the 1901 Census.

From the Courier, 1 June 1917: *Mrs Dunn, 114 London-road, has received a letter from her only son, Private J Dunn, Camerons Scottish Rifles, saying he was wounded on May 16th in the left shoulder by a German sniper. He is in a Military Hospital at Manchester. Before joining the Army in February, 1916 he was a motor driver. He has been in France eleven months.*

The Courier, of 8 November 1918 reported Lance-Corporal Dunn's death and noted that he was a motor driver for Mrs Gillingham, Tunbridge Wells, before signing up.

T Dunn

Private G/8523, 3rd Bn, Royal Sussex Regiment Labour Corps. Died 14 November 1918, age 32. Buried in Grevillers British Cemetery, Pas de Calais, France: Grave ref. XVIII.A.6. Son of William and Isabella Dunn, of 19 Wolseley Road, High Brooms.

The Armistice was signed, and hostilities ceased, on 11 November 1918, which makes the death date of Private Dunn all the more poignant.

John Levi Johnson was listed as resident at the same address.

Percy Duvall

Private 23135 6th Bn, Queen's Own (Royal West Kent Regiment). Died 10 March 1918, age 34. Buried in Merville Communal Cemetery Extension, Nord, France: Grave ref: I.C.19. Born at Chiddingstone, Kent and enlisted at Maidstone. Husband of Edith Emily Duvall, of 129, London Road, Southborough.

The Tunbridge Wells Advertiser of 18 May 1917 published the photograph on left with the following information: *Mrs Duvall, 28 Taylor-street, has received a letter from her husband, Pte P Duvall, Royal West Kent Regiment, informing her that he is suffering from poisoned hands and legs. He joined the Army in October, went out to France in January this year, and was employed by Mr Ashby, butcher, before joining up.*

The Courier, 11 August 1916, had carried news of Percy's wedding: *At St Peter's Church, on Saturday last, wedding of Mr Percy Duvall, youngest son of Mr & Mrs Alfred Duvall, of 59, Springfield-road, Southborough, and Miss Edith Emily Goddard, of 131 London Road. The bride's dress was of silver-grey, and she wore a wreath and a veil. The bridesmaid was Miss Alice Goddard, sister of the bride.*

And of his death: *Private P Duvall ... died of wounds ... Mrs Duvall has received a letter from a Chaplain of the BEF ..."I buried him yesterday in the British Cemetery, Merville, and can assure you that his grave will be tenderly cared for"...* Private Duvall was home in January of this year for 14 days' leave.

Frederick Charles Eggleson

Sergeant 1333561, 463 Sqdn, Royal Air Force Volunteer Reserve. Died Sunday 2 January 1944, age 21. Son of Frederick James Eggleson and Louisa Kate Eggleson. Commemorated on the Runnymede Memorial, Surrey, England: Panel 228.

Chris McCooey's book *Voices of Southborough and High Brooms* records the following memory: *George Funnell used to live in Forge Road ... he remembers: One of my friends was Fred Eggleson who lived at 16 Forge Road. He was a good swimmer and used to go to the Monson Road Baths. After leaving St Peter's School he went as an assistant to Leslie Moon, the butcher. When he was eighteen, he joined the RAF and rose to become a flight sergeant; his brother Edward served in the Royal Navy and a third brother worked on the land. In December 1943, Fred and I went for a drink at the Beehive in Modest Corner. Two weeks later, on January 2nd, he went missing in action.*

From the website www.raafmuseum.com.au: *463 Squadron was formed in England on 25 November 1943 from personnel and aircraft allocated from 467 Squadron. The unit began operations immediately when six Lancasters participated in an attack on Berlin. As 463 Squadron received more aircraft and personnel the weight of its attacks steadily increased. Operating against strong German fighter opposition and well organised anti-aircraft defences, squadron missions often resulted in considerable losses. In the lead up to the Allied invasion of Europe, 463 Squadron attacked targets throughout France, concentrating on enemy batteries along the Normandy coastline. After the landings the Squadron flew an increasing number of daylight bombing missions as the German fighter defences became progressively disorganised and less effective. 463 Squadron regularly supported the activities of the RAF Film Unit, and aircraft assigned to this unique role were modified with cameras mounted in their front turret and near the crew access door.*

Clive Maier's research shows that Sgt Eggleson took off from Waddington in Lancaster 1 bomber JO-Q bound for Berlin. The aircraft and its crew of seven were lost without trace.

William Saunders, who is also commemorated on the Southborough War Memorial, and who perished in the Hythe disaster of 28 October 1915, also lived at 16 Forge Road.

Roland Eldridge

Private 1945, 19th Bn Australian Infantry, AIF. Died 11 November 1916, age 31. Buried at Heilly Station Cemetery, Mericourt l'Abbe, Somme, France: Grave ref V.E.3. Son of Ellen Eldridge of 21 Forge Road, Southborough.

Clive Maier's research reveals that Roland Eldridge emigrated to Australia at the age of 21 and worked as an agriculturist at Surrey Hills, Sydney, New South Wales. He had served with the Kent Volunteers in England. He embarked at Sydney on HMAT A54 Runic on 9 August 1915.

From the Courier, 24 November 1916: *Mr and Mrs Eldridge of Forge-road have received the following letter from a Chaplain of the Australian Forces:* "I am very sorry to say that your boy was brought in here last night hopelessly wounded. He was unconscious, and did not live long after leaving the ambulance. I have just buried him in our little cemetery, where so many of our brave lads lie. His grave will be marked with a cross." *Private R Eldridge is the fourth son of Mr and Mrs Eldridge, and he joined the 19th Battalion Australian Forces in December 1914. He was twice wounded while serving in the Dardanelles. It is a coincidence that he should have been killed four days after Sergeant Parker (whose death was reported last week) with whom he went to Australia about seven years ago. Mr and Mrs Eldridge have three other sons serving in the Army.*

Arthur Thomas Ellis

Private 204008, 9th Bn, Norfolk Regiment. Died 8 October 1918. Commemorated on the Vis-En-Artois Memorial, Pas de Calais, France: Panel 4.

From CWGC information on the Memorial: *This Memorial bears the names of over 9,000 men who fell in the period from 8 August 1918 to the date of the Armistice in the Advance to Victory in Picardy and Artois, between the Somme and Loos, and who have no known grave. They belonged to the forces of Great Britain and Ireland and South Africa; the Canadian, Australian and New Zealand forces being commemorated on other memorials to the missing.*

Southborough War Memorial

Information from the website www.firstworldwar.com/onthisday gives the following campaign detail for 8 October 1918: *Western Front: Great Allied (3rd and 4th British Armies; 30th USA Division and French) three-mile advance on St Quentin-Cambrai 20-mile front; over 10,000 prisoners and 150 guns. North of Scarpe British take Fresnes-Rouvroy line.*

From the Courier, 1 November 1918: *Mrs Ellis, of 30, Charles-street, has received news that her husband, Private AT Ellis, was killed in action on the 8th October. He was the fourth son of Mr and Mrs John Ellis, of 11, Napier-road, and was formerly employed by Mr Adams, farmer, of Southborough. He was an old St Mark's School boy.*

Arthur Ellis died on the same day as **Charles Edward Malpass**, who is also commemorated on the Southborough War Memorial.

E A Ellis

Edward Alexander Ellis, Private G/4345, 8th Bn, Queen's Own (Royal West Kent). Died 26 September 1915. Commemorated on the Loos Memorial, Pas de Calais, France: Panel 95 to 97.

The Courier of 29 October 1915 carried the photograph on left and report: *News has been unofficially received of the death in action of Private EA Ellis, 8th Queen's Own (Royal West Kent Regiment), whose home was at 47, Springfield-road Southborough. The news was received from Pte L Drew of the 2nd Battalion Coldstream Guards, who found the body while acting as one of a search party, and identified Pte Ellis by two letters found on him. In one Pte Ellis had written to his mother saying how well he was in health, and the other was one that Pte Ellis had received from his mother. Pte Ellis joined the Army last November, and was formerly employed at Penshurst, and previous to that was with Messrs Harrison, seed merchants, of Maidstone, for six years. He was 24 years of age. We have to record a very sad sequel – the death of his mother on Sunday last. Mrs Ellis, who was aged 60, was in ill-health, having had a stroke some few months ago, and was naturally greatly distressed at the news of her son's death. She was out on Friday last, and was taken ill late in the same evening, and passed away on Sunday about mid-day, her death having no doubt been accelerated by the shock of her son's death. The funeral took place on Wednesday. Deceased was only at the Front seven weeks.*

Confusingly, a later Courier report says: *Pte EA Ellis, No 4345, D Company, 8th, Royal West Kent Regiment, of Southborough, who, as we stated two months ago, was reported killed in the Battle of Loos, has since been reported wounded. This later report was received from the Infantry Records Office, Hounslow, by his brother, some weeks ago, and he is unable to hear anything further. This report gave the initials and number wrongly, describing him as Private JH Ellis, 14345. Mr P Ellis, of 47 Springfield-road, Private Ellis's brother, would be glad to hear from anyone who could give any information of his brother, or could identify the Pte Ellis described in the second communication, should this refer to someone else.*

There are two men under the name of Private EA Ellis recorded by the CWGC in the Royal West Kent Regiment. The other named is:

EA Ellis, Private G/1816, 1st Bn, Queen's Own (RWK) who died on 3 October 1917. Buried in Zantvoorde British Cemetery, Zonnebeke, West-Vlaanderen, Belgium: Grave VI.G.2.

W J Ellis

Private W Ellis, 20084, 1st Bn Queen's Own (Royal West Kent Regiment). Died 1 June 1918. Buried in Tannay British Cemetery, Thiennes, Nord, France: Plot 4, Row A, Grave 9.

Arthur Emery

Private 65357, 4th Bn, Royal Fusiliers. Died 28 May 1920, age 35. Buried in Southborough Cemetery, England: Grave ref 1.295. Husband of Charlotte Emery, of 22 Meadow Road, Southborough.

The Courier, 5 February 1915, reported the following, which may refer to Private Emery's brother: *Saddler J Emery, of the Meerut Division, Ammunition Column, RFA, Indian Expeditionary Force, has been in England this week on seven days' leave from the Front, and visited his brother, Mr A Emery, at 46 Meadow Road. Saddler Emery went to India seven years ago, and went straight to the Front from India.*

From the Courier, 4 January 1918: *Private A Emery arrived home on Christmas Eve after serving for twelve months in France. He joined the Buffs in August 1916 and was transferred after reaching France in December 1916.*

From The Courier, 4 June 1920: *We deeply regret to have to record the death of Mr Arthur Emery, of 22, Meadow-road, Southborough, which took place last Friday morning, at the age of 35 years. Mr Emery had been in poor health for several months and had to take to his bed some six weeks ago. He appeared to be progressing favourably, until he had a relapse last Tuesday week and passed away on Friday. He came to Southborough from Chatteris, Cambs, seventeen years ago, and the whole of the time, with the exception of the time he was on military service, he has been a valued employee of Mr A Dee, at the Reliance Press. He served two-and-a-half years in the Army, in the "Buffs" (East Kent Regiment) and the Royal Fusiliers, over two years of his service being in France, where he saw much fighting, and after the Armistice he went into Germany with the Army of Occupation and remained there until his demobilization in February, 1919. He was well-known in sports circles and was particularly indentified with football during the whole of his residence in the town, being Captain of Southborough Reserves for several years. He gave up active participation in football some years ago and continued a staunch supporter of the Club and a member of the Committee. He served on the Committee of the Cricket Club and on the Sports Committee, and was also a member of the Kent RE Old Comrades' Club. Quiet and unassuming, he was highly regarded by all who knew him. He leaves a widow and one daughter, Gladys. Mourners included his sisters Mrs WS Muggridge and Mrs Skinner.*

Alan Douglas Mead Emmer

Captain 129418, 8th Bn, Royal Fusiliers (City of London Regiment). Died Wednesday 22 September 1943, age 27. Buried in Salerno War Cemetery, Italy: Grave ref. VI.A.6. Son of Andrew Frank and Emily Emmer, of 71 Yew Tree Rd, Southborough; husband of Violet Nina McIntosh Emmer, of Salisbury, Southern Rhodesia.

From the Courier, 22 October 1943: *News has been received of the confirmation of the death in action of Captain ADM Emmer, Royal Fusiliers, only son of Mr and Mrs AF Emmer, of "Windies", Southborough. Capt Emmer was educated at Rosehill School, Tunbridge Wells, from which he went to Bedford Grammar School. After passing out of Bedford with distinction he joined the staff of the National Provincial Bank. He was an all-round sportsman and was very popular among his friends in Tunbridge Wells and Southborough. He was married only a few months before his death.*

William Henry Everest

Lance Corporal WH Everest of the Buffs (East Kent) is commemorated on the Southborough War Memorial. William Everest enlisted at Canterbury from Southborough in 1912 and was given the

Army No. L/9985. He joined the 1st Battalion of the Buffs, and served in France from 1914 as a Lewis Gunner. William was wounded four times (reported in the Kent & Sussex Courier) and killed in action on 15 April 1917, aged 22.

William was born at 1 Holden Road, Southborough, to Henry Everest, Upholsterer, and Annie Everest née White. He had three brothers, Edward, Frederick, and Alfred, and three sisters, Beatrice, Gertrude and another who died in her teens. His father Henry Everest had premises in Holden Road with a workshop at the back, and later he had a shop at the corner of London Road and Holden Park Road (opposite what is now Costcutters). The family was probably living at 86 or 88 Springfield Road at the time of his death, having exchanged houses with the Valentine family who lived next door.

All William's brothers were in the Army; his brother Frederick (father of AJ Everest) was one of six men who survived his company. Frederick was at school at St Peter's, and it is likely William attended there too. When they started school, they were living in cottages at the top of Hand & Sceptre Hill, then next to the smithy and the wheelwright's. Fred was in the Queen's Own Royal West Surreys, (No 60735, MM) and was fighting only a few hundred yards away from his brother when William was killed, but their mother knew of William's death before Fred, such was the confusion in communications at the time. Fred, like so many of his generation, never spoke of his wartime experience to his family.

However, there is no record of William's death at the National Archives, and he has no known grave. He was known by the family to have left home and joined the colours under an assumed name but the mystery as to why he did so has never been fully resolved by them. His nephew Mr AJ Everest, who was born and bred in Southborough, being resident in Elm Road and Kibbles Lane before moving latterly to East Sussex, believes that his uncle may have changed names with a resident of High Brooms who joined up at the same time and who was called W Dunnings. He has a letter in his family papers from Capt WR Birrell MC, giving the address In the Field and dated April 19th 1917, sent to Mrs H Everest, which reads as follows: *It is with the deepest feeling of sorrow that I inform you of the death of your son No. 9985 L/C Everest, who was killed in action on April the 15th 1917. We lose by his regrettable decease one of the few of us of the remaining Expeditionary Force, who came forward so nobly at their country's call, and* who have laid down their lives ungrudgingly with heroic self-sacrifice. Your son who set an example to all was one of our keenest and most efficient Lewis Gunners, and was admired by all. The Commanding Officer, the Commissioned Officers, the Non-Commissioned Officers and men of the First Battalion The Buffs tender you their sincere sympathy at your sad bereavement. Captain and Ajutant WR Birrell, 1st Buffs, The Buffs.

The Courier of 4 May 1917 reported (note the typographical error in death date in penultimate sentence): *News has been received by Mrs Everest, 86 Springfield-road, that her son, L-Corporal W Everest, 1st Buffs, was killed in action on April 15th. He had been wounded four times before, and it is a coincidence that his last wound should have been received on April 16th, 1915, and he was killed on August 15th of this year. He joined the Buffs in 1912, and has been in France since September 1914, all the time being spent in the thick of all the hard fighting.*

Mr AJ Everest has been in correspondence with the Commonwealth War Graves Commission, who said that although under normal circumstances the details given would be more than sufficient for them to trace the casualty, they do not have a Lance Corporal W H Everest in their records. However they do have a Lance Corporal W Dunnings, whose details correspond with WH Everest, in Army Number, and date of death, birth place, enlistment details etc but not with the surname. W Dunnings is buried in Plot 3, Row A, Grave 7 in St Patrick's Cemetery, Loos, Pas de Calais, France. Furthermore, a local Tonbridge collector of Kent war memorabilia has the death plaque of William Dunnings, 1st East Kent Regiment, L9985. The CWGC concede that it was often the case that many servicemen during the First World War enlisted under different names, and they have contacted the Ministry of Defence Army Records Centre re the records of WH Everest and WH Dunnings to see if some concrete evidence could be provided about their identities, but their records were amongst those destroyed by enemy air action during the Second World War.

The family papers include, as well as the above letter, a death certificate for WH Dunnings, but none for WH Everest. So, sadly, given that no death certificate seems to exist for WH Everest, the family have to accept that while his remains are most likely to be those lying in the grave marked W Dunnings in St Patrick's Cemetery, the CWGC cannot at this moment in time see their way to changing the name on the tombstone, or listing William Everest's name amongst those Soldiers who Died in the Great War.

W F M Ewen

Private 137229. Machine Gun Corps. Died 22 February 1919, age 19. Buried in Southborough Cemetery, England: Grave ref: 4.230. Son of Mrs Alice Ewen, of 62 Springfield Road, Southborough.

From the Courier, 6 September 1918: *News has been received by Mr and Mrs Ewen of 57 Springfield Road, that their only son, Private W Ewen, Machine Gun Corps, was very seriously wounded on August 23rd, and was admitted to the General Hospital, Rouen. Later news says that he has been sent to England, and is in the 5th Southern General Hospital at Portsmouth. He is only just turned 19 years of age, and before joining the Army in June 1917, he was in the Kent (Fortress) Cadets for some years. He has been in France since April.*

And from the Courier, 9 March 1919: *The funeral took place on Friday last, at the Cemetery, with full military honours, of the late Pte W Ewen, Machine Gun Corps, only son of Mr and Mrs Ewen. Pte Ewen was seriously wounded on the 23rd August last year, and has been in Hospital ever since. He was awaiting another operation, but caught a chill and died from the effects of his wounds, combined with weakness, at the 5th General Hospital, Portsmouth, on February 22nd. The coffin, covered with the Union Jack, was conveyed from the house to the Cemetery on a gun carriage. The chief mourners were his father, mother and sister.*

Harold Fenner

Driver KF 2230, 1st/3rd Kent Field Coy, Royal Engineers. Died 28 October 1915 in the Hythe disaster, age 17. Commemorated on the Helles Memorial, Gallipoli Peninsula, Turkey: Panel 23 to 25 or 325 to 328. Son of Mrs E Fenner, 23 High Brooms Road.

Harold Fenner attended the Royal Victoria School, and before signing up worked at the Co-operative Society in Silverdale Road, High Brooms. He is also listed on the Tunbridge Wells Memorial and in St Mark's Church. GA Fenner, at the same address, was listed in August 1914 as serving with the Royal West Kent Territorials.

Walter Harold Fisher

Flying Officer 123937, 227 Sqdn, Royal Air Force Volunteer Reserve. Died Monday 26 April 1943, age 35. Commemorated on the Alamein Memorial, Egypt: Column 268. Son of Walter Henry and Elizabeth Fisher, of Tonbridge, Kent.

From the Courier, 7 May 1943: *Pilot Officer W Harold Fisher, son of Mr and Mrs WH Fisher, of 10, High-street, Tonbridge, has been reported missing, believed dead, during air operations in April. Pilot Officer Fisher, together with Sergeant Pilot R Harvey, who is also missing, formed the crew of a Beaufighter and went together to the Middle East. Pilot Officer Fisher joined the RAF in November 1940 as a volunteer, and trained as observer-navigator and also took a radio operator's course. He went to the Middle East in 1942. He was manager of the Southborough branch of his father's drapery business, the main establishment being at Tonbridge. An Old Juddian, he was a member of the Southborough Cricket Club and the Tunbridge Wells Hockey Club, besides being treasurer of the Shipbourne-road Boys' Club, on several occasions joining them at their holiday camps. Pilot Officer Fisher's brother, Flight-Lieut. David Fisher, DFM, is at present serving in England, being attached to Bomber Command.*

The RAF website gives the following information about 227 Squadron: *No 227 Squadron was formed on 1 April 1918 at Pizzone from part of No 67 Wing. Its basis was No 499, 550 and 551 flights of the Caproni Squadron established by the RNAS before it was absorbed by the RAF. Intended to become a day bomber unit, it did not become operational before the end of the war and was disbanded on 9 December 1918.*

The number 277 appears to have been allotted to a detachment of Beaufighters in the Middle East whose aircrews were absorbed by No 272 Squadron on 27 June 1942. A ground echelon arrived at Aqir to service the Halifaxes of No 10 Squadron but on 7 September No 10's detachment amalgamated with those of Nos 76 and 462 Squadrons and the 227 Squadron ground echelon was dispersed.

On 20 August 1942, a detcahment of Beaufighters of No 235 Squadron at Luqa Malta was designated 227 Squadron and was operational immediately. After being engaged in escorting Beauforts and attacking enemy shipping from Malta, the squadron moved to Egypt and Libya for sweeps over the Eastern Mediterranean from March 1943. In August 1944, it moved to Italy but was renumbered 19 Squadron, South African Air Force on 12 August 1944.

Gavin Ewart's ironic Second World War poem, *When a Beau Goes In*, is on the subject of the loss of a Beaufighter.

Harold Arthur Fletcher

Private 10599, 2nd Bn, Royal Scots Fusiliers. Died Friday 19 July 1918, age 25. Buried at Caestre Military Cemetery, Nord, France: Grave ref. I.D.IA. Son of Mrs Kate Fletcher, of Southborough.

The Tunbridge Wells Advertiser, 25 September 1914 names Harold Fletcher, Royal Scots Fusiliers, as resident at 36 Taylor Street. From the Courier, 30 July 1915: *Pte Fletcher, of the Royal Scots Fusiliers, who has been in hospital wounded, has been spending a few days' leave with his mother at Southborough before returning to France. Pte Fletcher, who enlisted five years ago, in his father's old Regiment, has seen service in India and South Africa, and came with his battalion to France last September. He has been through all the heavy fighting with the glorious Seventh Division, and has been several times wounded, but fortunately, only slightly, until the attack at Neuve Chapelle, when he was severely wounded in the back and legs by shrapnel. From a slight bayonet wound to the unpleasant experience of being gassed, Pte Fletcher has had his share of German "frightfulness", and had several narrow escapes before the shrapnel enforced his retirement from the firing line. Pte Fletcher considers his escape on so many occasions just a matter of wonderful luck, as he has had comrades on each side of him shot down. When he was wounded he remained a couple of days in a corn-field which divided the British and German trenches, and he considers it luck that he had this shelter, as the Germans do not hesitate to finish off the British wounded with the bayonet. They even settle their own wounded in the serious cases.*

Pte Fletcher's Division has been chiefly facing the Prussian Guards, who are most determined fighters, although he has fought at various parts of the British lines and has also faced the Saxon Regiments, who are not so bad as the Prussians. The Christmas Day truce, when both sides came out of the trenches, was the only interlude in the fighting, which has been most desperate. In fact, the temper of the British troops is hardening against their foe, owing to the many atrocities of which they are guilty. However, Pte Fletcher thinks the Germans have done their worst. If they could not break through last Autumn, when the British were nothing like as well prepared as they are now, and suffered terrible losses at the hands of the Germans, the enemy is certainly not going to break through now. Hitherto, the Germans have in many details been much better equipped than the British, but now the opposing forces are more on even terms, and our men can more than hold their own. As regards the gas, Pte Fletcher had his respirator stained a greenish hue by the terrible fumes, and he states that we have now got the mastery of the gas by our precautions. There is no doubt that, by the changes in the wind, the gas often did as much damage in the German lines as in our own. We have not retaliated with gas. Pte Fletcher had, among other souvenirs, a fragment of a gas shell, and he described the peculiar way in which the green cloud of gas expanded until it settled in a dense fug on the trenches. The respirators are, however, proving efficient.

In the fighting at Ypres, Pte Fletcher had 21 days in the trenches of continuous fighting without rest, owing to the overwhelming forces which the Germans brought to the attack. They fight in close formation, and their firing means a denser hail of bullets than the English fighting in open formation. But the English are the best shots, and the British artillery finds its mark better than the Germans. Our artillery does not waste ammunition, and its shooting is magnificent. Pte Fletcher had his officer shot just in front of him in the heaviest fighting, and he describes the emotion of General French at the sight of the decimated British Battalion when they marched back past him. Pte Fletcher saw Lord Kitchener at the famous conference, and also Mr Asquith, and he speaks of the great confidence of the British Army in Lord Kitchener. Private Fletcher has also frequently seen the Prince of Wales, and described how popular he is, particularly as he fully shares the day's hardships and dangers. The Prince is also experiencing the physical benefits of soldiering, and will come back a stronger man than when he went out. The work of the Flying Corps is also spoken of with enthusiasm by Pte Fletcher. The men go up in the midst of bursting shells, and their reconnaissance work has saved hundreds of British lives.

The coolness of the drivers of the Red Cross ambulances under fire is also gratefully acknowledged. The wounded are driven with the greatest care along roads full of holes from "Jack Johnsons", and the drivers in the heaviest fire are careful of the sufferings of the wounded men in their charge. The German disregard of the Red Cross is very noticeable. British hospitals are shelled without the least excuse. Where they are the only buildings in a district, and distinguished by the red flags by day, and the red light by night, the Germans still shell them, and it is nothing uncommon for the wounded to be moved to the cellars. The refugees fleeing from the Germans are relieved at the hospitals, and the British soldier is always ready to share his food with them. The stories they tell of German cruelty are really terrible. The clever dodges resorted to in warfare by the Germans were also described by Pte Fletcher, and one of the most remarkable was the following:-

For some time a German sniper had been very troublesome, and could not be located. It was at last found that he was painted green all over, of a tint not distinguishable from the field in which he had stationed himself. In the midst of all dangers the British soldier retains his sense of fun. He has named his trenches and dug-outs after London streets, and they have quite a Metropolitan geography. The long stay in the trenches has resulted in their being made much more comfortable and "home-like". Sandbags are particularly welcome, and too many cannot be sent out.

The Courier of 6 September 1918 reports of a younger brother, pictured left: *News has been received that Private B Fletcher, whose mother resides at 36 Taylor-street, has been in Hospital in France as the result of being gassed. Private Fletcher was well-known in Southborough, and joined up in the early days of the war in the Royal Scots Fusiliers, being a machine-gunner. Before joining up he was on the staff at the "Kent and Sussex Courier". Mrs Fletcher has already suffered the loss of her eldest son in France.*

It seems likely, though no house number is given, that the following report refers to another son, pictured below:

News has been received by Mrs Fletcher, Taylor-street, that her youngest son, Rifleman Victor Fletcher, POR, was wounded at Cambrai on December 2nd. He was taken to the South African General Hospital, France, and is shortly expecting to be sent to England. He joined the PO Rifles in August, 1916, and went to France in December. Before joining he will be remembered as having been telegraph boy at Southborough Post Office, afterwards being promoted to postman at Tunbridge Wells.

Stanley Nelson Follington

Able Seaman Stanley Nelson Follington, J/51664, HMS Lord Clive, Royal Navy. Died 17 October 1918, age 22, of pneumonia. Son of Mr & Mrs Follington of 32 Park Road, Southborough. Buried in Haslar Royal Naval Cemetery, Hampshire, England: Grave ref. E.34.12.

HMS Lord Clive was launched on 10 June 1915 and remained in service until she was sold for scrapping in October 1927. She and another Monitor class vessel, General Wolfe, were armed with 18 inch (457mm) guns with the longest range in the Navy.

From the Courier, 25 October 1918: *Great sympathy will be felt for Mr and Mrs Follington, Modest Corner, in the sad death of their youngest son, Able-Seaman Follington. He joined the Navy a little more than two years ago, and he has been to West Africa for two years, afterwards returning to Gosport, where he died on October 17th at the Royal Naval Hospital, Haslar. He was only 21 years of age.*

His mother travelled to see him while he was ill with pneumonia, and was with him until he passed away on the 17th.

John Henry Fountain

Stoker 1st Class, P/KX 602676, HMS Capel, Royal Navy. Died Tuesday 26 December 1944, age 19. Son of Charles and Bertha Sarah Anne Fountain, 13 Elm Road. Commemorated on Panel 85, Column 3 of the Portsmouth Naval Memorial, England.

John Fountain was born in 1925 and attended Southborough Church of England Boys' School from 1933 – 1939 (1939 photograph of St Peter's School Class, shows, in back row, John fourth from right, and his friend George Rowswell, far right). The Head Master was Mr HW Lyman, who lived in Doric Avenue, Southborough. After they left school in 1939, George Rowswell did not see John again until they met when both were on leave together some time in 1943. George had gone on from school to the Royal Navy Electrical College, Marlborough, and Vickers Armstrong in Canada. He recalls that Mr Lyman was a wonderful Headmaster, and that many boys found, when they came to take their service exams, that they scored higher than many others who had had the benefit of a private education, such was the quality of that provided by the school at St Peters'.

John received his Royal Navy training, after signing up, at HMS Duke, Great Malvern, Worcestershire, as a Stoker 2nd Class. His posting was to the Flower Class Corvette HMS Capel. John, George recalls, fell in love with a young lady from Devonport, and brought her home to get engaged early in 1944. He and George were both on a short leave at this time, and met only briefly. It would have disappointed the Admiralty to know that John and George both knew where they were next off to, as well as the convoy number! They made arrangements to meet in Gibraltar at the Trocadero Bar when possible, they shook hands, and that was the last time they saw each other.

The Flower class corvettes were the mainstay of convoy escorts, lightly armed with a single 4" (102mm) gun on the forecastle, and light anti-aircraft weapons amidships (known as Pom Poms). They carried 72 depth charges which were fired from four launchers or dropped over the stern from 2 rail tracks. Their top speed was 16.5 knots. HMS Capel had been laid down by Boston Navy Yard on 11 March 1943 and launched as DE-266 Wintle on 22 April, but never commissioned into the US Navy, being renamed HMS Capel after sent to Britain on lend/lease on 16 August.

Commander FJ Walker, on HMS Starling, was the Escort Commander in January 1944. He sank six U boats in the Bay of Biscay. He was greatly admired by those who sailed under his command. Sadly he died in 1944 and was buried at sea. During Gibraltar convoys air cover was normally given by coastal command Liberators, but the U boats worked in packs and preferred to attack at night from the surface, then submerge where they could not be detected.

HMS Capel was torpedoed and sunk by U-486 north-east of Cherbourg, France, commanded by Oblt Gerhard Meyer. The website www.uboat.net gives the following information about U-486: *On Christmas Eve 1944, U486 torpedoed the SS Leopoldville in the English Channel just 5 miles from the port of Cherbourg, France. The troopship was transporting 2235 American soldiers from regiments of the 66th Infantry Division. The ship finally sank 2½ hours later. Everything that could went wrong; calls for help were mishandled, rescue craft were slow to the scene and the weather was unfavourable. 763 American soldiers died that night, making this the worst loss an American Infantry Division suffered from a U-boat attack during the war.*

The Allied authorities were embarrassed by the incident and decided to bury the case. Many loved ones were told the men were missing in action although they were already dead by then, later to be classified as killed in action. It was not until 1996 that the files were opened to the public.

U486 had not said her last word, as she sank the British frigates HMS Affleck and Capel only two days later in the same area before returning on 15 Jan, 1945 to Bergen, Norway. U486 was herself sunk 12 April, 1945 in the North Sea north-west of Bergen, Norway, in position 60.44N, 04.39E by torpedoes from the British submarine HMS Tapir. 48 dead (all hands lost).

Mrs Ruth Marshall and her late husband moved to Southborough from Canterbury in 1947, and found lodgings for 4 years with Mrs Bertha Fountain, John's mother, known to all as Birdie, and to Mr & Mrs Marshall as Auntie Birdie. She recalls that Mrs Fountain kept John's photograph on the wall, and his name was later inscribed along the side of her grave in Southborough Cemetery, where there was also an urn, which was paid for by John's friends. John, she told them, had always liked boats, and used to take his parents rowing on the river at Tonbridge. He worked for the butchers on the corner of Norton Road and Western Road, until 2008 occupied by Mr Kevin Major, local butcher, but now a private residence.

The following report from the Courier, 24 November 1944, doubtless refers to a relative of John: *The name of P/O Ronald C Fountain, son of Mr and the late Mrs C Fountain, of 13 Elm-road, appears in a recent list of those mentioned in dispatches "for courageous determination during a series of successful attacks on enemy-escorted envoys off the coast of France". He is 32, and before joining the Royal Navy in 1941 was employed as a slaughterman. An Old Boy of St Paul's School, he has one brother, also serving in the Royal Navy, and one sister.*

Reginald Albert Edward Francis

Private 6354955, 7th Bn, Parachute Regiment, AAC. Died Tuesday 6 June 1944, age 20. Buried in the Ranville War Cemetery, Calvados, France: Coll. Grave VIA.C.1-25.

The 1940 Kelly's Directory gives two entries for Francis in Southborough: Harry Francis at 14 Charles Street and Mrs Francis at 51 Forge Road.

The CWGC website gives the following information about Ranville, which clearly refers to the action in which Private Francis was killed: *The Allied offensive in north-western Europe began with the Normandy landings of 6 June 1944. Ranville was the first village to be liberated in France when the bridge over the Caen Canal was captured intact in the early hours of 6 June by troops of the 6th Airborne Division, who were landed nearby by parachute and glider. Many of the division's casualties are buried in Ranville War Cemetery and the adjoining churchyard.*

Ernest William Funnell

Private 978870, South Staffordshire Regt, attached 13th (2nd/4th Bn, The South Lancashire Regt) Bn, Parachute Regiment, Army Air Corps. Died Saturday 19 August 1944, age 24. Buried in the Putot-en-Auge Churchyard, Calvados, France: Row B. Grave 5. Son of Percy William and Rose Funnell, 22, Wolseley Road, High Brooms.

Jerry Jones of High Brooms, a childhood friend of Ernie, recalls he was one of a large family, and that before his war service, Ernie worked for Frank (Dick) Dunn, at his piggery in Powdermill Lane. Ernie's older brother Frederick is also commemorated on the Southborough War Memorial. Another High Brooms resident, Pete Simmons, recalls that Ernie's younger brother was called up after the end of the war and killed in Korea.

Mr H Kershaw of Hove, East Sussex, after visiting the village of Putot-en-Auge and seeing the War graves there, was inspired to research the history of the 5th Parachute Brigade's action on D Day, which included the capture of the famous Pegasus Bridge. Ernie Funnell was killed during the assault of Hill 13 at Putot-en-Auge on 19 August, and was buried in the village cemetery along with 25 of his comrades. Mr Kershaw's letter to the Courier, 7 March 2003 includes the following:

At 16 minutes past midnight on the night of June 5 and 6, 1944, gliders landed near the bridge over the River Orne and the Caen Canal. The latter became famous as the Pegasus Bridge. Three minutes later the men of the 5th Parachute Brigade started to land. The gliders and the parachutists had to capture the bridges. Although lightly armed, they succeeded. It has been said that had these bridges not been captured and held, the Normandy landing may have been jeopardised.

After weeks of action near the coast, the Germans withdrew to the high ground overlooking the River Dives. This area included the village of Putot. The 5th Parachute Brigade was quickly in pursuit and arrived near Putot-en-Auge late on August 18. They launched a dawn attack and by 8.45am, against strong opposition, Putot was captured.

The brigade suffered many casualties who were temporarily buried in Putot churchyard. The War Graves Commission wanted to move these men to one of the large war cemeteries. The village opposed this, saying that these men died for us, so they should stay with us. A plaque displayed among the beautifully cared-for graves states: "The little town of Putot on Auge receives the parents, relatives, and friends of the soldiers lying in this cemetery with sympathy and gratitude."

Mr Kershaw's detailed account of the Battle also includes the following:

On the night of the 17 August ... the 6th Airborne Division pursued the Germans as quickly as possible and on the evening of the 18 August the 3rd and 5th Parachute Brigades arrived at Goustranville – some 4200 fighting men. The 3rd Parachute Brigade was ordered to attack at once and to clear the enemy from the land between Goustranville and the small river passing by Putot-en-Auge. This they did and in the small hours of the morning of 19 August the 5th Parachute Brigade was ordered to pass through the 3rd Brigade, cross the river and capture Putot-en-Auge. The 5th Brigade which included the 7th, 12th and 13th Parachute Battalions were the troops primarily engaged here.

In the early hours of the 19 August the 13th Parachute Battalion was ordered to lead the advance and to cross the river by the northern bridge. They were late in reaching the bridge because the land between Goustranville and the bridge had not been completely cleared of enemy troops. When they arrived at the bridge they found that it had been so heavily damaged that it was not possible for the entire Brigade to cross. The Battalion therefore halted without crossing and turned to the south. In the meantime, the 7th Battalion, which had been following, learned that the northern bridge could not be used and also that there was an undamaged footbridge to the south. They therefore changed direction, headed for, and crossed by this footbridge, followed by the 12th Battalion and finally by the 13th Battalion when it arrived.

The 7th Battalion crossed the railway line by the Putot station at 0500 hours and met very heavy fire in the rectangular field to the east of the station. They were held up for some time but reached their objective, an orchard to the north of Putot, by 0700 hours.

The 12th Battalion followed behind, and to the right of the 7th Battalion, but because of the delays caused by the failure to cross the northern bridge, they did not arrive at the Form Up Point until 0500 hours. They were then ordered to attack up the hill towards the Church, a task originally intended for the 13th Battalion. The village was captured by 0700 hours on 19 August. For the remainder of that day the Battalion stayed in the village suffering heavy casualties from mortar and shell fire which also caused heavy destruction to buildings in the village.

The 13th Battalion, the last to cross the footbridge, was originally intended to capture the village. Because of the delay in their arrival they were ordered to pass through the positions held by the 7th and 12th Battalions, and attack the high ground, known as Hill 13, on the far side of the village. The first crest of this hill was captured and held against German counter attack. The second crest was captured but could not be held. It was finally captured by another Brigade of ground troops on the night of 19 August. The 13th Battalion suffered very heavy casualties during this attack. This engagement at Putot was the first major battle to be fought during the German retreat, which eventually ended in Germany.

The following is an extract from the War Diary of the 13th (Lancashire) Battalion, The Parachute Regiment:

Shakespeare wrote: "*They win or die who wear the rose of Lancashire*" – This motto was taken up by this Lancashire Battalion and shortened to 'Win or Die'. To this was added one other saying, this was, '13th Battalion, unlucky for Huns'. The Battalion lived up to their motto.

On the 17 August the Battalion was enjoying a rest at Ranville when the whole German front retired and on the 18 August the Battalion was dispatched, with the rest of the 6th Airborne Division, in pursuit. Moving as fast as they could by Motor Transport and route marches the Battalion came up to the Germans who were in contact with the 3rd Parachute Brigade at Goustranville...

The night was very dark and the approach march, across the enemy front, to ford the stream by the mined railway bridge, was most difficult. Arriving at the ford it was found that unexpectedly, the river was tidal and the water was too deep to cross. The Battalion therefore turned about in its tracks and made back as fast as possible in the pitch dark, to join in at the end of the now delayed Brigade attack. Morning therefore found it still not across the river, sheltering under a bank in full view of the German observation posts. They were shelled and mortared but not a man moved and there were no casualties. Orders were then received to cross the open and attack through the 12th and 7th Battalions up the hill, known as Hill 13, at Putot.

The whole Battalion formed up and rushed the thousand yards with such dash that there were only 5 casualties. Hardly pausing, they reorganized and stormed up the hill, taking the first crest and reaching the summit of the second where they were strongly counter attacked by the Germans, who had just been reinforced. Major RM Tarrant, MC, leading his company in the assault in support of A Company, was mortally wounded and the second crest was lost, a counter attack by C Company making no progress. The German counter attack on the first crest was firmly held. That night the 4th Special Services Brigade passed through and captured the final crest.

Note: The 13th Battalion landed with the rest of the 5th Brigade at 0050 hrs on D Day. They were given the task of attacking and capturing Ranville, which they did by 0230 hrs.

Frank Funnell

Corporal 719, 1st/3rd Kent Field Coy, Royal Engineers. Died 28 October 1915 in the Hythe disaster, age 23 years. Commemorated on the Helles Memorial, Gallipoli Peninsula, Turkey: Panel 23 to 25 or 325 to 328.

From Frank Stevens' book *Southborough Sappers of the Kent (Fortress) Royal Engineers*: Before formation of No 3 Coy he had joined the RE Cadet Unit and was in their band, upon joining No 3 he also played in the band, a photograph shows him equipped for playing the bass drum. He originally was at 147 London Rd Southborough but he married in February 1915 a girl who lived in Strood and he set up home at 87 Kitchener Rd, Strood. His normal work was as a fireman on the London Brighton South Coast Railway. He drowned just offshore of Gallipoli at a time when his brother serving in the Royal Marines was also there, his parents were still at 147 London Rd.

Dee's Directory 1915 gives the address as 143 London-road. From the Courier, 1914: *Pte Thomas Horace Funnell, of the Royal Marine Light Infantry, has just been home on a brief furlough, after a terrible baptism of fire in the trenches at Antwerp. Pte Funnell is only 17½ years of age, and he joined the RMLI only seven months ago. He went through the historic siege of Antwerp, and had the terrible experience of being in the trenches 60 hours at a stretch. On one occasion Mr Winston Churchill greatly encouraged the men by walking down the trenches and chatting to the men. He spoke to Pte Funnell, and delighted the soldiers with remarkably appropriate gifts in the shape of "House of Lords" cigarettes. Pte Funnell saw the oil tanks set on fire at Antwerp, and he brought home several interesting souvenirs in the shape of a blue Belgian mug, a Belgian medal, bearing the Royal Arms of Belgium, and a Prayer Book printed in Flemish which he found in a farmhouse that had been set fire to by an incendiary shell. The volume has the name of "Maria de Voegt" written on the flyleaf at the end. Pte Funnell is the son of Mr and Mrs Funnell, 143, London-road, Southborough. His father is an ex-soldier, having served in the Army Service Corps, and he is now busy with the Southborough "Last Ditchers". Another son of Mr & Mrs Funnell in the merchant service is coming home from the West Indies this week to join Kitchener's Army; while a third son, Corporal Funnell, is in the Terriers.*

There were two other Funnells, brothers, in the same company as Frank, who were drowned in the Hythe disaster and commemorated on the Helles Memorial in Turkey. Though they are not named on the Southborough War Memorial, they are remembered in Frank Stevens' book, which again gives the following detail:

Alfred George Funnell KF 2234. *(pictured left) …also a St John's boy, 19 years of age … up to three months ago working with his father as carman and contractor, but he came home one evening and told his family he was about to join his brother in the Engineers, and in spite of the earnest entreaties of his father, who had another son, Driver Charles, in the Engineers, now about to leave for the Front, Alfred said it was his duty and went. Only on Monday morning his mother*

received a letter from him (after the notification of his death), in which he asked for cigarettes, and saying that they had had a good voyage up to the time of writing, having just passed Gibraltar, where he said it was a treat to see land again … "I don't know how it is going to finish up."

Driver Henry George Funnell, KF 900, age 21. Son of Mrs Funnell, 59 Southview Road, High Brooms.

Henry Funnell (pictured left) joined the company pre-war at a time when he was employed by WG Harris of Grosvenor Rd, Tunbridge Wells. He was educated at St John's.

Frederick George Funnell

Private 6343102, 4th Bn, Queen's Own Royal West Kent Regiment. Died Sunday 26 May 1940, age 25. Buried at Le Grand Hasard Military Cemetery, Morbecque, Nord, France, grave reference 5.C.7. Son of Percival (Percy) William and Rose Funnell, of High Brooms. Husband of Mary Helen Funnell and brother of Ernest Funnell.

From the Courier, 5 September 1941: *News received by Mr & Mrs PW Funnell, 22 Wolseley-road, High Brooms, of the death in France of their son Private Frederick Funnell of the Royal West Kents. Private Funnell, who was married, was reported missing in June of last year. His father and brother are also serving.*

Stephen Alfred Funnell

Private L/9872, 2nd Bn, Royal Sussex Regiment. Died 10 September 1914, age 20. Son of Stephen and Emily Funnell, of 18 Springfield Road, Southborough. Buried in Montreuil-Aux-Lions British Cemetery, Aisne, France: Grave ref. II.C.10.

A clipping from October 1914 includes: … *killed in action at Priez, France, on September 10th, is the son* of Mr and Mrs Funnell, 30, Springfield Road ... having seen three years' service with the colours. His parents received no news of him, and only learned of his death on Friday last, when the official notification from the War Office and the message of sympathy from the King and Queen was sent to them.

Stephen Funnell is remembered on his parents' grave-stone in Southborough Cemetery, as is their eldest daughter Emily Elizabeth Jones, who died on 8 June 1930 aged 42.

George Frederic Furley

Private 808603, 31st Bn, (formerly 137th Bn) Canadian Infantry (Alberta Regt). Died 8 November 1917, age 41. Buried in Lijssenthoek Military Cemetery, Poperinge, West-Vlaanderen, Belgium. Son of Henry Furley (late Rector) of Kingsnorth, Kent, and Helen Mary Furley. Born at Heydown, Lincs.

The Rev Henry Furley lived at 44 Pennington Road in 1916. George and his brother Robert Furley are also commemorated on the Memorial Plaque in Kingsnorth Church. Private Furley was born on 31 December 1875, was resident in Calgary, Alberta, and had been in Canada for 13 years, his occupation given as farmer. He enlisted at Calgary on 16 February 1916. He was unmarried and 6'4" tall.

The family may have been relations of Robert Furley, who in 1830 founded the firm of solicitors practising in Ashford today and now under the name of Hallett & Co. This Robert Furley was the son of a prominent family of lawyers and bankers in Canterbury. He became a Magistrate, known for his willingness to give deserving paupers a second chance, and his contrasting advice to more "idle, frivolous and thriftless young gentlemen" to join the army or the navy. He campaigned against the closure of the 'casual ward' for tramps in Tufton Street, and took an interest in the Industrial School at Kingsnorth, an early kind of approved school, where boys were sent for training.

Robert Basil Furley

Second Lieutenant 1st (Bucks) Bn, Oxford and Bucks Light Infantry (formerly 16th Battalion, London Regiment). Died 25 January 1916, age 27. Buried in Hebuterne Military Cemetery, Pas de Calais, France: Grave ref. I.A.10. Son of Henry Furley (late Rector) of Kingsnorth, Kent and Helen Mary Furley.

Enlisted in the 16th London Regiment (Queen's Westminsters) in the summer of 1915 and left for the Front on 6th January 1916. The Southborough War Memorial gives his rank as Lieutenant.

Albert Victor Gainsford

Sapper 34381, Railway Operating Division, Royal Engineers. Formerly L/7412 Queen's Own (Royal West Kent Regiment) (47th BGO Coy). Died Thursday 18 July 1918, age 31. Buried in Ligny-St Flochel British Cemetery, Averdoingt, Pas de Calais, France: Grave ref. I.F.8. Husband of Laura Gainsford, 75 Auckland Road, Tunbridge Wells.

From the Courier, 4 September 1914: *Of the three Tunbridge Wells members of the Salvation Army at the Front, Private A Gainsford, of Southborough, was wounded at Mons, and is now in Netley Hospital. In a letter to Adjutant Wright, he states that "the roar of the German Artillery, the cloud of smoke and the numbers of dead and wounded made up a terrible spectacle".*

And a week later on 11 September: *Corporal Albert Victor Gainsford, another of the heroes of the Royal West Kent Regiment, wounded at Mons, arrived at his home in Honnington Cottages, Vauxhall Lane, Southborough, on Tuesday from Netley Hospital. He was in the thick of the fight and was hit by bullets and shrapnel, sustaining several wounds in the lower part of his body and the legs. He has made a remarkably rapid recovery, and is now home on 14 days' leave. Prior to his departure for the Front, Corporal Gainsford was a shunter at the South East Goods Station. He is a well-known member of the Salvation Army, and at the Wednesday evening meeting at the Varney-street Citadel, he gave a touching address upon the value of his religion to him at the Front. Corporal Gainsford's father, by the way, served for 12 years with the Royal Horse Artillery.*

From the Tunbridge Wells Advertiser, of the same date: *He has also gained a reputation as a racing cyclist, being a member of the Tunbridge Wells St John's Motor, Cycle and Athletic Club and the Southborough Athletic Club … he received his papers on returning from the Ticehurst sports on Bank Holiday. Like a good many heroes, Lance-Corporal Gainsford is very modest and much more willing to talk about his cycling trophies, his swimming and his football than he was of his shrapnel-torn limbs. "Yes, it does seem quiet and peaceful here after what I have been used to for the last five weeks. I particularly noticed it when I was hobbling home through the fields last night. I thought of the old 'boys' then; some in the thick of the fight, and others lying in mud and water. As you say, a modern battle is a terrible experience. And, mind you, we are fighting a relentless foe. I got knocked over too soon to have had a great deal of experience, but some of the tales the wounded 'Tommies' tell of German cruelty makes one's blood run cold ... What does it feel like before a battle starts? Well I can hardly tell you, for as a matter of fact we were having our tea when the first shell burst over us. It was quick work then, I can tell you. We were near a river, and the Germans got very close to us before opening fire with their deadly machine guns ... Yes, it was a sight to be remembered, as you say, but curiously enough it did not affect me half as much as the leave-takings I saw in England on my way to the depot. The sight of fathers saying good-bye to their families would melt anyone with a heart of stone ..."* with that the young NCO gripped my hand and made straight for a shaggy Airedale, who all along had resented my intrusion into Honnington Cottages. *"Poor old chap,"* the soldier went on, *"you wanted to come to the war with me, didn't you?"*

Southborough War Memorial gives Albert's rank as Sergeant, Machine Gun Corps. Frank Stevens writes that Corporal AV Gainsford was never in the Machine Gun Corps. In the Spring Offensive of 1918 when everyone was called upon to repel the Germans, he went forward with his Lewis gun and was not seen again. He died while serving in the 47 Broad Gauge Operating Company, Royal Engineers.

George Arthur Gainsford

Corporal, MSM, Royal Engineers. KF 1632, later 540822.

George Arthur Gainsford is commemorated on the Southborough War Memorial under the Second World War listings, but he is not listed on the CWGC site. He joined up in 1915 but did not go to Gallipoli or Egypt. Eventually he went to France, possibly with 3rd Kent Coy but eventually to Signals of 14th Brigade of the RGA. Awarded the Meritorious Service Medal (some reports – see below - give the award as the Military Medal).

From the Courier, 19 April 1918: *Mrs Gainsford, 25 Meadow-road, has received a notification that her husband, Corporal George Gainsford, RE, has been recommended by his Commanding Officer to receive the Military Medal. Corporal Gainsford joined the K(F)RE in 1915 and has been in France since April, 1917.*

And from the Courier, 18 October 1918: *Mrs Gainsford, 25 Meadow-road, has received a letter from an officer suggesting that her husband, Corporal George Gainsford, Signals, RE, was seriously wounded in France on*

October 4th. His officer was wounded by the same shell. Corporal Gainsford is the holder of a Military Medal.

After the First World War it is possible he joined the local Searchlight unit of RE in Speldhurst Road because of the rank of Corporal. However, he died on 26 June 1933 and is buried in Southborough Cemetery with a civilian marker making no mention of rank or decoration. He may have been related to Albert Victor Gainsford.

F T Gammon

Sergeant 200032, 2nd Bn, Queen's Own (Royal West Kent Regiment). Died 20 December 1918, age 35. Buried in Baghdad (North Gate) War Cemetery, Iraq, Grave ref: XIII.A.1.

Tunbridge Wells War Memorial lists him as Frederick Thomas Gammon, and a plaque at St James' Church as Frederick F Gammon.

C Gibbs

Private, Royal Fusiliers. Died in World War 1.

Kelly's Directory 1916 for Southborough lists only one Gibbs – A Gibbs, resident at 1, Holden Place. Of the 435 Gibbs listed on the CWGC site, none of those with the Royal Fusiliers has any mention of a connection with Southborough.

John Frederick Gilks

Private 30502, 1st Bn, Essex Regiment. Died Thursday 12 October 1916. Born Walthamstow, Essex; enlisted Tunbridge Wells; resided Southborough. Buried in Bancourt British Cemetery, Pas de Calais, France: Grave ref. IX.J.3.

Bancourt is a village approximately 4 kilometres due east of Bapaume. Information from www.firstworldwar.com/onthisday gives the following for 12 October 1916: *British attack on four-*

mile front between Eaucourt and Bapaume-Peronne road, line advanced 500 to 1,000 yards.

From The Courier, 24 August 1917: *News has been received by Mrs Gilks, The Gardens, "Broomhill", that her husband, Private John F Gilks, who was first reported as having been "missing" since the engagement on October 12th, 1916, is now believed to have died on that date or since. He was the eldest son of Mr WJ Gilks of Oxhill, Kineton, Warwickshire, and before joining the Essex Regiment on May 30th was in the employ of Sir David Salomons, and proceeded to France on September 20th, 1916. He had three brothers, who enlisted in the autumn of 1914, one having fallen in action on the 1st July 1916, and the other still remains in England, while the youngest is now in France. His loss will be sadly felt by his wife and two young children.*

Thomas Godsmark

Driver (Bugler) 2233 1st/3rd Kent Field Coy, Royal Engineers. Died 28 October 1915, age 21, in the Hythe disaster. Commemorated on the Helles Memorial, Gallipoli Peninsula, Turkey, Panel 23 to 25 or 325 to 328.

Thomas was born on 22 June 1895 at 34, Charles Street, Southborough. His father William Godsmark was born in Newhaven, Sussex in December 1859, married Eliza Ellen Hook, a native of Tunbridge Wells, in St John's Church, Tunbridge Wells in January 1882, and died in December 1930 at 25 Gordon Road, High Brooms. Mrs Godsmark died in September 1942. William Godsmark worked as a farm labourer in his childhood and later as a labourer, and at the time of the First World War, they were living at 25 Gordon Road.

Eliza already had a daughter, Ada, born in Tonbridge Workhouse, when she and Thomas's father married, and they went on to have seven more children: William Henry (also commemorated on the Southborough War Memorial), Annie Sarah, James Henry, Florence, Olive Ellen, Thomas and Charles.

Thomas died a week after his brother William. Thomas was believed by his family to have drowned when the Hythe went down because he would not leave his horses.

William Henry Godsmark

Serjeant 5056, C Bty, 52nd Brigade, Royal Field Artillery. Died 21 October 1915, age 31. Buried in Grave I.B.26A at Lijssenthoek Military Cemetery, Poperinge, West-Vlaanderen, Belgium.

William was the older brother of Thomas Godsmark. In the census 5 April 1891, William, aged 8, was living with his parents at Burlington Cottage, Southborough. William Henry Godsmark married Phoebe B T Holloway in January 1911 in Alton, Hampshire, where she was born. His name appears on the Headley War Memorial in Hampshire as well as the Southborough War Memorial. William and Phoebe had two children before he died: John FW Godsmark, born 11 June 1912 in Alton, and Edward A Godsmark, born October 1913, Alton. Two years after his death, Phoebe married Sydney Wilson in Alton registration district in Hampshire during the 3rd quarter of 1917. Her address on the CWGC site is given as Washford Lane, Linford, Bordon, Hampshire.

From the Tunbridge Wells Advertiser, 5 November 1915: *Battery Sergt-Major W Godsmark, son of Mr and Mrs W Godsmark, 25, Gordon-road, High Brooms, has died in a clearing hospital as the result of wounds received a fortnight ago. In writing to the deceased soldier's wife, the chaplain said: "I regret to inform you that your husband died in this hospital last night. He came to us in a very shattered condition, and in spite of all we did for him he passed away. He will be buried today in the Military Cemetery, 1½ miles South of Poperinghe, Belgium, in a grave marked by a wooden cross bearing his name and number. May God strengthen you to bear this sad blow, made easier, I hope, by the memory of a brave man who died in a righteous cause." Sergt-Major Godsmark was 35 years of age, and had been in the Royal Field Artillery for 17 years. He went to the Front five months ago. He has two brothers in the Army, Jem being in the Royal Field Artillery and Tom in the Kent (Fortress) Engineers. The former went to the Front with the First Expeditionary Force, and was home on leave for six days about a fortnight ago. Both were old High Brooms School boys, but Sergt-Major Godsmark was educated at Southborough National School.*

Harry Goldbaum

Sapper 1149, 1st/3rd Kent Field Coy, Royal Engineers. Died 28 October 1915 in the Hythe disaster, age 17. Commemorated on the

Helles Memorial, Turkey, Panel 23 to 25 or 325 to 328. Son of Charles and Sonia Goldbaum, of 24, High St, Stepney, London.

From *Southborough Sappers of the Kent (Fortress) Royal Engineers*: *Born in Edinburgh 23 February 1898. The family moved to London, and at the time of his death his mother and father were living at 24 High St, Stepney, but his address was 13 Edward St, Southborough. He lived in the area for a long while as he had risen to Sgt Bugler in the Cadet unit although some reports say Boys Brigade. He was only 17 so had taken the opportunity to join up when war was declared. He was the Trumpeter for the unit which places him with the Transport Section; he gained the place because Gerald Baker's mother would not let him go as being underage. The names of his parents were Charles and Sonia Goldbaum, nee Trager.*

Further research by Frank Stevens records that Harry was the fourth son of Solomon and Sarah Goldbaum (daughter of Harry Trager) of 26 Marron Street, Stepney (perhaps anglicised to Charles and Sonia?). Educated at Beth St Council School, Harry was believed to have worked on the Salomons estate. *Soldiers Who Died in The Great War* gives his forename as Henry. His brother Private Philip Goldbaum 3499, 1st/10th Bn, London Regiment (son of Sarah and Solomon Goldbaum) was killed in action 23 July 1916, age 19, and is buried in the Suez War Memorial Cemetery (Grave Reference: B.71.) in Egypt.

Harry Mark Goodsell

Private 200833, 2nd/4th Bn, Queen's Own (Royal West Kent Regiment). Died 4 November 1917, age 21. Buried in Beersheba War Cemetery, Israel: Grave ref. G.40. Son of Mary Jane and the late Henry Goodsell, of 26 Great Brooms Road, High Brooms.

Harry was in the same company, died on the same day, and is buried in the same cemetery, **as Cecil Shoesmith.**

The CWGC information on the Memorial includes the following: *By October 1917, General Allenby's force had been entrenched in front of a strong Turkish position along the Gaza-Beersheba road for some months, but they were now* ready to launch an attack with Beersheba as its first objective. On 31 October, the attack was carried out by the XXth Corps (10th, 53rd, 60th and 74th Divisions) on the west, and the Desert Mounted Corps on the east. That evening the 4th Australian Light Horse Brigade charged over the Turkish trenches into the town. The cemetery was made immediately on the fall of the town, remaining in use until July 1918, by which time 139 burials had been made. It was greatly increased after the Armistice when burials were brought in from a number of scattered sites and small burial grounds.

James Edward Goodwin

Private 24720, 13th Bn, Canadian Infantry (Quebec Regt). Died 22 April 1915, age 22. Commemorated on the Ypres (Menin Gate) Memorial, Belgium: Panel 24-26-28-30. Son of James and Ada Goodwin, of 3 Forge Road, Southborough, later of Charles Street.

Born in Southborough on 27 April 1892, James Goodwin enlisted at Valcartier, Quebec on 23 September 1914. He was unmarried and gave his occupation as baker. The Courier, 4 June 1915, reported: *Mr and Mrs Goodwin have this week received official notification that their son is missing. They last heard from him on April 11th, and as far as they know he took part in the fight for "Hill 60". Private Goodwin joined the Canadian contingent at the outbreak of the war, and came to England with the first contingent in September, and went into training on Salisbury Plain. He went to the Front early in February. Mr and Mrs Goodwin have another son, Private R Goodwin, who was in the Royal Sussex Regiment and was wounded in the hand some months ago and has been invalided home.*

From the Courier of 12 March 1915: *Private Robert Goodwin is home from the Front, where he was wounded on January 29th. Pte Goodwin joined the 2nd Royal Sussex Regiment (Special Reserve) two years ago last December, and was called up at the beginning of the war. He has seen most of his service in the neighbourhood of La Bassee, and had a narrow escape with his life. He was carrying a tin of biscuits on his shoulder along a communicating trench, and came in for the attention of German snipers posted in the trees. One bullet cut off the middle finger of his right hand, and it was afterwards found that half-a-dozen bullets had embedded themselves in the tin of biscuits, which shielded his head and no doubt saved his life.*

On another occasion Pte Goodwin had a narrow escape. His Company went into a factory for a few hours rest, and a shell went clean through the building without injuring anyone. Pte Goodwin was sent home from the Front to the American Women's War Hospital, Paignton, Devon, and speaks highly of the kindness and attention he received. Mr and Mrs Goodwin have another son at the Front, who has been in the firing line, but came through unscathed, and is still doing his bit for his country.

Dee's Directory 1915 lists a J Goodwin, perhaps the third son referred to above, serving with the Royal West Kents.

James' brother-in-law is shown in the photograph on the left, which was published with these words: *Mrs Goodwin, of 3 Forge Road, has been informed that her son-in-law, Pte J Sherlock, Royal West Kent Regiment, was wounded on April 19th in Egypt. Pte Sherlock joined the colours in 1915. He was before then employed by Messrs Dee, contractors, of Tonbridge.*

William Groombridge

Corporal KF 727, 1st/3rd Kent Field Coy, Royal Engineers. Died on 28 October 1915 in the Hythe disaster, age 22. Commemorated on the Helles Memorial, Turkey: Panel 23 to 25 or 325 to 328. Son of Mr and Mrs Joseph Groombridge of 6 Forge Road.

From *Southborough Sappers of the Kent (Fortress) Royal Engineers: His number shows he was the 13th man to join No 3 Coy, at the time living in Southborough where he had been born. He was a Corporal and known as a "rough-rider" so was with the horses of the Transport Section. He received schooling at St Peter's School. William was living at Court Styles (Stiles) Cottages, Cranbrook, with his wife and one (or two) children; next door to Bert Holmans, also of the unit.*

Frederick James Grove

Lieutenant 312377, 6th Bn, Queen's Own Royal West Kent Regiment. Died Friday 13 April 1945, age 22. Buried in Faenza War Cemetery, Italy: Grave ref. II.D.1. Son of Frederick Francis and Sophia Grove, of Beckenham, Kent.

Kelly's Directory of 1940 lists only one Grove resident in Southborough – Wm Grove, 17 Powder Mill Lane.

George Henry Hackett

Corporal 432182, 49th Bn, Canadian Infantry (Alberta Regt). Died 2 June 1916, age 30. Buried in Oosttaverne Wood Cemetery, Heuvelland, West-Vlaanderen, Belgium: Grave ref. VIII.D.18.

From the Courier, 7 July 1916: *Corporal GH Hackett, Grenade Platoon of the Canadian Expeditionary Force, the second son of Mr F Hackett, butcher, of London-road, was killed in action on June 3rd at Ypres. The news was only received by his parents on Saturday last. Corporal Hackett, who went out to Canada five years ago, enlisted at the outbreak of the war, and after training in England went out to France in September of last year. His friends were expecting him home on leave when the sad news of his death came. He leaves a widow and four children.*

Clive Maier's research adds: *According to his attestation paper, George Hackett was born on 24 November 1895 (sic – 1885?) at Oxford, Kent. Perhaps this should be Otford. He was married to Bessie Hackett of 64 Clark Street, Edmonton, Alberta. He enlisted at Edmonton on 5 January 1915 and gave his occupation as butcher. He had previously served for one year in the West Kent Yeomanry.*

Thomas Frederick James Handley

Driver 2225, 1st/3rd Kent Field Coy, Royal Engineers. Died 28 October 1915, in the Hythe disaster, age 19. Commemorated on the Helles Memorial, Turkey: Panel 23 to 25 or 325 to 328.

Thomas was born on 25 April 1896 and is pictured left with his parents Thomas Richard Handley (a railway porter in 1897 when Thomas's sister Ada was born) and Eliza Handley (formerly Eliza Dear). The family lived at 27 Lower Bland Street, Newington, in the district of St Saviour, Southwark. Thomas Handley Sr fought and died in the Transvaal (Boer) War (No 1431, 1st East Surrey Regiment). He was killed in May 1900 at Mooi River, and his wife Eliza received an allowance from the

Transvaal War Fund for Widows, Orphans, and other Dependents of Officers and Men losing their lives in the War in South Africa. She had also been granted a life annuity of £10 a year from the Daily Telegraph Shilling Fund for Our Soldiers' Widows and Orphans. However, in a letter dated 26 June 1901 from the Royal Commission of the Patriotic Fund, 53 Charing Cross Rd, London, Eliza was informed that as she was to receive a state pension of five shillings a week for herself and eighteenpence a week for each of her three children, she would no longer receive her Transvaal War Fund allowance. Her son Thomas, on the death of Queen Victoria, received a portrait and a donation of one sovereign from the Fund.

In 1901 Eliza walked with her three children (Thomas, Ada Elizabeth and their sister Mary Ann) in a pram, all the way from London to Tunbridge Wells to make a new home there.

Thomas attended High Brooms' Boys' School. At the time of his death, the family were living at 19, Nursery Road, High Brooms. Frank Stevens writes: ...*he enlisted 25/5/1915 and did not have six months service at the time of his death ... he gained employment with the Co-Operative Society Tunbridge Wells until joining the army. A keen footballer, he was in the St Luke's Football Club.*

From a newspaper report of the time: *Mrs Handley received a letter from the Sapper on Monday (after notification) saying he was quite well and had had a good voyage.*

Thomas's sister Ada married Charles Berry, who was born Antonio Cocorochio in 1896 in Cassino, Italy, moving at the age of 12, to Swindon. He worked as a warehouseman and was naturalised on 18 November 1919. He had fought in the British Army in World War 1, and had decided on the name Berry after seeing it on a fruiterers' sign in Brighton. Between the two wars he had an ice-cream factory in Sevenoaks, and later he had a greengrocers and fruiterers business in Tonbridge High Street. In their wedding photograph above, Thomas is pictured in the front row, far left, with a small boy on his knee.

Hubert Harrowing

Leading Seaman Z/1860, Howe Bn, RN Division, Royal Naval Volunteer Reserve. Died 14 November 1916. Buried at Varennes Military Cemetery, Somme, France: Grave ref. I.E.59. Son of Walter John Harrowing, of 29 Vale Road, Southborough.

From the Courier, 24 November 1916: *Official information has been received by Mr and Mrs Harrowing, Vale-road, that their only son, aged 20, has died at a Casualty Clearing Station in France from wounds caused by a shell, on November 14th. Leading Seaman Hubert Harrowing joined the Naval Division 18 months ago. Before joining he was serving an apprenticeship with RW Weekes, Tunbridge Wells. He was educated at Judd's School, Tonbridge.*

Thomas John Harvey

Private 4806, 1st Bn, Queen's Own (Royal West Kent Regiment). Died 21 July 1916, age 32. Buried in Caterpillar Valley Cemetery, Longueval, Somme, France: Grave ref. XIV. F. 40. Son of Thomas John and Louisa Marian Harvey, 67 Colebrook Road, High Brooms; husband of Esther Louisa Harvey, 68 High Brooms Road.

Private Harvey had five siblings: James Henry Harvey, Albert Edward Percy Harvey (67 Colebrook Rd); Mrs Alice Fuller (Southview Rd), Mrs Rose Tingley (10 High Brooms Rd), and Mrs Daisy Jane Manktelow (67 Colebrook Rd). His children were Doris Tickner (step-daughter, born 2 December 1901), Mabel Louisa Rose (born 15 August 1904); Gwendolin Alice (born 14 October 1906); and Thomas James (born 6 February 1909). He was a brick-maker with the High Brooms Brick Company, and enlisted on 7 December 1914. He served at home until 21 April 1915, and thereafter with the BEF until his death. He received the 1914-1915 Star, BWM, and Victory Medal.

His wife received the following letter from 6258, Sgt A Rogers, Stretcher Bearers' Headquarters, 1st Royal West Kent Regiment, BEF, dated 9 August 1916: *"Dear Mrs Harvey, I meant to have written to you before, but could not find time, but I expect by now you have had the sad news of your husband's death, which I am sure must have come as a great blow to you. I am sorry to say he had the misfortune of getting wounded the night we were going to the trenches,* and he died the following morning, but I am pleased to say he suffered no pain as he was unconscious up to the time he died. I gave him every attention I possibly could, but am very sorry to say nothing could save him as the bullet had penetrated his head. I buried him in a quiet spot behind the firing line, and erected a cross over his grave with his name, regiment, and the date he died. I am extremely sorry for your great loss, Mrs Harvey, for I am sure he will be greatly missed. I come from Tunbridge Wells, but I did not know your husband personally to speak to. I have handed his books and photos in, which I hope will be forwarded on to you safe. Yours sincerely, Sgt A Rogers."* Sadly, Sgt Rogers himself died on 9 April 1917, and is buried in Nine Elms Military Cemetery, Thelus, Pas de Calais, Grave ref. III.C.13.

Clement Hawkins

2nd Corporal 741, 1st/3rd Kent Field Coy, Royal Engineers. Died 28 October 1915, in the Hythe disaster, age 34. Commemorated on the Helles Memorial, Turkey: Panel 23 to 25 or 325 to 328.

Clement Hawkins' mother Sarah Hawkins lived at 13 Castle Street, Southborough at the time of his death. His brother Thomas Hawkins was born at 4, Percy Place, Sevenoaks. Clement's other siblings were Mrs Jane Elizabeth Saunders, of 31 Bedford Road, Southborough, and Mrs Clara Eliza Clifton of New Lodge Farm, Marden. His nieces included Lilian Gardner of 31 Bedford Road, Caroline Jenner and Maria Whitehead. Clement and his wife Ada Mary Ann lived at 19, Western Road, Southborough. Their son Frederick Arthur was born on 8 July 1909. Clement stood 5'9¼", with grey eyes and brown hair. He worked as a painter. He was a friend of **Frederick Somers.**

He joined up at Maidstone for the Boer War on 4 February 1901 with the 1st Volunteer Battalion of the West Kents, No 6965, served until 1902, and was awarded the following medals: QSA (Queen's South African) with four bars – Cape Colony, Orange Free State, Transvaal and 1902. He joined up again on 1 March 1914, and was awarded the BWM (British War Medal) and the TFM (Territorial Force War Medal).

From a local newspaper: *Hawkins was one of the first members of the Company when it was formed, and had previous to this seen service in the South African War, being one of the volunteers from the Tunbridge Wells district who took part in that campaign. He had been promoted 2nd Corporal since the outbreak of the war.*

Allan Sydney Hayfield

Second Lieutenant 7th Bn, The Buffs (East Kent Regiment). Died Friday 6 October 1916, age 29. Buried in Puchevillers British Cemetery, Somme, France: Grave ref. III.B.3. Son of George Henry and Mary Ann Hayfield, of 21, Prospect Road, Southborough.

Clive Maier writes that Allan Hayfield died of wounds received at Schwaben Redoubt near Thiepval. From the Courier, 13 October 1916: *Second Lieutenant AS Hayfield has died from wounds in Hospital in France. His mother, Mrs Hayfield, of Prospect-road, last received a letter from her son dated September 30th, and has since received a letter from the nursing sister stating that he was admitted to the Hospital with very serious injuries, and that everything possible was done for him. Mrs Hayfield has two other sons serving, including a younger one in the same Regiment.*

From the Courier 12 April 1918 regarding Allan Hayfield's brother: *Among those recently gazetted as having received a second bar to the MC is T-Capt Cyril Dudeney Hayfield, MC East Kent Regiment, son of Mrs Hayfield, 21 Prospect-road. The award was for the following good work – "When sent forward to reconnoitre the situation, he went to within a few yards of the enemy post. Though two men with him were killed, he completed his reconnaissance, and returned with valuable information. He had previously marked out the assembly position with great skill, moving about continually in a most exposed position."* Captain Hayfield was awarded the Military Cross in November, 1916, and the first bar was gazetted in April, 1917. He was later awarded the DSO in November 1918, and was twice Mentioned in Despatches.

G Hayman

Private, 2nd Battalion Coldstream Guards.

The Tunbridge Wells Advertiser of 14 August 1914 lists, under Local Men on Service, G Hayman, 58 Nursery-road, High Brooms, in the Coldstream Guards. It is possible that the name is misspelt here and on the Memorial, as it is likely that the man commemorated is the following:

Private James George Haymon, 7574, 7th Company, 2nd Battalion Coldstream Guards. Died 20 May 1915, age 27. Commemorated on

the Le Touret Memorial, Pas de Calais: Panels 2 and 3. Son of the late Amos and Eliza Haymon of Colebrook Road, High Brooms; husband of Mary Louise Haymon of 164A Portland Street, Walworth, London.

From the Courier 4 December 1914, with picture as shown: *Pte. Haymon, of the 2nd Coldstream Guards, writes to Mrs Haymon, at High Brooms, as follows: "We did not stick long in Belgium the first time we came here, but we mean to stick it this time, and wear the Germans out. They are not bad soldiers, but they ought to be Suffragettes from the way they like burning people's houses down. It is very cold here, but the Germans will get warmed up if they wait long enough. We are pretty close to them now – only a few hundred yards separate us – and we keep driving them back. – is now billeted in a house in Belgium for a few days' rest. They have received fur coats, which make them look like Teddy Bears hopping about."*

J Hazelden

Lance Corporal G/795, 7th Bn, Queen's Own (Royal West Kent Regiment). Died 27 May 1917. Buried in Rookery British Cemetery, Heninel, Pas de Calais, France: Grave ref. C.26.

The CWGC gives this information about the Cemetery: *Heninel village was captured in a snowstorm on 12 April 1917 by the 56th (London) and 21st Division and the 50th (Northumbrian) Division, advancing from Heninel on the two following days, captured Wancourt Tower. Rookery British Cemetery (named from a group of trenches) was made by the 18th and 50th Division Burial Officers in April-June 1917 and used until November 1917.*

The photograph shown was published in the Courier on 15 June 1917 with the caption: "L-Corporal Hazelden, Rusthall, Killed".

Dee's Directory 1915 lists, under Men Serving, HWG Hazelden, Kent Cyclist Bn, and AW Hazelden, KFRE, both living at 35 Prospect-road. Kelly's Directory 1916 lists an AW Hazelden at 2 Edward-street. There may be a possible link between J Hazelden and the above.

Jesse Heasman

Sapper 1037 1st/3rd Kent Field Coy, Royal Engineers. Died on 28 October 1915 in the Hythe disaster. Commemorated on the Helles Memorial, Turkey: Panel 23 to 25 or 325 to 328.

Jesse Heasman died in the Hythe disaster at the age of 19, with his brother William (both listed as Driver on the Southborough War Memorial). They had both joined at the formation of the 1st/3rd Kent Field Company before August 1914, and were members of the KFRE band. Their parents were James Henry Heasman and Mary Ann Heasman of 54 Springfield Road, Southborough. Mrs Heasman later remarried, and at the time of CWGC listing, was named Mrs Mary Ann Stringhill, of 32 Springfield Road.

William Heasman

Sapper 786 1st/3rd Kent Field Coy, Royal Engineers. Died on 28 October 1915 in the Hythe disaster, age 22. Commemorated on the Helles Memorial, Turkey: Panel 23 to 25 or 325 to 328.

William Heasman worked in St John's Sanitary Laundry as an engineer before the war, and after signing up he was batman to Captain Salomons.

The Courier reported: *The War Office letter stated that Sapper William Heasman had been drowned, but no mention was made of his brother, Sapper Jesse Heasman, who was serving with him. The news of the former's death came as a terrible blow to his mother, who has unfortunately been seriously ill for nearly twelve months. On Saturday the blow fell with renewed force, for news was then received of the death of his brother Jesse.*

Frank Bernard Hemsley

Corporal 6345633, 4th Bn, Queen's Own (Royal West Kent Regiment). Died Tuesday 28 May 1940, age 19. Commemorated in Le Grand Hasard Military Cemetery, Morbecque, Nord, France:

Sp. Mem. 'A'. Son of Frank Hemsley, and of Mercy Freda Hemsley, of 65 Nursery Road, High Brooms.

Frank Hemsley was in the same regiment, died on the same day, and is commemorated in the same cemetery, as **Frank Sutcliffe** (also on the Southborough War Memorial), **Charles William Barton** (added 2009) and Fred Scrace (who is not). Frank was a mechanic at Nightingale Farm and Dairy before he joined up.

From the Courier, 12 February 1943: *Much sympathy will be extended to Mrs F Hemsley, of 65 Nursery-road, who has now been notified that her only son, Cpl FB Hemsley, RWK Regiment, was killed in action on May 28, 1940 at Hazebrouck, France. Cpl Hemsley, who was previously reported missing on June 15, 1940, was an old Royal Victorian schoolboy, and was only 19. This is the second time tragedy has befallen Mrs Hemsley and her daughter, for it will be remembered that a short while ago Mrs Hemsley's husband, the late Mr Frank Hemsley, met his death by accident at the Tunbridge Wells Gas Company, where he had been employed for 23 years as a water gas operator. An old soldier, Mr Hemsley played his part throughout the last war and saw service in Egypt and France with the Australian Forces.*

On 29 September 1916, a Private F Hemsley, an old St John's School boy of Tunbridge Wells, (pictured right) who joined the Australian Infantry, was reported killed in action in France in the Courier. He had three brothers serving, and may perhaps have been Frank Bernard Hemsley's uncle.

Ernest Henry Hobbs

Sapper 15099, 12th Field Coy, Royal Engineers. Died 22 April 1915. Buried in Bailleul Communal Cemetery (Nord), Nord, France: Grave ref. K.10.

A newsaper report of 30 April 1915, includes the following: *We regret to record the death of Sapper Ernest Henry Hobbs, RE, son of Mr and Mrs J Hobbs, of 19 Meadow-road, Southborough, who was wounded in the head on*

Wednesday last and died the following morning in the Clearing Hospital. Sapper Hobbs, who was aged 32, was born in Tunbridge Wells, and the family afterwards moving to Southborough, he received his education at St Peter's School, Southborough. At the age of 23 he joined the Royal Engineers at Chatham, and went to Hong Kong with his Company, where he was stationed for three years. Then he came out of the Army and joined the Reserve, soon after emigrating to New Zealand, where he was when war broke out. He was re-called to his regiment, and arrived in England at the end of November. Since then he has been stationed at Chatham and Felixstowe, and went to the Front with the 12th Company, RE at the end of February. The news of his death was sent by a nurse at the hospital, who wrote a kind and sympathetic letter to his parents.

Albert E Hodges

Sapper 2212 1st/3rd Kent Field Coy, Royal Engineers. Died 28 October 1915 in the Hythe disaster. Commemorated on the Helles Memorial, Turkey: Panel 23 to 25 or 325 to 328.

Rank given as Driver on Southborough War Memorial. From a newspaper report of the time: *Last week we recorded that his brother was among the saved, and no news had up to then been received of Driver A Hodges ... The following letter has been received by Mrs Hodges, late of No 10 Vernon-road, Tunbridge Wells:*

1/3rd Kent Field Coy RE, Mediterranean Expeditionary Force, 13th November 1915

Dear Mrs Hodges

The news of the death of your son, Driver A Hodges (No 2212) of my Company, will have reached you before this is posted. You would perhaps like to hear from me something of how he died. We had left the intermediate base on the afternoon of that 28th October all as cheerful as could be at the prospect of getting at last to the Front, and had almost reached our journey's end when a large vessel loomed out of the darkness, and before we could avoid it, crashed into the forepart of our vessel, bringing down the foremast. Alas! In that part of the vessel all our drivers were gathered, some of them already putting on their equipment so as to be ready to disembark. Only eight out of some 48 drivers were rescued, so I fear that many must have been killed or injured in the collision. What happened to your son after the collision I do not know, but it is enough he died doing his duty in the service of his King and Country. May *that thought and the sympathy of those of us who were fortunate enough to escape be a comfort to you in your loss. Yours very truly, A J RUSTON, Major"*

Driver AE Hodges was an Old Victoria School Boy, and enlisted with his brother (who is saved) on May 25th last. At the time of enlisting he was employed as a groom by Miss Woodhouse, of 9, Nevill Park, Tunbridge Wells, and would have been 22 in January next.

Albert's brother, William Samuel Hodges, Sapper/Driver 2211 541306 is pictured left. From Frank Stevens' book *Southborough Sappers of the Kent (Fortress) Royal Engineers*. Known throughout his life as "Jockey" from his small stature, he was rejected several times for this reason but eventually was allowed to join with his brother Albert on 25 May 1915. He describes his rescue and the events leading up to it which can be found in *The Unfinished Journey* in Tunbridge Wells Library. His story says that he was landed on Gallipoli along with other men who did not belong to the RE and was there ahead of the advance party, 30 Oct, and the main body Nov. Because of his injuries and experience he was invalided home to recover at the Kent Depot Maidenhead. He had caught dysentery and it is believed that he only survived because of attention by Len Everdell. Prior to the war he had been employed by Winston Scott, horse trainer. He died at the age of 88 and his age in 1915 is given as 26, so this puts the year of his death as 1977. Maxwell Macfarlane believes this calculation is incorrect, as he recalls interviewing "Jockey" Hodge in December 1979, and believes he died in 1980 or 1981.

Edward Hollamby

Lance Corporal G/1027, 1st Bn, Queen's Own (Royal West Kent Regiment). Died 5 May 1915, age 31. Commemorated on the Ypres (Menin Gate) Memorial, Belgium: Panel 45 & 47. Husband of Elizabeth Hollamby, of 44 Charles Street, Southborough.

From the Courier, 28 May 1915: *Although he received his discharge from the Army 10 years ago as "unfit for foreign service", Pte Edward Hollamby, of Southborough, re-enlisted on August 11th last, a week after the outbreak of war, and his widow has just received the news that he was killed in action* on May 5th. Pte Hollamby resided at 42, Charles-street, Southborough. He was 31 years of age and a native of Tunbridge Wells. Prior to enlisting nine months ago he was employed in the Telephone Department, and was very popular among his colleagues. He had previously served for three years in the Royal Sussex Regiment, and saw two periods of service in India. He was then discharged as unfit for foreign service, but in spite of this fact he joined the 1st Battalion Royal West Kent Regiment after the European War was declared, and went to France on December 7th. From that time to the date of his death he experienced a lot of strenuous fighting in the grim struggle which has been taking place in France during the past few months. Pte Hollamby leaves a widow and a young daughter, and much sympathy is felt for them in their great bereavement.

George T Hook

Lance Corporal, L/8644, Royal Sussex Regiment. Died 27 December 1919. Buried in Southborough Cemetery, England: Grave Ref. 1.224.

The following from the Tunbridge Wells advertiser, 5 October 1917, refers to George Hook's brother: *Official news has been received by Mr and Mrs Hook, 96, Springfield-road, informing them that their eldest son, Sapper CA Hook, RE, was wounded on September 19th by bullets, which pierced his arms, thigh and shins. He is now in hospital at Folkestone, where he is progressing as well as can be expected. Sapper Hook joined the Army in November, 1915, and proceeded to France in January 1917, being later transferred to the North Staffordshire Regiment. Mr and Mrs Hook have two other sons serving in India.*

From the Courier, 2 January 1920: *A SOLDIER'S DEATH We regret to have to record the death of Lance-Corporal George Hook, 1st Battalion Royal Sussex Regiment, which took place at Kitchener's Hospital, Brighton, on Saturday, at the age of 31 years, the cause of death as disclosed at the post-mortem examination being blood-poisoning. The deceased, who was the youngest son of Mr and Mrs J Hook, of 96 Springfield-road, Southborough, had recently come home to England after 13 years' foreign service, and during the war he took part in the campaign on the North-West Frontier, and also against the Afghans. He was a well-known sportsman, he and his four brothers having played for the Southborough Football Club at various times in years past. He was also a well-known hockey and football player in the Army, and played for the local Football Club on December 8th against Hildenborough. The funeral took place yesterday (Thursday) at Southborough.*

Earl Houser

Private 7784, Royal Canadian Dragoons. Died 23 September 1915, age 19. Buried in La Plus Douve Farm Cemetery, Comines-Warneton, Hainaut, Belgium: Grave ref. II.C.13. Son of Levi Houser, 88 Huron Street, Brantford, Ontario.

Rank of Trpr on Southborough War Memorial. Clive Maier's research shows that the attestation paper gives the address of Levi Houser as 176 Grey Street, Brantford, Ontario. Earl was born in Beamsville, Ontario on 19 January 1895; his occupation being given as electrical worker. He enlisted at Brantford on 5 February 1915.

A letter from Trooper HA Spencer to Houser's parents was reported in the Brantford newspaper: *He wrote from the trenches only two days after Houser's death. Spencer remarks that in the tent before leaving for the trenches, Houser several times said, "Do you know, I feel it in my bones I will get it this trip." Spencer reports that Houser was bombing between the German lines when he was hit in the head by a bullet. He was unconscious and died ten minutes after he was carried to the dressing station. He was buried at Ration Farm near Neuve Eglise. A memorial service was held for Houser at Marlboro Street Methodist Church, with the Reverend JE Peters officiating.*

The Courier, 8 October 1915 reported: *We regret to have to record that Trooper Earl Houser, whose wife recently came to live at 8, Pennington-road, Southborough, was killed in action at the Western Front on September 22nd. Trooper Houser was born in Canada, and joined the Royal Canadian Dragoons, landing in England last January. After further training in England he went to the Front on June 8th. Trooper Houser was married on June 3rd (five days before leaving for the Front) and the deepest sympathy will go out to his widow. Before her marriage Mrs Houser was a member of staff of the "Tonbridge Gazette". The following is an extract of a kindly and appreciative letter from Roy Nordheimer, Lieutenant, B Squadron, RCD: " ... he had made many friends, and was a fine fellow in every way. He was one of our bombers sent out with two other men as a listening post in front of our trench. He was hit in the forehead by a bullet, and death was instantaneous".*

A letter from his chum: "Just a line to express my greatest sympathy for you. Earl and I had been bombing together for about a week. Everything went along smoothly until the night of the 22nd. It was our turn on listening post, and about 10pm the bullets began to spit about us; mind you, not bullets aimed at us, but stray bullets from away on our left. The German trenches are the shape of a horse-shoe, and as luck would have it, we were at the toe of the shoe, and therefore enfiladed with fire from both sides of the German trench. About 10 o'clock a bullet whizzed by my ear and struck my dear friend. Take it from me Earl never knew what hit him: he never as much as said 'Oh!' We sent for the doctor in case there was any hope and we bandaged him up. He was breathing very hard for half-an-hour or so, and it was all over. He went to a better land, where we are all going some day."

George T Huggett

G (George) Huggett, SD/5827 (South Downs) Private, 7th Bn, Royal Sussex Regiment. Died 5 April 1918. Buried in Bouzincourt Ridge Cemetery, Albert, France: Grave ref. II.M.19.

The War Memorial gives GT Huggett's rank as Lance Corporal in the MFP (Military Foot Police). Born in Sussex, and enlisted in Tunbridge Wells. Frank Stevens gives his No as 10705 and says that he lived at 4, Meadow Road, Southborough. There was news in the Courier on 12th and 19th January 1917 of what may have been a family member: *Gunner Harold Huggett, 127th Battery, City of Bristol RGA had been in hospital in France for more than a month before being sent to England, ... in Hospital at Shrewsbury, suffering from trench fever. He is the youngest son of Mr and Mrs Huggett of 6 Meadow-road.*

And from the Courier, 13 September 1918: *Mr W Huggett of Windmill Farm Cottages, Frant Forest, has received news that his brother, Pte G Huggett, of the Royal Sussex Regiment, was killed in action on the 5th April. He joined the Colours on the 14th April, 1916, and went out to France in August of the same year. He came home gassed after twelve months' fighting in September last year, and went out again in November.*

On 31 May 1918, the Tunbridge Wells Advertiser (see picture left) had reported: *Pte W Huggett, of the Dorset Regiment, brother to Mr T Huggett, tobacconist, of Grove Hill-road, and Miss Huggett, of 71, Woodlands-road, has been gassed, and is in hospital overseas. Pte Huggett joined up in 1916, and has been in the Dardanelles, Egypt and France. He went to school at High Brooms and Southborough, and was home on leave before Christmas. He has five brothers serving.*

Albert Leslie Hunter

Private 13047826, Pioneer Corps. Died Friday 19 July 1946. Buried in Southborough Cemetery, England: Grave ref. Sec. 11. Grave 380. Son of Thomas Edward and Harriet Ethel Mildred Hunter; husband of Doris Mabel Ellen Hunter, of Southborough.

From www.royalpioneercorps.co.uk: *During WWII the Corps were, among other places, at Dunkirk, Salerno, Anzio, North Africa, Normandy, Burma, India, Iceland and Faroe Islands, for the Pioneers were not only engaged on labour tasks behind the lines but in all the big landings also. Army Commanders in every theatre of war paid full tribute to the work of the Corps without which they freely admitted that the war could not have been won.*

From the Courier, 26 July 1946: *On July 19th, at 20 Taylor-street, Southborough, Albert Leslie, devoted husband of Doris ME Hunter, passed peacefully away after much suffering, patiently borne, aged 33.*

Joseph Guy Huntrods

Captain, 157691. Died Monday 22 January 1945, age 57. Buried in Southborough Cemetery, England. Sec 11, Grave 387.

Joseph Guy Huntrods (known as Guy) was of Yorkshire ancestry. There were Huntrods recorded living in Whitby in the mid-16th century, and Guy's grandfather hailed from Yorkshire, but at the age of eighteen Guy's father Joseph walked to Workington, on the Cumbrian coast, and spent the rest of his life building up a ship's chandlers business there. Guy was the last child of Joseph Huntrods' first wife Elizabeth, who died when Guy was four. His father married again and had two more sons, Oliver and Richard. He despatched them around the world to make their way, and Guy was sent to Sicily at eighteen to learn the wine trade for several years, then spent some time in Canada before returning to Workington.

Guy joined the Border Regiment, and after fighting in the trenches in France, was commissioned into the Green Howards (6th Yorkshire) as a 2nd Lieutenant. In October 1916 he received a skin wound to the throat. On 9 October 1917 the family received news that

Guy lay dangerously ill in hospital in Boulogne, severely wounded in the lungs and in a critical condition after having been in action at Passchendaele. He had lain, wounded, in a shell-hole for ten hours before rescue, and put in a tent with the dying. Someone came round asking if the men would like anything, a last kindness, and Guy said, "I'd give anything for a glass of champagne". Amazingly, one was somehow produced, and sipping it revived Guy sufficiently for the doctor who was looking the wounded over to think he could be saved. (The photograph below shows, L to R, Oliver, Eva, Richard & Guy Huntrods.)

Guy married Ethel in 1917 and they lived in West Hartlepool, Co Durham. Towards the end of the war he was declared unfit for action. His first child Margaret, born in 1919, died in infancy. He then went on to work for the family business in Workington. In 1921 his first son Joseph Wilfred William was born, and in 1923 his father died just before his second son Guy was born, and the business was left to him and his half brother Oliver.

Guy was very methodical and precise, and had tremendous integrity, but in spite of his best efforts, the business went under, as did so many, in the 1929/30 world-wide economic crash. His father had tied up all his money in trusts until 1938, and Guy wanted his sons to be given a good education so, lacking available funds, he moved south, to Felstead in Essex. He bought a small cottage and some land and went into poultry production; the boys went to Felstead School. The family stayed there until 1936, when they moved to Hastings for a year, and to Southborough in 1938. Son Guy went to board at Kings', Rochester, and the older son, Wilfred, went into the City. The Huntrods rented a house in Pennington Road, part of a former mansion owned by Lady Lushington, which was hit during the war by a V2 rocket. The family was lent a house in Littlegates after this, behind the playing fields.

Wilfred joined the Territorial Unit, Artists Rifles before the Second World War began, and at the outbreak of war was commissioned 2nd Lieutenant in the Green Howards, his father's old Regiment, and despatched with the British Expeditionary Force to France. He went out to the Middle East late 1940/early 1941, and was taken prisoner by the Italians at Bir Hacheim; he was mentioned in dispatches. He was later shipped to Germany, and was a prisoner of war in Kassel until released by the Americans in 1945.

His younger brother Guy joined the Royal Navy as a rating. He served on HMS Duke of York, which took Winston Churchill over to Washington just after Pearl Harbour in 1941. He was recommended for a commission and was Midshipman at 19, and went into Combined Operations, Assault Landing Craft. He took part in various allied landings in Sicily, and one day stood on the stage of the Theatre Massimo, where his father as a young man had once seen Caruso booed off the stage. After further landings in Italy and then Normandy he joined a light cruiser in the Far East as a lieutenant.

Guy Huntrods (Senior) volunteered to serve at the outbreak of the Second World War, and, having been an infantryman in the First World War, he was signed up for the Royal Artillery, and trained on searchlights at Shrivenham. However, with his past experience of speaking Italian, and being still fluent, he was by 1940 sent to Ruthin in Wales, and then back to Tonbridge, to serve as translator in the Italian prisoner of war camp there, to which Italian soldiers captured in North Africa had been sent. Captain Huntrods was much respected by the prisoners, and when he died of angina, and was to be given a military funeral, they asked for permission to carry his coffin to the grave.

His son Guy was present at the funeral, and recalls that there was thick snow and brilliant sunshine on the day. **Flight Lieutenant Rigg**, a friend of his, was buried next to Captain Huntrods three months later.

Kenneth Lotherington Hutchings

Lieutenant 4th Bn, attached 12th Bn, The King's (Liverpool Regiment). Died 3 September 1916, age 33. Commemorated on Thiepval Memorial, Somme, France: Pier and Face 1 D 8 B and 8 C.

Clive Maier's research includes the following: *KL Hutchings was a dashing right-hand bat who at his peak was one of the most exciting players to watch in England. He loved to drive anything over-pitched, and when his eye was in he could hit the good-length ball off the front foot very hard indeed. He had exceptionally strong forearms and wrists, and it is said that when he came into bat, mid-on and mid-off automatically dropped back a few yards, such was the power of his driving. For defence he relied entirely on back-play, and overall his style was considered unique. He was also a superb fielder both at slip and in the deep. After a stellar schoolboy career at Tonbridge – he made several centuries including a double hundred against strong opposition – he debuted for Kent the year after he left school. After playing a full season in 1903 he was seen only occasionally for the county until 1906, his greatest year. He made nearly 1500 runs, with four centuries, and averaged over 60, playing quite brilliantly, and leading Kent to the County Championship. He was less successful in 1907, but was chosen to tour Australia.*

From the Courier, 4 June 1915: *Lieutenant Kenneth L Hutchings, who received a commission in the King's Liverpool Regiment, and was transferred to the Royal Welsh Fusiliers, writes as follows: -*

"I have been near to death two or three times already, but it is very hard to realise how near one has been to it when you look round and see your surroundings. In the first place, we discovered an enemy patrol the other evening right up in our barbed wire, cutting them, so we got our machine-gun ready and about 20 men on the parapets. We then sent up a flare and spied them about 100 yards away, and let them have it.

"I was on the parapet directing the fire of my small squad of men, and keeping my head only just above the top, just enough to be able to see in front. All of a sudden I felt a loud crack (a bullet near you makes a crack like the snapping of a branch) just by my right ear. I thought it must have been pretty close, and then discovered that the bullet had actually hit and ripped away the top of the sandbag on which I was resting my head.

"The other shaves were even closer, and I and the three officers with me cannot make out why we were not hit – it is simply miraculous. We were talking about being wounded, when all of a sudden I thought I heard a shell coming. I shouted, "Look out!" Before we had time to throw ourselves down on the ground the shell burst clean over our very heads; in fact, when we found we were not hit we looked up, and there was the smoke of the burst shell not twenty feet above our heads ...

"We had not got twenty yards before I heard the bang of another gun. We listened for a second, heard the thing coming along, and threw ourselves into a ditch, which, luckily, was pretty deep, but had a lot of water in it. This time the shell burst ten yards to our left, but we then had managed to get practically under cover, and once again we got off.

Our trenches and dug-outs are wonderful, with flowers, roses, pansies, ferns, etc, which we have grown all along our lines.

Dee's Directory 1915 lists, under Men Serving, KL Hutchings, 1st King's Liverpool, and Sgt JS Hutchings, 7th Royal West Kent, both resident at 71 London Road, Southborough.

From the Courier 28 July 1916: *Lieutenant JS Hutchings, 4th Kings Liverpool Regiment, was wounded on July 19th, sustaining a shrapnel wound in the thigh. He is now in Reading Hospital, progressing favourably. He joined the Army in September 1914 and went to the Front in February 1916.*

And from the Courier, 15 September, 1916: *It was with widespread sorrow that the news was received on Saturday that Lieutenant Kenneth Lotherington Hutchings had been killed in action in France while leading his men, on September 3rd. The son of Dr and Mrs Hutchings, "Highbury", he was born in Southborough on December 7th, 1882, and was the great-grandson of Mr Thomas Lotherington, of Holden House, and grandson of the much-beloved Dr Henry Colebrooke. He was educated at Tonbridge, where he broke all the cricket records, was in the XI five years, Captain for two years, and held the Dale Cap three years in succession, and scored the highest individual score of 205 runs. He played in one match for the County the year he left school, and again occasionally until 1906, when he became a regular member of the Eleven. There his brilliant cricket and extraordinary unselfishness and sympathetic consideration for the other members of the team won for him the admiration and affection of everyone. Like a true sportsman, he offered himself at once when the war broke out, and obtained a commission in the 4th The King's (Liverpool) Regiment, and was gazetted full Lieutenant at the end of last year. He went out to France in the Spring of 1915, and returned to England in December, having been in the firing line the whole time he was out. He then had to undergo an operation, and went out again in July of this year, and had been in the thick of the fighting for some time. In the Army, as in the cricket field, he won the love and respect of all with whom he came in contact, as the many letters from his brother officers and friends from far and near will testify. His charm of manner and unfailing courtesy to all classes will always be* remembered affectionately by those who knew him. Mr KL Hutchings' three brothers are serving their country. The eldest is in France, one is in England recovering from wounds, and the other is expecting to be sent out at any time.

According to a message received at Liverpool from an officer where, prior to the war, he had been engaged in business, Lieutenant Hutchings had a presentiment that he was about to be killed. It appears that he was struck by a shell and killed instantaneously.

Harold Henry Isted

Rifleman C/3955, 17th Bn, King's Royal Rifle Corps. Died Sunday 3 September 1916. Buried in Ancre British Cemetery, Beaumont-Hamel, Somme, France: Grave ref. V.F.38.

Rifleman Isted was killed on the same day as **Kenneth Lotherington Hutchings**.

The CWGC website includes the following information about the Ancre British Cemetery: *The village of Beaumont-Hamel was attacked on 1 July 1916 by the 29th Division, with the 4th on its left and the 36th (Ulster) on its right, but without success. On 3 September a further attack was delivered between Hamel and Beaumont-Hamel and on 13 and 14 November, the 51st (Highland), 63rd (Royal Naval), 39th and 19th (Western) Divisions finally succeeded in capturing Beaumont-Hamel, Beaucourt-sur-Ancre and St. Pierre-Divion.*

The 1916 Kelly's Directory lists a Henry Isted resident at 81 Albion Road, Tunbridge Wells.

From the Tunbridge Wells Advertiser, 27 October 1916: *Private Harold Henry Isted, of the King's Royal Rifle Corps, has been reported missing since the 3rd of September. Private Isted, who was only 22 years of age, was a native of Groombridge, and received his education at St Thomas' School, Groombridge.*

William Alfred James

The Southborough War Memorial lists a Sapper W James, Kent Field Coy, Royal Engineers. Dee's Directory for 1915 gives the address as 4 Speldhurst Road, Southborough.

Local author Frank Stevens can find no record of this man in 3rd Kent, but there is a record on the CWGC site of the following casualty:

Sapper William Alfred James, 19446, 7th Div Signal Coy, Royal Engineers. Died on 9 May 1915, age 25. Commemorated on the Le Touret Memorial, Pas de Calais, France: Panel 1.

He was the son of Mrs L James of 15, Ewart Road, Chatham, and the husband of Emily Pratt (formerly James), of Ash Street, Ash, Sevenoaks, Kent. William James was born in Chatham and enlisted there. He died on the same day as **Herbert Avard** and **Robert Bassett**, who are also commemorated on the Southborough War Memorial.

George Arthur Jenner

2nd Corporal 540134, 497th Field Coy, Royal Engineers. Died 15 April 1917, age 22. Buried at Tilloy British Cemetery, Tilloy-Les-Mofflaines, Pas de Calais, France: Grave ref. I.E.29. Son of George and Jane Jenner, of 82 Taylor Street, Southborough.

Tilloy-Les-Mofflaines is a village 3k south-east of Arras, on the south side of the main road to Cambrai. The village was taken by British troops on 9 April 1917. Information from the website www.firstworldwar.com/onthisday gives the following campaign detail for 15 April 1917: *Western Front: British repulse German attack on Bapaume-Cambrai road; severe fighting at Lagnicourt. British capture Villeret (north-west of St Quentin).*

Frank Stevens' book *Southborough Sappers of the Kent (Fortress) Royal Engineers* includes the following: *KF 715 540134. The first man to enlist in No 3 Company, he survived the Hythe sinking and went on to France, after Gallipoli, and was killed on 15 April 1917; the report says hit in the throat by a gas shell. He was an employee of a local newspaper. He was also Captain of the Southborough Third Football Team.*

From the Tunbridge Wells Advertiser, 26 October 1917: *Leading Seaman H J Jenner, RN, son of Mr & and Mrs Jenner, 82 Taylor Street, is home on ten days' leave before proceeding to a foreign station for two or three years. He joined the Navy seven years ago, and has seen some big battles at sea, and had some nerve-racking experiences. He was also in the recent air raid on Chatham.*

Harold Jesse Jenner was George Arthur's brother. He joined the Navy on 27 June 1910 and served in the Antrim, Endymion, Formidable and Lennox among other ships. On the first day of the war he saw the mine-layer Koenighouse sunk off Harwich by the Lance and Amphion.

In the battle of Heligoland Bight he was serving on the Lennox, which picked up 95 survivors from the Cressy, Aboukir, and Hogue (see **Alfred Assiter**).

Arthur Charles Johnson

Of the two men named A Johnson who served with the 2nd Bn, Hampshire Regiment, it may be more likely that Arthur Johnson is the one referred to on the Southborough War Memorial. Abram Johnson's details are included for interest.

Private Arthur Charles JOHNSON 8235, 2nd Bn, Hampshire Regiment. Died 9 August 1916. Born in Bidborough, resided in Southborough. Buried in the Potijze Burial Ground Cemetery, Ypres, Belgium, Grave ref: T1.

From the Courier, 25 August 1916: *Mr and Mrs Johnson have received the sad news that their youngest son, Private Arthur Johnson, died in France from gas poisoning on August 9th. Private Johnson joined the 2nd Hants Regiment eight years ago, and was in India at the commencement of the war. He came to England Christmas, 1914. He was twice wounded in the Dardanelles, and was also frost-bitten while there. He had been in France about two months.*

(Also see **Private A Avis**, likely the step-brother of Private Arthur Charles Johnson, and resident at 11, Taylor-street.)

Private Abram Johnson 14341, 2nd Bn, Hampshire Regiment. Died 18 May 1915. Commemorated on the Helles Memorial, Turkey: Panel 125-134 or 223-223 228-229 & 328.

The Royal Hampshire Regiment's website tells the story of a young 15 year old soldier, James Lock, who was in the 2nd Battalion's campaign in the Dardanelles in May 1915, and these extracts may give some idea of what Abram Johnson might have experienced: *Military Citation Gallipoli Number 10418 : Private James Lock 2nd Battalion Hampshire Regiment . Took part in Gallipoli landings with 2nd Battalion Hampshires. 29th Division, 89th Brigade. Went out on King Edward, later sunk in landing. Landed Suvla Bay. About six hours before got off beach. Held up mainly by machine gun fire - no cover from fire. Captain Day, Platoon Commander killed. Second in command Corporal Bright killed. Senior soldier took over section. Eventually pushed into hills towards Achi Baba. Dug in as much as possible with entrenching tool and use of captured enemy trenches. There was barbed wire. Existed on iron rations. Turks counter-attacked the first night, but were driven off. Lock himself was in the reserve* section. *Gradually re-organised and after 3 weeks Lock was wounded by machine gun fire in hip and head. Evacuated to Egypt and then to the UK on Hospital Ship Asturias ... The position taken up by the force to which Lock was attached was found to be untenable and they re-embarked to go further down the Peninsula. They arrived off the coast near Achi Baba and went ashore at night to move into the trenches. Of this manoeuvre Lock said, in 1915, "We were aboard ship in the evening, and next morning we were defending the first line trenches. Had to land at night because of the shelling in the day time".*

His force returned to Suvla Bay for another landing: "It was just a case of tumbling overboard into the mud and wading ashore as best we could. Full kit, of course. We got some way inland before they spotted us, and then the fun began". Later they returned to Achi Baba. This was a disastrous battle for the 2nd Hampshires and their losses were heavy. Lock was wounded six times by shrapnel and a bullet from a Turkish sniper struck him behind the right ear. Along with other wounded he was shipped to Alexandria where he remained for two days before being sent on to England. Here the bullet (eventually made into a brooch for his mother) was finally extracted.

John Levi Johnson MM

Lance Sergeant G/4078, 7th Bn, Queen's Own (Royal West Kent Regiment). Died 12 October 1917. Commemorated on the Tyne Cot Memorial, Zonnebeke, West-Vlaanderen, Belgium: Panel 106 to 108.

From www.firstworldwar.com/onthisday for 12 October 1917: *British attack north-east of Ypres on six-mile front from French right to Ypres-Roulers railway. Some progress all along line, but rain stops big advance.*

From the Courier, 3 August 1917: *Mrs J Johnson has received official notice that her husband Sergeant JL Johnson was wounded in the left thigh on the 18th of July, and is in hospital at Le Treport. In a cheerful letter to his wife he tells her not to worry, for "it is nothing serious this time"... He was wounded in the right leg in October, 1916, and was sent to Netley Hospital, and went back in France in May of this year. He has served six years in the Navy, and previous to the war worked as a platelayer for the SE Railway Company. He is an old Victoria School boy.*

From the Courier, 16 November 1917: *News of the death of her husband has been received by Mrs Johnson, of 19, Wolseley-road, High Brooms. He* joined the Colours on September 25th, 1914, and his ability soon earned for him the rank of Sergeant. He went to France on the 5th of August, 1915, and he won the Military Medal during the Battle of the Somme, on July 1st 1916. He had seen a great deal of fighting, and had been wounded twice, the first time in September, 1916, and the second on July 15th, 1917. On his recovery from his second wound he went back to his post in the trenches, and was killed by a bullet almost at once. He leaves a widow and three children to mourn their loss. Mrs Johnson has two sisters who both have lost their husbands in the war. She has now four brothers serving, two in France and two in India. Lieutenant Allchin, in a letter to Mrs Johnson, says that the late Sergeant Johnson was a good fellow, and one of the bravest men in the Company. He had served with the Battalion ever since it had been formed, and it was very unfortunate that he should have met his death so soon after he had re-joined from Hospital.

Edwin Malcolm Jones

Private 353, "B" Coy, 6th Bn, Queen's Own (Royal West Kent Regiment). Died 19 July 1915, age 24. Buried in Poelcapelle British Cemetery, Langemark-Poelkapelle, West-Vlaanderen, Belgium: Grave ref. LVI.D.8. Son of John and Harriet Jones; husband of Ada Wren (formerly Jones), of 83, St James Park, Tunbridge Wells. Born at Tunbridge Wells.

On the same page in the Courier of 30 July 1915 were featured, ironically, both a letter from Private Jones (in the column LETTERS FROM LOCAL MEN ON ACTIVE SERVICE) and the report of his death. Firstly: *FROM CAMDEN ROAD TO THE TRENCHES Pte EM Jones, of the Machine Gun Section of the Royal West Kent, writes to the "Courier" from "Somewhere in France". "During the lull in the firing I now – as a lad from 111, Camden-road, Tunbridge Wells, have pleasure in sending you a narrative of 'Trench Warfare' which I shall be pleased to see published for the benefit of the readers. Perhaps you wonder what the trenches are like. This is just a brief idea. The first thing that meets the eye is one long, zig-zag line. In front of this line is another, and so on, ad lib. A nearer view shows you a deep cutting or trench divided into bays, each with a* ledge inside on which to stand when firing. The depth may be from seven to nine feet, counting from the top of the innumerable sandbags. The trench should be deep and narrow, with dug-outs in the square bays opposite the firing steps. This is the main trench. Smaller ones are dug leading out of these, either backwards or forwards, to trenches behind or in front, respectively. These are the communication trenches, up which the rations, ammunitions, etc, are brought. There is something very fascinating about the field of action. Take a peep over the parapet at night, when a star shell flares up. You see just the trees and hedges, as in England, only the trees are spread with wicked barbed wire, as well as being torn and grotesque. Not a soul is to be seen, but with the ground alive with men, each with death in their hands. There is a continuous crackle of snipers' rifles, the 'zip' and 'whine' of bullets. In the distance a gun might boom, a shell may scream overhead, to be lost in the night, or it may burst, with a flash and a roar, which is followed, in the case of shrapnel, by the swish of falling iron, or, if high explosives, by a cloud of falling earth and bricks. Inside the trench are sleeping men. 'Familiarity breeds contempt'. For instance, you may be making tea. Suddenly you hear a dull boom, followed later by a whistling noise as the revolving bullet rushes towards you. 'Look out!' says your pal, 'another of the beasts'. You bend low and wait. Crash! 'Near', says your pal, 'Come on with tea', sometimes to find it spoilt by lumps of fallen earth. Further up the line may come the call 'Stretcher-bearers, forward'. The person with the tea looks up. 'Wonder who it is?' says he, and goes on with the tea. A Tommy is very cool.

We relieved the -------- on Friday, and times without number we have had miraculous escapes. We have twice had the gas alarm, but the precautions taken keep us all right. It is awful stuff – like a low, white mist creeping towards you. Then your eyes begin to tingle, your throat aches, and you wait with 'smoke-helmets' or 'respirators' on until it has passed. There was a heavy bombardment the other night. For nearly an hour guns belched forth death, and everything used during war-time was in occupation. All that time we got covered in earth, sand etc and the earth shook. The noise was intense. Up to the time of writing we have had few casualties, and I myself am in the 'pink'. There were many who prayed that night, and many an answered prayer. You know it is quite exciting at times, this game, and at times very gruesome. Souvenirs galore, 'if' you can get them, but it doesn't do to worry."

Further down the page, friends and relatives must have been distressed to find the following: *The news of the death at the Front of Pte Edwin Malcolm Jones, of "B" Company, 6th Service Battalion, Royal West Kent Regiment, has been received with deep regret at High Brooms, where he was very popular. His widow is now residing with her husband's mother, Mrs. H Jones, at the Home Club, Camden-road, Tunbridge Wells, and the sad news of their bereavement has brought many messages of genuine sympathy during the week. Pte Jones, who was 24 years of age, had lived in High Brooms all his life, and was much esteemed by his numerous acquaintances. He was an old scholar of High Brooms Council School, was* formerly a member of the Wesleyan Sunday School at High Brooms, and has been employed as a clerk in the office of the High Brooms Brick Company. He joined the Army last August, and went to the seat of warfare in France on June 1st. He had rapidly become an efficient soldier, and was much liked by his officers and comrades. He met his death exactly seven weeks after arriving at the Front. Letters to the family included the following: "Pte Jones was on guard with a Machine Gun Section in one of the trenches, when, happening to show his head above the parapet, he was immediately marked by a German sniper and shot through the head, death being instantaneous. He was buried with military honours on the following day, Tuesday of last week, at a quiet little spot in Flanders ... carried out just as reverently as if he had been buried in England." and "Knowing the fact that he died while fighting for his King and Country. It will help you to bear what must naturally be a great loss to you. I am sending you his cap-badge, which I took from his cap as he was being carried from the trenches, knowing that you would like to have it. Hoping you are as well as can be expected under the circumstances. With deepest sympathy, yours very sincerely, Lance-Corporal HW Moon, Machine Gun Section, 6th R, West Kent."

George Alfred Prime Jones

Captain, Royal Flying Corps, also 8th Bn, The Buffs (East Kent Regiment). Died 28 May 1916, age 21. Born Bolotwa, South Africa. Buried in Southborough Cemetery, England: Grave ref. 5.160.

Listed RAF on Southborough War Memorial. From the Courier, 8 October 1915: *Lieut GAP Jones, 8th Buffs, of Ampthill, Southborough, was wounded at the Front on Sunday week last (September 26th) during the British advance, but we are glad to report his wound is not serious. He had an extremely narrow escape, a bullet striking his belt and glancing off, inflicting a flesh wound. A few minutes after – before he had recovered from the shock – a shell burst just behind him and rendered him unconscious for half-an-hour from concussion. Lieut Jones is well-known in the neighbourhood, particularly as a sportsman. He is a keen cricketer and footballer, and in the latter game, has played for Tunbridge Wells, Southborough, and several times for the Rangers, and his prowess as a goalkeeper is envied by every custodian in the district. Standing 6ft 4ins, his reach is a great asset, and he knows how to make the best use of it. Lieut Jones is the son of Mr and Mrs WC Prime Jones, of Whittlesea, South Africa, his father being the Government*

Magistrate there, and a grandson of the late Capt Richard Walker Jones, of Park Place, Sevenoaks Common. He obtained a commission in the 8th Buffs soon after the war broke out, and went to the Front on August 31st.

The Tunbridge Wells Advertiser also reported that he was asked to play for Tottenham Hotspur, and soon after joining the Army turned out for Brighton and Hove Albion.

From the Courier, 2 June 1916: *We deeply regret to record the death ... as a result of an aeroplane accident in Kent on Sunday morning ... Capt Jones resided with his aunts at 'Ampthill', 46, Pennington-road, and was the second son of Capt WC Prime Jones, late of the Cape Mounted Rifles; his grandfather was Capt Richard Walker Jones; and his great-grandfather was Capt Richard Jones, RN, of Warehorn, Tenterden. He was in the Battle of Loos in September last year and was promoted to his Captaincy on 27th September. He was attached to the Royal Flying Corps about three months ago, and entered into the study and practice of aviation with the same enthusiasm that he has shown in everything else. He had gained his pilot's certificate, and in about a fortnight or three weeks would probably have gained his "wings". His brother officers speak very highly of him, and were convinced he would have made a first-class airman. He was educated at Skinners' School, Tunbridge Wells, and was a member of the Officers' Training Corps of the School.*

The Inquest was held on Tuesday evening. The first witness was Mr Raymond Walker Prime Jones, uncle and guardian of the deceased, who gave evidence of identification ... the next witness was the Police Constable on duty. He stated that at about 11am on Sunday he was in a field used by the authorities as a landing place. He saw the biplane descend with Lieut Tennant acting as pilot, deceased being in the observer's seat. They got out, had a smoke and a chat, and were both very cheerful, commenting on the fine morning. They stayed about a quarter-of-an-hour, and then prepared to return. The machine was not more than 100 feet up, when it appeared to gradually turn to the left, and then side-dipped, taking a nose-dive to the ground. Witness got to the spot two or three seconds after the machine fell, and found that Lieut Tennant had been thrown two or three feet clear of the machine, and was apparently badly injured, but was still living. Capt Jones was still in the machine, but was quite dead. It took about three-quarters-of-an-hour to get him out. Witness described his injuries, and said death was absolutely instantaneous. His wrist watch was still going when he was got away from the machine. In answer to questioning, witness stated that there was a gusty, south-west wind blowing. The machine bounced eight or nine feet before it finally came to rest.

Captain Uriah Cook said he saw the bi-plane arrive, and also saw it start on its way back and come down. He considered the machine was in perfect order, and the engine was running when it struck the ground. The air was fairly still on the ground owing to the surrounding trees, but the machine may have struck a gust when clearing the trees.

Second-Lieutenant Frederick Russell Hardie, attached to the Royal Flying Corps, was the next witness. He said the machine was one he usually used, and in his opinion was in perfect order, and had been previously flown that morning. He sent Lieut Tennant out for a practice flight from the aerodrome and back again. Capt Jones was not included in the order, and probably went with him voluntarily. Lieut Tennant had never been to that particular field. Witness heard of the accident about noon, and immediately flew to the ground. He found the wrecked machine and saw Lieut Tennant being attended to. Capt Jones had been removed when he arrived. He had since seen Lieut Tennant, who said he experienced a bad "bump" when ascending, and the machine side-slipped, and was too near the ground to recover. He was trying to do a gradual turn. Witness considered Lieut Tennant was a competent man; he had done twenty hours' flying as pilot. There had been a Court of Inquiry held that morning by the Military Authorities, and they had found that the accident was due to the causes above enumerated. The Jury brought in a verdict of "Death by Misadventure", and expressed their sympathy with the relatives.

THE FUNERAL

Captain Jones was laid to rest ... on Wednesday afternoon with military honours. The body was brought back to Southborough by the military authorities, and conveyed from the house to the cemetery on a gun-carriage drawn by six black horses, the coffin being covered with the Union Jack. The cortege was headed by the Band of the Buffs, who played the "Dead March" in "Saul"; the firing party of the same Regiment, officers and men of the Royal Flying Corps, and also the Skinners' School OTC followed as mourners. Six officers of the Buffs acted as bearers. The boys from the National Schools were drawn up on either side of Victoria-road, and the girls were close to the Cemetery entrance. A large number of people were present at the Cemetery to reverently pay their last respects to one who had given his life for his country as much as though he had died on the battlefield. The whole of the service was held at the graveside, conducted by the Rev TAE Williamson, and the Rev FG Knott (Headmaster of Skinners' School), the clergy of the town being also present. The firing party fired three volleys over the grave, and the fifes and drums played the salute, thus ending an impressive service.

The mourners were Mr and Mrs RW Jones (uncle and aunt), Miss Florrie Jones, Miss Leila Jones and Miss Maud Jones (aunts), Mrs Nicolas, Mr Walter T Fremlin, Rev and Mrs FWB Ford, and officers and men of the Flying Corps. Several other members of the family would have been present, but were unable to arrive in time owing to the short notice.

Robert Ernest Joyce

Private G/37769, 7th Bn, The Queen's (Royal West Surrey Regiment). Died 27 February 1917, age 32. Commemorated on the Thiepval Memorial, Somme, France: Pier and Face 5D and 6D. Husband of Agnes Gertrude Joyce, of 17 Taylor Street, Southborough.

Information from www.firstworldwar.com/onthisday gives the following campaign detail for 27 February 1917: *Western Front: Ligny (east of Le Barque) and Gommecourt occupied by the British. Also the western and southern defences of Puisieux. East of Armentieres British raiders seriously damage three lines of enemy trenches and take 17 prisoners.*

Frederick James Kates

Private T/24830, 112th HT (Horse Transport) Coy, Army Service Corps. Died Thursday 3 October 1918. Buried in Taranto Town Cemetery Extension, Italy: Grave ref. III.C.7. Husband of Edith Mary Kates, of 8 Millcroft Road, Cliffe-at-Hoo, Rochester. Born in Southborough, enlisted at Aldershot, when resident in Rochester.

Southborough War Memorial gives Frederick Kates' rank as Lance Corporal, RASC – MT. Dee's Directory for 1915 gives his address as 7 Elm Road, Southborough.

From the Courier, 25 October 1918: *Mrs Manktelow, of London-road, Southborough, has been informed of the death of her son, Driver Frederick James Kates, Army Service Corps, aged 30, on October 3rd. Driver Kates, who was an Army Reservist, was called up on the outbreak of war, and was in the retirement from Mons, 1914. He was transferred to Egypt, and subsequently journeyed to Salonica, returning to England on 21 days' leave on August 23rd last, after three years' absence. It was while on his way to rejoin his unit that he succumbed at Taranto, Italy. He leaves a widow and two young children, residing at Cliffe.*

It might be surmised, given the date, that Frederick Kates may have 'succumbed' to the 1918 influenza pandemic, which claimed the lives, it is estimated, of between twenty and forty million people.

J Kelly

Private, Royal West Kent. Died in World War I.

From the Courier, 30 July 1915: *Pte J Kelly, who enlisted in the West Kent Regiment at the outbreak of war, is reported killed in action. Mr Kelly, who leaves a widow, was a well-known local compositor among the typographical fraternity in Tunbridge Wells and Tonbridge, who have learnt with regret of his death.*

On 23 July 1915 the Courier had reported that Mrs Kelly had received a War Office intimation that her husband was killed in action a month ago. The author thinks it possible that the following details may refer to this casualty – they are the nearest match she can find on the CWGC site.

Private G R Kelly S/39, 1st Bn, Queen's Own (Royal West Kent Regiment). Died 27 June 1915. Buried in the Voormezeele Enclosures No 1 and No 2, Voormezeele, Belgium, Grave Ref. I.B.5. Husband of Rosanna Kelly, of 5, Albion Square, St John's, Tunbridge Wells.

Stanley Arthur Kimber

Sapper 1024 1st/3rd Kent Field Coy, Royal Engineers. Died 28 October 1915, in the Hythe disaster. Commemorated on the Helles Memorial, which stands on the tip of the Gallipoli Peninsula in Turkey. Panel 23 to 25 or 325 to 328.

Frank Stevens' book *Southborough Sappers of the Kent (Fortress) Royal Engineers* includes the following: *His number shows that he enlisted before the war and it is likely that he came through the Cadets. His civilian job was engine cleaner on the London Brighton – South Coast Railway, and he was 19 years old. He lived with his mother at 32 Southview Road, High Brooms, and had earlier attended the High Brooms School. He was her only son.*

Southborough War Memorial

Charles James King

Rifleman 3211, 2nd Bn, Rifle Brigade. Died on Tuesday 18 April 1916. Buried in Becourt Military Cemetery, Becordel-Becourt, Somme, France: Grave ref. I.L.4.

CJ King was born in Faversham. Dee's Directory 1915 listed Rifleman King and his brother E King, Royal Sussex Regiment, resident at 7 Speldhurst Road, Southborough.

From the Tunbridge Wells Advertiser, undated: *Rifleman C King, 2nd Batt Rifle Brigade, arrived home at Southborough this week, after having spent several weeks in various hospitals recovering from a wound received after the Battle of Neuve Chapelle. A representative of the Advertiser had the pleasure of a chat with the rifleman on Tuesday. He has spent five years in India, coming home from that country in October. He left England for the Front on the 5th November. Landing at Havre, the Rifle Brigade proceeded to Hazebrook, where they had three days' rest.*

"We entered the trenches at Pinkington", said the rifleman, "and we spent the winter in the trenches round about there. We moved on the 4th of March to a place near Estaires, where we rested until the 9th. Then we marched to Neuve Chapelle. We knew something big was on the move, and at 7 o'clock in the morning, we heard the guns commence. Everything had been as usual during the night, and when the 350 guns roared out upon the morning stillness it was like hell. Every gun, from 4.7's to 15in, was brought into play, and they wrought terrible havoc. The Germans were absolutely blown out of their trenches, and we saw arms and legs and other parts of their bodies flung in all directions. At 7.35 the whistles sounded, and we leapt from our trenches eager to come to grips with the enemy. The Berks were on our right, and the Lincolns on our left. We were in support of the Berks, and the Lincolns were supported by the Irish Rifles. The Berks and Lincolns had to take the trenches facing them, and our duty was to go through them, and, together with the Irish Rifles, rush the village. And we did it, but not without hard fighting and heavy losses. We went right through the village, and set up our parapet on the other side. Whilst engaged in that work we discovered we were being fired on from behind, and under the leadership of a corporal a number of us went back to find where it came from. Our search was successful, and we found ten Germans in a cellar. They were all wounded, and we made them prisoners. Altogether our battalion must have taken about 400 prisoners. The artillery kept pounding away, and in the afternoon we made another move forward, but had to retire in the face of heavy machine gun fire. The Manchesters made another gallant attempt in the evening, but were no more successful.

Rifleman King is naturally very proud of his regiment, which claims two gallant VCs, Serg-Major Daniel and Corpl Noble. "I actually saw those two men win the coveted Cross," he said. "It was when the Germans were preparing for a counter-attack. I saw them climb out of the trench, knowing what a perilous job they were on, but they succeeded in cutting the barbed wire entanglements. I also saw them both brought back – wounded. The Sergt-Major is recovering from his wound, but Corporal Noble died the same night." Shortly after that notable incident, Rifleman King was wounded, being struck in the jaw with a piece of shrapnel. With a number of comrades who had suffered the same fate, he succeeded in reaching the ambulance after dashing across a bullet-swept open space. He was conveyed to Estaires, where his wound was attended to. After passing through Merville and Boulogne, he eventually reached Le Treport, where he went under an operation. On returning to England he landed at Bristol, where he remained for five days before going to the Countess of Suffolk's Hospital.

Thomas King

Private G/1603, 12th Bn, Royal Sussex Regiment. Died on 24 July 1917, age 27. Buried in Essex Farm Cemetery, Ypres, West-Vlaanderen, Belgium: Grave ref. I.Q.4. Son of Mrs Emma King, of 3 North Farm Road, High Brooms.

The land south of Essex Farm was used as a dressing station cemetery from April 1915 to August 1917. It was here that Lieutenant-Colonel John McCrae of the Canadian Army Medical Corps wrote the poem *in Flanders Fields* in May 1915.

From the Tunbridge Wells Advertiser, 16 August 1917: *Mrs King, of 3, North Farm-road, High Brooms, has received news that her son, Pte Tom King, was killed in action at the end of July. Pte King, who was 26 years of age, joined the Royal Sussex Regiment nearly three years ago, and has been in France 17 months, and in a letter to his mother said he was shortly expecting leave. He was an old St John's School boy. Mrs King has two other sons with the colours, one in France and one in India.*

"Dear Madam – I am writing to sympathise with you in the loss of your son, Pte King of this Battalion, and tell you how greatly he will be missed. I was out with him at the time he was killed, but it will relieve you to know that he suffered no pain, his death being instantaneous. As platoon commander of No 6 Platoon for over three months, I came into daily contact with him, and have always found him a splendid *soldier, particularly on long marches, when he kept everybody cheerful by his quaint humour. In the line as a sniper he carried out his duties thoroughly and patiently, and was always ready to help a pal. Again sympathising with you in your great loss, I remain yours sincerely, SS Honeyman, 2nd-Lt".*

John Vincent Kirsten

Private 14875, 1st Bn, Scots Guards. Died Sunday 14 January 1917, age 20. Buried in Combles Communal Cemetery Extension, Somme, France: Grave ref. II.E.8. Son of John George and Marie Kirsten, of 13, Rue Van Hulthem, Ghent, Belgium.

From the Courier, 2 February 1917: *Mr and Mrs Kirsten, Grove House, have received information from the War Office that their eldest son, John Vincent Kirsten, Scots Guards (attached Machine Gun Corps) was killed in action on January 14th. Private Kirsten joined the Army in November 1915, joining as a Private in preference to taking a commission which was offered him. He was educated at Beech House, Eastbourne, and by the Reverend JB Hyland, Combe Storey Rectory, Taunton.*

The following, from the Courier of 1 November 1918, may refer to Private Kirsten's sister: *Military wedding reported at St Peter's of Miss Marie Marguerite Kirsten, daughter of Mr and Mrs TG Kirsten, Southborough, and Lieutenant S Moore Gilbert. The bride was given away by her brother Private Jack Kirsten, Royal Highlanders (Black Watch). The best man was Captain SF James, Kings' Royal Rifle Corps.*

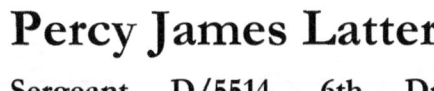

Percy James Latter

Sergeant D/5514, 6th Dragoon Guards (Carabiniers). Died 18 April 1918, age 25. Buried in St Sever Cemetery Extension, Rouen, Seine-Maritime, France: Grave ref. P.XI.L.1A. Born and lived in Southborough. Son of Mrs Francis Eveleigh, of 170 Lower Hythe Street, Dartford, Kent.

Percy Latter had been injured earlier in the War. The Courier of 13 November 1914 reported: *Corporal P Latter, 6th Dragoon Guards (The Carabineers) is now in hospital at Wandsworth, London, with* bullet wounds in the head. He is the grandson of Mr & Mrs Pounds, 21, Speldhurst Road, Southborough, and has seen 4 years' service with the Colours. In a letter home he stated that his regiment had been in a number of heavy engagements, in several of which they gallantly charged the enemy. Corporal Latter was wounded in the middle of October, and arrived in England on October 28th. He had been on duty so long that he and several of his comrades fell asleep in the saddle. Orders were given to dismount, and the tired men lay down beside their horses. Shortly after the Germans attacked, and Corporal Latter was shot through the head.

And on 18 December 1914: *Corporal Latter has had four horses shot under him at different times, and also at Passy was knocked down by the force of a shell explosion, which killed four men and wounded six others with whom he was standing. It was whilst reconnoitring on October 20th, during the battle of the Aisne, that he received the severe wound which was the cause of presence in these parts now. A shrapnel shell burst near him, and a piece struck his head, inflicting a severe wound. He has spent the time since in Hospital and at home on a month's furlough. Being a cavalryman, Corporal Latter was spared those weary vigils in the trenches, but had to be ever on the qui vive for the order to charge. The men while away the time by playing football with bully beef tins in the rear of the trenches. Corporal Latter, however, participated in numerous exciting and dangerous reconnoitring movements entrusted to the Dragoons, and it was in one of these that he was wounded. He relates how the infantry in the trenches would indulge in impromptu concerts during lulls in the fighting, and how they and the Germans would "sauce" each other when the trenches were close enough by means of messages engraved on turnips, which were slung across.*

From the Courier 3 May 1918: *Mr and Mrs Pounds have received news of the death of their grandson and adopted child, Sergeant P Latter. He joined the Army eight years ago, and has seen service in South Africa. At the outbreak of war he was drafted to France, and had been through all the principal battles from Mons onwards. He was wounded on April 1st, and he died in a Base Hospital after an operation for the amputation of his leg.*

Patrick John Lawford

Private S/8794, 2nd Bn, Queen's Own (Royal West Kent Regiment) attached Royal Dublin Fusiliers. Died 6 October 1916, age 21. Son of W Douglas Lawford and Annie E Lawford, of Southborough. Buried in Lahana Military Cemetery, Greece: Grave ref. II.C.11.

From the CWGC website: *Lahana is a village on the old Thessalonika-Seres Road, about 56 km north-east of*

Southborough War Memorial

Thessalonika. The cemetery lies 1km west of the village. It was begun in July 1916 for burials from the 27th Casualty Clearing Station, to which sick and wounded men were brought from the Struma front. After the Armistice, 41 of the graves in Plots II and III were brought in from the two front line cemeteries at Paprat (about 12 km north-west of Lahana). www.firstworldwar.com/onthisday gives the following campaign detail for 6 October 1916: *Southern Front: Gradual withdrawal Bulgarians from valley of Struma to mountains beyond Demirhissar and Seres.*

From the Courier, 20 October 1916: *News has been received by Mr & Mrs Douglas Lawford, Southborough, of the death of their son, Patrick John Lawford, in Serbia, who joined the 3rd (Special Reserve) Royal West Kent Regiment in 1913, and volunteered for draft for the Front in November, 1914. He fought throughout the winter campaign in Flanders, 1914 and 1915, and was invalided home with severe frost-bite in March, 1915. After four months in Hospital he re-joined his Regiment, and in September left with a draft which landed in Salonika. He fought in the winter campaign of 1915 and 1916 in Serbia, and died of wounds received in action on October 6th. Mr and Mrs Lawford have three other sons serving their King and Country.*

Dee's 1915 Directory listed, under Men Serving, *AP Lawford, 16th Lancers*, and *PR Lawford, RWK Sp Res, resident 14 Church-road*. The Queen's Own Gazette of February 1917, page 3597, included the following under the heading Information Wanted: *Any information regarding S/8794 Private PT Lawford, who was reported as having Died of Wounds received in action on October 6th, 1916, whilst attached to the Royal Dublin Fusiliers, will be thankfully received by his father, Mr Douglas Lawford, Southborough, Tunbridge Wells.*

Patrick's brother, Private A.B. Lawford, was with the Machine Gun Corps, and the Courier, 8 June 1917, reported that he: *... has been wounded while acting as guide to a relieving party. The OC of his Squadron writes that after receiving attention at the aid post Private Lawford then conducted the relieving party up the line, and from there was sent back on a limber in the dressing-station and field ambulance.*

George Thomas Leaney

Corporal 5232, 1st Bn, Queen's Own (Royal West Kent Regiment). Died 22 February 1915, age 34. Husband of Louisa Leaney, of 52 Highams Road, Tunbridge Wells. Born at Lamberhurst. Commemorated at the Tuileries British Cemetery, Ypres, West-Vlaanderen, Belgium: Special

Southborough War Memorial

Memorial B.3. Eighty of the nearly one hundred 1914-18 War casualties whose graves were made in this cemetery are represented by special memorials as the graves were destroyed by shell fire during the war.

From the Courier, 19 March 1915: *Corporal George Leaney, of the "B" Company, Royal West Kent, was killed in action on February 22nd. The deceased, who leaves a wife and two children, was in the second reserves, and within a few days of his expired time when he was called up, and went out in September with the Expeditionary Force and took part in several engagements. Leaney had previously been through the Boer War, and for the past six years had been rural postman at Lamberhurst, where he was greatly esteemed for the faithful discharge of his duties. He recently sent home to his wife the Christmas presents from the King and the Princess Mary, which he had received in common with the troops at the Front, and of which he was very proud. The widow has received the expression of Royal sympathy which Lord Kitchener is sending out to the widows of those who fall in action. This is the first death among the Lamberhurst contingent, and the greatest sympathy is felt for the widow and family.*

Jesse Leaney

Private 204969 Ist Bn, Royal Scots Fusiliers. Died 12 April 1918. Commemorated on Panel 1, Ploegsteert Memorial, Berks Cemetery Extension, Belgium.

Dee's Directory for 1915 lists J Leaney, serving with the Royal West Kent Regiment, resident at Birling Farm (also the address of **George Luck**), and J Leaney is listed with the RWK on the War Memorial

From the Courier, 13 September 1918: *Private J Leaney, son of Mrs Leaney of Birling Farm, Powder Mill Lane, is reported missing since April last. He is an old King Charles School boy, and was employed by Messrs Rock, Thorpe & Co.*

Co-incidentally, there were two J Leaneys reported in the Tunbridge Wells Advertiser of 13 September 1918. The other was: **Lance Corporal James William Leaney, G/31351, 6th Bn, Queen's Own (Royal West Kent Regiment). Died 9 August 1918, age 26. Born at Ticehurst. Son of Emily and James Leaney, of 35 Napier Road, Hawkenbury, Tunbridge Wells. Buried at Morlancourt British Cemetery No2, Somme, France: Grave ref: A.12.**

Southborough War Memorial

The row of photographs above shows Private J Leaney on the left, and Lance-Corporal JW Leaney on the right.

Harry Ernest Lipscombe

Acting Bombardier 81503, 308th Siege Battery, Royal Garrison Artillery. Died 31 October 1917. Buried in Menin Road South Military Cemetery, Ypres, Belgium: Grave ref: III.H.23.

From the Tunbridge Wells Advertiser of 30 November 1917: *Mrs Lipscombe, of 39, Bedford-road, has been notified by the War Office of the death in France, on October 5th, of her husband, Bombardier HE Lipscombe, of the RGA. He joined up in May, 1915, and proceeded to France in September, 1917. He leaves a widow and four young children to mourn their loss.*

Rank is given as Bombardier on Southborough War Memorial.

Albert Edward Lorne

Ordinary Seaman LT/JX 129163, HM Trawler Cobbers, Royal Navy Patrol Service. Died Monday 3 March 1941, age 29. Buried in Southborough Cemetery, England: Grave ref. Sec. 6. Grave 84. Son of William and Alice Maud Lorne; husband of Gladys Rose Lorne, of High Brooms.

Albert was one of a very large family, and lived in Groombridge, at Mott's Mill. His father had formerly been in the Navy, and latterly worked as a sweep. Albert worked at John Brown's

121

Dairies, on St John's Road, in Tunbridge Wells, before the War. He and Gladys had one daughter, Ann Maude.

The trawler Cobbers was attacked by enemy aircraft and sunk off Lowestoft on 3 March 1941. Of the crew of fifteen, four were saved and nine known to be killed. The other two were missing and presumed dead.

George Luck

Donkeyman SS Poljames (London), Mercantile Marine. Died 2 October 1918, age 27. Son of George and Amelia Luck (nee Knee) of Birling Farm, Powder Mill Lane, Southborough. Commemorated on Tower Hill Memorial, London.

George Luck's rank is given as AB, Royal Navy on Southborough War Memorial. Donkeymen were stokers & engine room artificers, and their duties included operating & maintaining the small engines on board the trawlers manned by the RNR & MFA. Some of those very small ships would not have carried enginemen, so the donkeyman would have run the main ship engines also.

The SS Poljames was torpedoed by enemy submarine UB112 and sunk six miles south from the Lizard, Cornwall, with thirteen lives lost. Some of the survivors rowed to shore at Falmouth.

The CWGC website includes the following information about the Tower Hill Memorial: *The Tower Hill Memorial commemorates men and women of the Merchant Navy and Fishing Fleets who died in both World Wars and who have no known grave. It stands on the south side of the garden of Trinity Square, London, close to The Tower of London.*

In the First World War, the civilian navy's duty was to be the supply service of the Royal Navy, to transport troops and supplies to the armies, to transport raw materials to overseas munitions factories and munitions from those factories, to maintain, on a reduced scale, the ordinary import and export trade, to supply food to the home country and - in spite of greatly enlarged risks and responsibilities - to provide both personnel and ships to supplement the existing resources of the Royal Navy. Losses of vessels were high from the outset, but had peaked in 1917 when in January the German government announced the adoption of "unrestricted submarine warfare". The subsequent preventative measures introduced by the Ministry of Shipping - including the setting up of the convoy system where warships were used to escort merchant vessels - led to a decrease in losses but by the end of the war, 3,305 merchant ships had been lost with a total of 17,000 lives.

Southborough War Memorial

A W Luxton

The AW Luxton named on Southborough War Memorial as Lieutenant AW Luxton, Royal Navy is not listed on the CWGC site. Clive Maier's research reveals that he was the son of Mr and Mrs Luxton of 9 Park-road, Southborough. Curiously, another AW Luxton (listed with CWGC but not on Southborough War Memorial) was resident in Southborough, and his details are included here.

Rifleman R/35739, 2nd Battalion King's Royal Rifle Corps. Died 7 July 1917, age 20. Buried in Ramscappelle Road Military Cemetery, Nieuwpoort, Belgium: Grave ref. VC4.

A William Luxton, known as Willie, was the only son of William and Helena Luxton, both Prudence Assurance Company agents, who moved to Prospect-road, Southborough, some time before 1915. He had two younger sisters, Olive, who never married, and Helena Myra.

A brass plaque dedicated to Willie in St John's Methodist Church, Southborough, bore the words: *"His sun seemed scarcely risen, ere its setting gained him the entrance into perfect life."*

The Courier of 21 June 1940 reported the death of Willie's father: *Mr W Luxton of "Meldon", Chestnut Avenue, came to Southborough in 1911 ... keen worker in the Methodist Church, joined the Wesleyan Church in Southborough, which became St John's Methodist Church.*

Oscar Frederick Maier

Private 2448, 3rd/1st, West Kent Yeomanry (Queen's Own). Born Maidstone. Died 31 August 1916. Buried in Dantzig Alley British Cemetery, Mametz, Somme, France: Grave ref. I.B.17.

From the website www.firstworldwar.com/onthis day for 31 August 1917: *British gas attacks at Arras and Armentieres. Heavy German attacks between Ginchy and Bois Foureaux.*

The Maiers came to Southborough around 1895 and members of the family lived there until Clive Maier's mother died in 1995. The family lived in a wooden clapboard dwelling at 121 London Road. The site is now occupied by Hythe Close.

From the Courier (undated): *Mr & Mrs O Maier, 121, London-road, have received information from the War Office that their son, Private OF Maier, West Kent Yeomanry, is wounded and is in Hospital in France. They cannot yet gain any further information. In a letter that Mrs Maier received from her son's chum, he says he is sorry to say that Oscar was wounded while in the trenches. He (his chum) did not take part in this fight, as he had been busy taking the wounded to and fro each day. Oscar had just received their parcel when he was obliged to leave to go into the trenches. The letter goes on to state that Private Maier is being well looked after, and is going on nicely.*

And from a later edition: *Mr & Mrs O Maier, 121, London-road, have now received the information from the War Office that their eldest son, Private Oscar Maier, West Kent Yeomanry, was killed in action on August 31ˢᵗ. Mrs Maier received a notice from the War Office some weeks ago to the effect that her son was reported wounded on that date. The Red Cross Society have been trying to trace him, but were unable to do so, and until the official notice was received on November 29ᵗʰ his parents were hoping that he was still alive. Private Maier joined the Yeomanry some months ago, and was drafted to France in July.*

Clive Maier, whose father was Oscar's younger brother, and 16 at the time of Oscar's death, recalled his account of the arrival of news of Oscar's death: *"The only thing my father ever told me was that the telegram came on the morning of his sister's wedding. His father read the telegram, put it in his pocket, told no one and went through with the wedding. Only when the last guest had gone did he tell the family."*

Charles Edward Malpass MC

Captain, 11ᵗʰ Bn, Queen's Own (Royal West Kent Regiment), attached London Regiment (Artists' Rifles). Died 8 October 1918, age 23. Buried in the Rumilly-en-Cambresis Communal Cemetery Extension, Nord, France: Grave ref. I.B.2.

From the CWGC website: *Rumilly was captured by the 3rd Division on the 2 October, 1918. The dates of death of the 80+ 1914-18 war casualties commemorated on this site cover the first fortnight of*

October 1918. *Thirty German graves of this period have been removed to Cambrai East Military Cemetery.*

Charles Malpass was the only child of Charles and Edith Malpass of Leybourne, 35 North Farm Road, Tunbridge Wells. Local High Brooms man Jerry Jones says that Charles Malpass was Headmaster and Edith was a teacher at High Brooms Boys School. A memorial plaque to Captain Malpass in St Matthew's Church, High Brooms, records that he was killed in action at Niergnies. This village lies 6 km south-south-east of Cambrai.

From the Tunbridge Wells Advertiser, 11 June 1915: *Mr Charles E Malpass, who has just been posted as a 2nd Lieutenant in the 9th Battalion Royal West Kent Regt, is the son of Mr CM Malpass, Head Master of Southborough Council Boys' School. He was educated at Skinners' School and Clark's College, London, and was a member of Skinners' School Cadet Corps for three years.*

At the age of 17 he entered, as apprentice engineer, with Messrs Denny & Co, the celebrated shipbuilders and engineers, of Dumbarton. While there he was often engaged in Government work, and at the time of the declaration of war was engaged on the steam trials of HMS Legion, which played such a prominent part in the battle of Heligoland. On taking up his residence in Scotland he joined the Clyde Royal Garrison Artillery, in which he was soon promoted to Bombardier. Since the outbreak of war he has been on duty with his regiment at Portkil Battery, at the entrance to the Clyde, protecting that important estuary from the approach of German submarines and other hostile craft. He now proceeds to Glasgow to commence his training as an officer.

Frank Martin

Private 41225, 13th Bn, Royal Fusiliers. Died 23 April 1917. Commemorated on Arras Memorial, Pas de Calais, France: Bay 3.

www.firstworldwar.com/onthisday for 23 April 1917: *Western Front: British capture rest of Trescault and greater part of Havrincourt Wood – second phase of Battle of Arras begins. British attack north and south of the Scarpe (Arras), capturing two villages.*

Thomas Martin

Sergeant 11277, 6th Bn, East Lancashire Regiment. Died Monday 9 August 1915, age 24. Commemorated on the Helles Memorial,

Turkey: Panel 113 to 117. Enlisted Blackburn, Lancashire. Brother of **Walter Charles Martin**.

The eight month campaign in Gallipoli was fought by Commonwealth and French forces in an attempt to force Turkey out of the war, to relieve the deadlock of the Western Front in France and Belgium, and to open a supply route to Russia through the Dardanelles and the Black Sea. The Allies landed on the peninsula on 25-26 April 1915. On 6 August, further landings were made at Suvla, just north of Anzac, and the climax of the campaign came in early August when simultaneous assaults were launched on all three fronts. However, the difficult terrain and stiff Turkish resistance soon led to the stalemate of trench warfare.

The Courier of 3 September 1915 reported: *The sad news was received yesterday by Mr and Mrs TOP Martin of 14 Elm-road, Southborough, that their eldest son, Sgt Thomas Martin, of the 6th East Lancashire Regiment, was killed at the Dardanelles on August 9th ... formerly in the Cheshire Regiment, in which he served for about three years, and was discharged unfit for service owing to contracting ague in India. Soon after the commencement of the War, he joined the 6th East Lancashires at Accrington, and soon obtained promotion, rising to the rank of Sergeant. He came home on leave a fortnight before he sailed for the Dardanelles on June 6th.*

From the Courier, 10 September 1915, an account, from survivor Pte Gordon Staite, of Tunbridge Wells, of the landing of the British Force on the beach under a hail of shell and bullets: *He wonders that they came through alive ... he considers the fighting more difficult at Gallipolli than France, because the Turks are fighting in their own country, which at this part is very mountainous, and gives them great advantage in the defensive. The Turks are as stubborn fighters as of old, and will, says Pte Staite, "take some driving out."*

Walter Charles Martin

Private 633372, 20th Bn, London Regiment (formerly 2885, Queen's Own (Royal West Kent Regiment). Died 6 July 1917, age 21. Buried in the Bedford House Cemetery, Ypres, Belgium: Enclosure No 4. XIV. A.23. Son of Thomas O P and Lucy C Harriet Martin, of 14 Elm Road, Southborough.

The Courier, 20 July 1917, reported: Official news has been received by Mr & Mrs T Martin, 14 Elm-road, of the death of their only remaining son, Pte W Martin, London Regiment, who was killed in action in France on July 6th. Very great sympathy will be felt for them in this, their second, great loss, their other son being killed in August, 1915. Private Martin joined the West Kents in August, 1914, and was transferred to the County of London Regiment when he went to France in September of last year. He has been through some very severe fighting while in France. A letter was received from him by Mrs Martin two days after he was killed. Before enlisting he was apprenticed to Mr Newman, draper, and had just completed his time there when the war broke out.

William Roy McMillan

Private 7/400012, 3 Regular Australian Army. Buried in Busan United Nations Memorial Cemetery, South Korea: Grave ref 2920.

The Kent & Sussex Courier of 26 June 1953 reported that: *Private McMillan, age 24, twin son of Mrs EG McMillan and the late Mr Kenneth McMillan, of 'Rosebank', Church Road, Southborough Common, had been killed in Korea on 22 June 1953, whilst serving with the Australian Army after serving there for 12 months.*

He was educated at Skinners School, where he was a drummer in the cadet band. When he left school he studied agriculture and later joined the British Food Corporation on the ground-nut scheme in East Africa. When this ended he sailed for Australia with some friends, and it was while he was there that he enlisted, in 1951, in the Australian Army.

William Roy McMillan was known as Roy to his family. His twin brother Mr K I McMillan writes that The Courier was mistaken, in that Roy had nothing to do with the ground-nut scheme in East Africa. Mr McMillan continues: "Roy left for Australia in 1950 under the £10 Pom scheme, working his way across the country and finishing in Darwin, where he joined the regular Australian Army, who flew him back to Melbourne for training. He was sent to Japan, and Korea in 1952. Whilst patrolling the forward line against Chinese forces, his patrol clashed with another Australian patrol, resulting in casualties including Roy's tragic death by 'friendly fire'. Killed in action. Roy is buried in Pusan, South Korea, in the Australian section of the Commonwealth War Cemetery."

Southborough War Memorial

Denis Livingstone McPhee

Private 6412331, 1st Bn, Dorsetshire Regiment. Died 19 July 1943, age 20. Buried in Catania War Cemetery, Sicily: Grave ref. III.K.32. Son of Donald and Mabel McPhee of Southborough, Kent.

Pictured below: Denis McPhee and his sister June on far right, with their mother and family.

From a newspaper report of the time: Units from the Devon, Dorset and Hampshire Regiments in the spearhead of our advance in Sicily won their right to that place by years of patient, brave unacclaimed service in Malta. Most of these units had been in the island since 1938. Their combatant duties were only part of their work. They helped to build airfields and hangars, they filled up craters, unloaded ships; they were soldiers, navvies and general handy-men. But their severest test was not the Luftwaffe but the hardship they had to endure through shortage of food. Their daily toil, which a navvy would find exacting, had to be done on very spare rations indeed. For the last nine months in Malta there was simply not the food to allow more than a bare subsistence; something like a little more than a quarter pound of bully beef a day, a slice or two of bread, and a few locally grown vegetables.

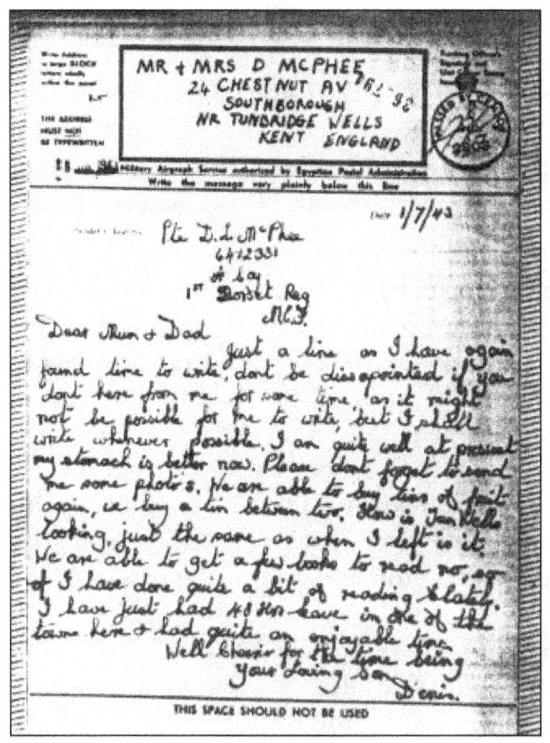

Pictured left: Denis McPhee's last letter home to his parents, dated 1 July 1943, which gives their address as 24 Chestnut Avenue, Southborough.

Extract from an uncredited account of the action which is held by Denis's brother Brian:

The 1st Dorsets landed in Sicily from Port Said on 10 July 1943 as part of 231 (Malta) Brigade. The Brigade's landing craft set off for the beaches at 1245 hrs, encountering a rough sea which caused much sea-sickness and resulted in many men being soaked to the skin before they left their landing craft. The 1st Dorsets were to land just north of the fishing village of Marzamemi. Some resistance was encountered from the Italian coastal defence troops in pillboxes protected by barbed wire, but they were heavily outnumbered, and in the face of determined attacks, the resistance soon crumbled. The Dorsets were counter-attacked by Italians in French tanks during the early afternoon but the attack had been anticipated and was repulsed.

During the period 19-28 July, 231 Brigade was involved in the attack by 1st Canadian Division on Agira. The 1st Dorsets were engaged in operations on the road to Agira on 19 July, and took several casualties.

On 2 November 1943 a Form D2 from the War Office informed:

Dear sir, I write to tell you that information has now reached us that your son 6412331 Pte DL McPhee of 1st Dorset Regiment is buried near Agira, 33 miles west north west of Catania, Sicily.

And on 10 October 1944 a Form E2B stated:

Dear Sir, I have to inform you that a later report has been received which states that your son, No 6412331, Private D L McPhee, 1st Bn Dorset Regiment, is now buried in Catania British Cemetery, Sicily, having been removed from the isolated grave in which he was buried near to where he fell.

Albert Miller

Private 35237, 9th Bn, The Loyal North Lancashire Regiment, formerly 2440 West Kent (Queen's Own) Yeomanry. Died 10 April 1918, age 28. Commemorated in Croix-du-Bac British Cemetery, Steenwerck, Nord, France: Special Memorial F.14. Son of Mark Miller, of 12 Meadow Road, Southborough.

Steenwerck is a village approximately 5 kilometres south-west of Armentieres. Croix-du-Bac is a hamlet 3.5 k south of Steenwerck. The cemetery was begun in July 1916 and used by field ambulances and fighting units until March 1918. On 10 April 1918, Croix-du-Bac was in German hands but was retaken by the 23rd Lancashire Fusiliers on 2 September. After the Armistice, the cemetery was enlarged when further graves were brought in from the battlefields. Of the 554 Commonwealth casualties buried or commemorated here, 263 of the graves are unidentified, and special memorials commemorate 140 known to be buried among them.

The Courier, 11 August 1916, reported that Private C Miller, 9th Royal Fusiliers, son of Mr & Mrs Miller of 36 Meadow-road, Southborough, was wounded and buried by the explosion of a shell on 3rd August, and was going on satisfactorily. It is possible he was a relative of Albert Miller (see also **James Vesey**).

Charles Moon MM

Corporal 653, 6th Bn, Queen's Own (Royal West Kent Regiment). Died 14 August 1916, age 21. Buried at Warloy-Baillon Communal Cemetery Extension, Somme, France: Grave ref. VII.C.4. Son of Walter and Anne Moon of 13 Western Road, Southborough.

Charles Moon died on the same day as his brother **John Moon**, who was only 18. Their brothers **Henry** and **Walter Moon** are also commemorated on the Southborough War Memorial. They were killed respectively in June and July 1916 at the ages of 22 and 23.

From a local news report at the time, headed *Southborough Family loses Four Sons*: *Very great sympathy will be felt for Mr and Mrs Moon in their terrible loss. They have indeed truly contributed their share in this great war, having now lost four sons in less than three months ... On Tuesday morning Mrs Moon received a letter from Capt E Williams of the 6th Battalion Royal West Kent, in which he says "It is with very deep regret I have to inform you of the death of your son Corporal C Moon, who died of wounds received in action. He was one of my best non-commissioned officers, and had been setting an exceptionally good example under fire, and I shall find it hard to replace him in the Company. Please accept my deepest sympathy in your great loss." Corporal Moon joined the 6th Battalion soon after the outbreak of the war. He was previously in the employ of Mr H Nicholson, of Bidborough Court, as footman. In a letter to his mother in June last, Corporal Moon enclosed a card he had received from the Major-General commanding the 12th Division, on which he stated his pleasure at hearing how Corporal Moon (then Private) had distinguished himself by his conduct in the field. The gallant soldier was the third son of Mr and Mrs Moon. Mr Moon has been ill himself for some months, and is now in Bath Hospital, where Mrs Moon will have to travel to break this terrible news.*

From the Tunbridge Wells Advertiser of 25 August 1916: *He joined the Army in August 1914, and went to the Front on the 1st June, 1915. Corporal Jenner, DCM, High Brooms, who is a stretcher-bearer, first brought news that Corpl Moon was wounded, as he picked him up and helped to carry him to the dressing station, he having lost a leg. He was home on special leave last April for his distinguished conduct in the field.*

Christopher Moon

Private 463135, 29th Bn, Canadian Infantry (British Columbia Regiment). Died 12 August 1917, age 25. Buried in Maroc British Cemetery, Nord, France: Grave ref. II.J.19. Son of John and Elizabeth Moon, of 11 Springfield Road, Southborough.

Private Moon's attestation papers show that he was born 12 December 1893 at Speldhurst. He enlisted at Vernon, British Columbia on 21 July 1915, was single, and gave his occupation as rancher.

Southborough War Memorial

Henry Moon

Gunner 83420, 4th Bde, Canadian Field Artillery. Born on 26 August 1893. Died 2 June 1916, age 22. Buried at Lijssenthoek Military Cemetery, Poperinge, West-Vlaanderen, Belgium: Grave ref. VII.A.34. Son of Walter and Anne Moon of 13 Western Road, Southborough.

From the Courier, 9 June 1916: *Gunner H Moon, of the 13th Canadian Field Artillery, second son of Mr and Mrs W Moon, Southborough, was severely wounded on Thursday week in Belgium, and he died in hospital the following day. He was 22 years of age, and was in Canada when war broke out, and he at once volunteered for service overseas. Before going to Canada, he belonged to the Southborough Company of the Kent (Fortress) Royal Engineers. He was educated at St Peter's Schools, and was afterwards a telegraph messenger at Southborough Post Office, and later was in the employ of Mr Pearson. He is the first member of the "Hand and Sceptre" Lodge of Oddfellows to give his life for his country ... letter from the Rev RF Thompson, Chaplain: "June 1st – I know you will be very much disturbed and anxious to hear that Harry has been wounded. He asked me to write and tell you about it, as he will not be able to write himself for some time. The Battery where Harry was was heavily shelled today at noon, and Harry, unfortunately, was hit by a small splinter on the lower part of the chest on the right side. Our Medical Officer was away when the word came to our Brigade Headquarters only a few hundred yards away. I got the Medical Sergeant, and we went over with a stretcher. We put a dressing on his wound and carried him on the stretcher down the road, where an ambulance and doctor met us. The doctor redressed his wound and sent him off to the Hospital, where I think they will operate to remove the splinter. He was very brave and bright, though he was suffering a good deal. He will probably be laid up for quite a while, but the doctors do not anticipate any danger. I am very sorry for both you and Harry, whom I have known for eighteen months now. He was a fine, Christian boy, and always did his duty well. I like him very much indeed. I got to know him first when his chum, Arthur Smith, was so sick in Toronto."*

Arthur Smith was another Southborough lad, the son of Mr and Mrs Jonathan Smith. A kindly, sympathetic letter was also sent by the Chaplain at the Hospital, who was with Gunner Moon when he died.

Mr and Mrs W Moon and family, and Miss Oxley, wish to express their grateful thanks for the many messages of sympathy they have received in their bereavement.

Gunner Moon enlisted at Toronto on 1 December 1914, giving his trade as Fixture Builder. He died on the same day as **Corporal GH Hackett**, 49th Bn, Canadian Infantry (Alberta Regt).

John Moon

Able Seaman London Z/3438, Anson Bn, Royal Naval Volunteer Reserve. Died 14 August 1916, age 18. Buried at Tranchee de Mecknes Cemetery, Aix-Noulette, Pas de Calais, France: Grave ref. H.14. Son of Walter and Anne Moon of 13 Western Road, Southborough.

From a local newspaper: *On Tuesday morning Mrs Moon received a letter informing her that Charles had been killed at the age of 21 … On Saturday Mrs Moon received further distressing news in a letter from Lieut J Gilliland, OC "C" Company, Anson Battalion, BEF: "Dear Mrs Moon, I am awfully sorry to have to write and tell you your son John was killed during a bombardment this afternoon. I know how terrible this news must be to you, but in your great grief it must be a consolation to you to know what a splendid soldier your son has proved. He joined us on the 22nd March, and we all very soon got to know his cheerful and manly disposition. It will console you, too, to know his death was instantaneous, and that he had no suffering. He will be remembered by his friends in "C" Company, who are very numerous." Mrs Moon also received the following letter from the Chaplain, Rev W E F Rees: "I am deeply grieved at the death of your son John, who was killed on the 14th August by a German shell in the front trenches. I took the funeral service, in which your son was accorded full military honours, and his comrades and officers attended. He was buried in a cemetery close behind our trenches, and his name has been placed above the grave. After the war we shall be able to tell you the exact spot of the grave. May God comfort you in your great loss."*

Mrs Moon has also received a letter from Lieut Moir, who speaks very highly of Able-Seaman J Moon, and one from Petty Officer H Gobling, who says how he and all the men of "C" Company greatly sympathise with Mrs Moon, and how much they all respected her son. Able Seaman J Moon is the fourth son of Mr and Mrs Moon, and joined the Royal Naval Division a week after his 18th birthday, and he is not yet 19 and had been in France some months.

From the Tunbridge Wells Advertiser of 25 August 1916: ... *he joined the Royal Naval Division last October. He went to Mudros in February, and was sent to France on the 22nd March.*

An earlier Courier, featuring this "Patriotic Southborough Family" states that John Moon was: *attached to the 5th Nelson Battalion in the Eastern Mediterranean Squadron, "somewhere at sea".* This account quotes John's platoon commander Sub Lieut DB Moir's letter: ... *It's too sad altogether to see a nice boy like your son called away. He was just a boy, and every man in his platoon liked and respected him, and to-day we are all cut up and sad at our loss. The poor boy was killed instantly, and didn't suffer in any way. So you mustn't grieve too much, for he died a man's death, the best in the world, for he offered and gave his life for his God and King, and I know that he would not like to think he was leaving pain behind, but would like his loved ones at home to feel proud that he has done his duty thoroughly. It's a sad, sad time for mothers, and I just hope that God will give you strength and help. I knew your son well, as I commanded his platoon since he joined us at Mudros. I send you a heart full of sympathy".*

This account gives a slightly different cause of death, as the letter from the Petty Officer stated that AB Moon was killed by a rifle-grenade. It also says that at the time of joining the Forces John was employed by Mr H Hemsley, bootmaker, Crescent-road, Tunbridge Wells.

Ronald William Albert Moon

Private 6351076, 2nd Bn, Parachute Regiment, AAC. Died Wednesday 20 September 1944, age 23. Commemorated on the Groesbeek Memorial, Gelderland, Netherlands: Panel 9. Son of William H and Winifred M Moon, of Southborough.

Allied forces entered the Netherlands on 12 September 1944. Airborne operations later that month established a bridgehead at Nijmegen and in the following months, coastal areas and ports were cleared and secured, but it was not until the German-initiated offensive in the Ardennes had been repulsed that the drive into Germany could begin.

Martin Kirkham was a friend of Ronald Moon's younger brother Patrick (Pat); they grew up together in Southborough in the 1940s and 1950s, Patrick Moon in Charles Street, and Martin Kirkham in Edward Street. Pat often talked to his friend Martin about Ron, who had been posted as 'missing in action' until the end of the war six months later, when it was confirmed that he had lost his life. Pat was deeply affected by his brother's death, and the uncertainty which preceded the news.

The following is from an account of the part played in the Battle of Arnhem in September 1944 by B Company of the 2nd Battalion, the Parachute Regiment, kindly sent to the author by Martin Kirkham:

What was left of the original British main force now pulled back and regrouped around Brigade and Battalion HQs and the adjacent houses. In this last position, Private Don Smith took cover in a house next to Hofstraat, the house of Dr Van Niekirk. By now, most of the remaining men of B Company had dug in, in the garden behind the house. Don Smith: "We defended the building with spasmodic fire fights developing. At about 2pm (I am uncertain about the time), Regimental Sergeant Major Jerry Strachan opened fire with a sub-machine gun from the top window aiming down the street. The Germans retaliated and all hell broke loose. The RSM rushed down the stairs and told us to get out fast. I rushed towards the rear window when there was a tremendous explosion. I felt myself being propelled through the air, in sort of a slow motion. Suddenly I hit the garden wall. Ronny Moon, who had been in the garden, came up to me and asked if I was all right. I said I was. I was only slightly wounded, and losing some blood. Ron then took his Bren gun, and ran towards the house. He was going in to a downstairs room when he was hit and killed instantly by a tracer bullet through the head."

Norman Dellar was also in the garden, and had taken cover in one of the slit trenches near the house. He remembers that when he looked up he saw Ronny Moon lying there. Dellar: "His hand seemed to reach out to me, quite peacefully. I seem to remember his hand, as he was wearing a remarkable ring."

Private Ronald Moon's body was never found after the war.

Walter Moon

Lance Serjeant 14152, 9th Bn, King's Own Yorkshire Light Infantry. Died Tuesday 4 July 1916, age 23. Buried at Heilly Station Cemetery, Mericourt-L'Abbe, Somme, France: Grave ref. I. D. 25. Son of Walter and Anne Moon of 13 Western Road, Southborough. Brother of **Charles, Henry** and **John Moon.**

The Courier, 18 February 1916: *HOME FROM FRONT Lance-sergeant Walter Moon, 9th Kings Own Yorkshire Light Infantry came home from the Front on leave on Sunday last. Sergeant Moon joined the*

Army on September 7th, 1914 in London, where he was employed with Messrs Upsop. He went to the Front on September 11th of the following year, and his first experience under fire was at the Battle of Loos, when his Battalion made three charges, and acquitted themselves most courageously. Soon after, Sergt Moon had a very narrow escape. While walking through a wood he paused a moment to speak to a Sergeant of the Canadians, and a German sniper fired at them. The bullet struck sideways on a pocket-book in Sergt Moon's breast pocket, was deflected by the frame of a miniature in his pocket book, and wounded the Canadian in the lung. Our representative was shown the pocket book and the miniature with the mark of the bullet. Sergt Moon is full of praise of the arrangements for the comfort and health of the men in the way of food, clothes and baths. He had only once been short of food, which was during the Battle of Loos, when it was impossible for the convoy to come up owing to the heavy fire. They had then to depend on the emergency rations carried with them, and Sergt Moon says that that meal of "bully beef" and biscuits was the best and most welcome he had ever had.

From the Courier, 21 July 1916: *Sergt Walter Moon, who was reported wounded, has since died at a Base Hospital ... the Rev George H Grossland, Wesleyan Chaplain, wrote: "I had many talks with him, both in England and out here, and very frequently saw him at services. I deeply regret his passing, but yet you may rejoice in the reality of his Christian life and character, and that he has given his life in so noble a cause. Private FA Horide, ASC, of Southborough, in a letter home, said he had made enquiries at the Hospital, and understood that Sergt Moon progressed favourably several days after being wounded, but had a relapse and passed away. Mr and Mrs Walter Moon and family, and Miss Bathurst, wish to express their grateful thanks for the many messages of sympathy they have received in their bereavement.* (Private F Horide, in Dee's Directory 1915, resided at 49 Forge-road).

William Alfred Henry Moon

Sergeant 540146, 9th Field Coy, Royal Engineers. Died Monday 2 September 1918, age 23. Buried in Vis-en-Artois British Cemetery, Haucourt, Pas de Calais, France: Grave ref. VI.B.I. Son of William and Harriet Moon, of 15 Bedford Road, Southborough; husband of Eveline Clara Watts Moon, of Woodbine Cottage, Warmington, Banbury, Oxon.

www.firstworldwar.com/onthisday for 2 September 1918 for the Western Front: *Battle on 23-mile front; Troops of First Army, supported by tanks, break through Drocourt-Queant "Switch" line, south of Scarpe, capture Cagnicourt and Villers, encircle and take Queant by nightfall; 10,000 prisoners. On Lys front British also gain ground, and north of Peronne, where Sailly-Sallisel and whole of St Pierre-Vaast Wood re-taken.*

Dee's Directory 1915 lists, under Men Serving, all resident at 15 Bedford-road, W Moon (Senr), East Kent Regiment; A Moon, 4th Royal West Kent; and Corpl LW Moon, KFRE.

From the Courier, 18 September 1918: *Sergt Moon joined the Kent (Fortress) Royal Engineers six years ago, and was called up at the outbreak of war, and had been in France a year. The following letter has been received from his Major: "I am writing a few lines to console with you in the loss of your husband, Sergt WAH Moon, who was killed on duty on September 2nd. Sergt Moon had not, as you know, been with this Company very long, but quite long enough for me to realise that by his death I and the Company have lost an excellent NCO, whom it will not be easy to replace. His Section Officer was wounded the same day, or would have written to you as well as myself."*

Local historian Frank Stevens' research shows that: *William Moon's original number was KFRE 749. He enlisted in February 1912 and was a training NCO at Maidenhead, where he may have met his wife. He served some time with 9th Bn Durham Light Infantry (Pioneer Unit), No. 76936, and that it seems he then went back to the Royal Engineers' 9th Field Company.*

H E Moore

Able Seaman KX/244, Howe Bn, Royal Navy Division, Royal Naval Volunteer Reserve. Died on 13 November 1916. Buried in Ancre British Cemetery, Beaumont-Hamel, Somme, France: Grave ref. I.B.28. In the same battalion as **Hubert Harrowing**, who died the day before.

www.firstworldwar.com/onthisday for 13 November 1916 for the Western Front: *Battle of the Ancre: British capture St Pierre Divion (south of Ancre) and Beaumont Hamel (north of Ancre) and nearly 4,000 prisoners. Fourth phase of the Battle of the Somme begins.*

Thomas A Morley

Sapper 540144, 497th (Kent) Field Coy, Royal Engineers. Died 5 March 1917. Buried in Grove Town Cemetery, Meaulte, Somme, France: Grave ref. III.C.36.

The Tunbridge Wells Advertiser, 16 March 1917 reported that Thomas suffered shot wounds to the knee, left thigh and a fracture.

From the Courier, 23 March 1917: *Mr & Mrs Morley, 7 Bedford-road, have received the sad news that Mr Morley's son, Sapper T Morley, (Fortress), RE, has died of wounds received in action. On Monday Mr Morley had a telegram to say that his son was badly wounded, and was at the Casualty Clearing Station, and on Friday another wire was received to say that he had since died. A letter was received from the Sister at the Hospital there stating that everything was done for him that could be done. Sapper Morley was in the Kent Fortress Engineers at the outbreak of war, when they were mobilized, and he was also one of the few who were rescued from "The Hythe".*

A letter has also been received from Major Reechton, who states that: "Deceased was one of a company who were carrying forward materials on the night in question, when a 'whizz-bang' exploded, wounding five, your son among them. He was taken as rapidly as possible to a Medical Aid Post, and everything was done for him that could be done. I have known him ever since he joined the Company, which was, of course, before this war. There are but few of those who came out on mobilization left, and I personally feel now that your son has gone one more link in the chain of old associations is broken. He was a good lad, who always did his best at whatever he was set to do, and we shall all miss him very much. We all feel deeply for you in your loss, which may perhaps be lightened by the thought that he died doing his duty." A letter has also been received by Mr Morley from the Chaplain.

A Morris

Private, Infantry Brigade. Died in World War I.

The author has not been able to identify any details of Private A Morris in her research. Dee's Directory 1915 listed a Corporal WG Morris, 1st West Kent Yeomanry, resident 17 Prospect-road; Kelly's

Directory 1916 gave two names of Morrises resident in Southborough: C Morris, 20 Western-road, and W Morris, 78 Springfield-road.

Though he is not commemorated on the Southborough War Memorial, 2nd Lieut Philip Henry Morris, 144th Battalion Machine Gun Corps, died on 9 October 1917, and is buried in the Poelcapelle British Cemetery, Langemark-Poelkapelle, West-Vlaanderen, Belgium, Grave ref. XIV.A.10.

He was born in Edinburgh, the son of the late Arthur Morris and Marion CS Morris of Glen Rosa, Southborough. He is commemorated in St Peter's Churchyard, Southborough, where a grave adjacent to the south gate carries this inscription: *In loving memory of Arthur Morris who died 14 October 1922 aged 74 years and Philip Henry Morris killed at Passchendaele 9 October 1917. Aged 26 years.*

George Thomas Mugridge

Private 75842, 7th Bn, Royal Fusiliers. Died 3 April 1918, age 19. Commemorated on the Arras Memorial, Pas de Calais, France: Bay 3. Son of George and Mary Ann Mugridge, of 26 South View Road, High Brooms.

Kelly's Directory and Dee's Directory 1915 give the name as Muggridge.

From the Courier, 26 April 1918: *Mr Muggridge of 26 South View-road has received notification of the death of his eldest son, Private "Dick" Muggridge, who was killed in action. Deceased joined on 19th April 1917, and went to France on March 17th, and was killed on April 3rd. He received his education at High Brooms Boys' School, and lived in the district until joining up. Deceased was only 19.*

And from the Courier, 3 May 1918: *At St Matthew's Church High Brooms on Sunday afternoon, a Memorial Service was held for five men, four of whom were recently killed in action in France, their names being George Muggridge, George Day, Eric Jarrett, Norman Russell. The fifth, Arthur John Webb, died in a Military Hospital from heart trouble, and was buried on Monday at Southborough with full Military Honours.*

Henry Oliver Muggridge

Private Henry Oliver Muggridge G/5314, 8th Battalion, Queen's Own (RWK). Died 26 September 1915. Commemorated on the Loos Memorial, France: Panel 95 to 97.

Name is spelt Muggeridge on Southborough War Memorial. From the Tunbridge Wells Advertiser, 25 February 1916: *PATRIOTIC SOUTHBOROUGH FAMILY. The reproductions below are of the five soldier sons and a grandson of Mrs Goldsmith, of Nightingale Farm Cottages, Southborough, and she is justly proud of their remarkable military service for King and Country. Their record is as follows: Pte Henry Muggridge, 8th Royal West Kent Regt. Enlisted at the beginning of the war. Wounded and missing at Loos, September 25th, and no information has been received since. – Gunner William Muggridge, RFA. Stationed in Scotland, and is an officer's servant. Previously served 21 years. Farrier-Corpl John Muggridge, RFA. Now in Flanders. Previously served 21 years. - Pte Thomas Muggridge. Now stationed at Faversham. Previously served 18 years in the Royal Sussex Regt. – Gunner Albert Muggridge, RFA. Enlisted at the outbreak of war. Went to the Front in January of last year. Wounded on the 9th of May. – Mrs Goldsmith's son-in-law, Pte William Stebbings, Essex Regt, had served in the Army before the war, but re-enlisted. – Her grandson, Pte RW Stebbings, has been in the Royal Marine Light Infantry about 12 months. – Her brother, Pte Edward Read, was also a soldier, having served 24 years in the Royal Sussex.*

(Pictured above, from left to right: Pte T Muggridge, Pte R Stebbings, Corpl J Muggridge, Mrs Goldsmith (mother), Gunner W Muggridge, Pte H Muggridge, Gunner A Muggridge).

With regard to Pte Tom Muggridge, it is interesting to note that two of his children, Jack and Dolly, received a letter from Queen Alexandra on the occasion of the death of King Edward. The facts were narrated in a Bexhill paper as follows:

"Mr Muggridge, it should be mentioned, is a member of the local detachment of the Engineers, and his little son is following in his father's footsteps in his loyalty to his King and country, and he never passes a flag but what he salutes it in real military fashion. When Master Jack was informed on Saturday morning, May 7th, that the King had died, he was bitterly upset. "Oh, mum, I am sorry the King is dead," the little fellow said, "I should have liked to have seen him." He then expressed the wish to send some flowers. His little sister was also enraptured with the idea of sending a token of their sympathy, and Mrs Muggridge accordingly despatched a spray of narcissi, forget-me-nots, and shamrock, addressed to "Her Majesty the Queen, Buckingham Palace."

The little wreath bore a card with the inscription: "A simple token of love to our dear departed King, and deepest sympathy to our loving Queen, from Jack and Dolly Muggridge." Pleased as they were at thus being able to pay a tribute to their dead King, Master Jack's and Miss Dolly's enthusiasm knew no bounds when a letter with the monogram, ER VII, addressed "Miss Dolly Muggridge, Park Gate Cottage, Hastings-road, Bexhill-on-Sea," was left by the postman. The contents read: Buckingham Palace, 9th May, 1916 – Miss Knollys is commanded by Queen Alexandra to thank little Dolly Muggridge very much for her kind sympathy and for the flowers she has been good enough to send.

George Henry Nickells

Leading Aircraftman 574428, Royal Air Force. Died Saturday 5 July 1941, age 18. Lost in SS Anselm. Commemorated on the Runnymede Memorial, Surrey: Panel 56. Son of William Albert Nickells, and of Florence Katie Nickells, of Southborough.

Information from the Wartime Memories Project website www.wartimememories.co.uk - *The SS Anselm was built in Dumbarton in 1935; a coal fired passenger ship, she was converted to a troop ship in 1940. The SS Anselm was sunk by U96 5 July 1941 about 300 miles north of the Azores while on passage from Gourock to Freetown carrying 1,200 troops. 250 troops and 4 crewmen were lost. The Monthly Anti-submarine Report for September, 1941, states that immediately preceding the attack, HMS Challenger and SS Anselm were in line ahead and were being screened by HMS Lavender and HMS Petunia. HMS Starwort, whose Asdic (anti-submarine detection equipment) was out of order, was stationed astern. The escorts had been keeping listening watch in thick fog, but at 0350 the fog cleared and both ships commenced transmitting. At this time, HMS*

Lavender and HMS Petunia took up screening positions on either bow of HMS Challenger and commenced a zigzag on a course just east of south at a speed of 11 knots. At 0426, in approximate position 44 30N, 28 30W, not far from the Canary Islands, the SS Anselm was struck by a torpedo on the port side amidships. The SS Anselm settled rapidly by the head and sank 22 minutes after being hit. All the lifeboats got away with the exception of No 6, which was damaged by the explosion. By skilful manoeuvring, HMS Challenger placed her bow alongside the SS Anselm's port quarter, and in this manner rescued 60 men. Unfortunately 254 men, including 175 RAF personnel, lost their lives, but it is probable that many of these were killed by the explosion of the torpedo which struck the ship immediately below the accommodation space.

James Hooper Dawson Nish

Corporal 71201, 27th Bn, Canadian Infantry (Manitoba Regiment). Died 16 September 1916 of wounds received the previous day at Courcelette, age 20. Buried in Albert Communal Cemetery Extension, Somme, France: Grave ref. I.O.52. Son of Robert Mackenzie Nish and Jamima Hooper Dawson Nish.

www.firstworldwar.com/onthisday for 15 September 1916: *Great British advance (third phase) on the Somme, a six-mile front to depth of 2 or 3,000 yards. Flers, Martinpuich, Courcelette and whole of High Wood taken. New heavy armoured cars (Tanks) used for first time, north of Pozieres to east of Guillemont.*

And the next day: *Somme near Courcelette the British front advanced 1,000 yards; "Danube" trench taken, and Mouquet farm (Thiepval) captured.*

James Nish was born 21 October 1894 at Wigtownshire, Scotland. He enlisted at Winnipeg in October 1914, giving his occupation as farmer. He was a member of the 79th Cameron Highlanders of Canada.

From the Courier, 29 September 1916: *Many connected with this neighbourhood have given their lives for King and Country, placing patriotism and the call of duty before selfishness and the love of ease. To the number of those who have set a noble example of self-sacrifice, and who have given their all for the honour of the Homeland and the Empire, must be added the name of Corporal James Nish, who had his life been spared, would have been 21 years of age next month. On leaving school, where he had always taken a leading part in games and sports, he proceeded to Buckhurst Place, the Boy Scouts' farm at Wadhurst, to prepare himself for the work of farming in Canada. Having finished his course he went out to the Dominion, where he joined Mr Carl Neild, a son of Dr Neild, on his farm near Strasburg. On the outbreak of the war he lost no time in enlisting in a Winnipeg Regiment (27th Batt, 6th Infantry Brigade), eventually coming back to the help of the Motherland, with the*

Southborough War Memorial

2nd Contingent of the Canadians. *After a short period of training at Shorncliffe he went to the Western Front, where for over a year he saw much hard fighting. His relations and friends in Tunbridge Wells had the pleasure of seeing him in the early summer, when he was granted a few days' leave. He had been given leave on an earlier date, but remained abroad to enable a man who was married to come home and see his family. Returning to France, he resumed his duties. He was wounded in action on September 16th, and passed peacefully away in hospital on the same day into the great Beyond.*

Albert Nye

Sapper 776, 1st/3rd Kent Field Coy, Royal Engineers. Died 28 October 1915 in the Hythe disaster, age 20. Commemorated on the Helles Memorial, which stands on the tip of the Gallipoli Peninsula in Turkey: Panel 23 to 25 or 325 to 328.

From Frank Stevens' book *Southborough Sappers of the Kent (Fortress) Royal Engineers*: *One of the early members who had joined the Company at its formation, and came through the ranks of the Cadets as he had nearly four years in the KFRE when he drowned. He attended St Peter's School and was the son of Mr and Mrs William Nye of 38, Charles Street, Southborough. He was an old boy of St Peter's School. His employment was as a gardener with Major Bertram Pott, a well-known local figure who had served in the Boer War.*

Dee's Directory 1915 lists, under Men Serving, Major RB Pott, of Bentham Hill, with the West Kent Yeomanry.

Herbert William Nye

Rifleman 47565, 16th Bn, Royal Irish Rifles, formerly (38201) Suffolk Regiment, and Essex Regiment. Died Saturday 23 March 1918, age 37. Commemorated on Panel 74 to 76 of the Pozieres Memorial, Somme, France.

Herbert Nye was the son of George and Emily Harriet Nye, and husband of Sarah Florence Nye, 17 London Road. His father worked at the Powder Mills in Leigh. Herbert had a tiny antiques shop in Southborough. It is possible that Herbert Nye was killed in the Battle of St Quentin, which took place in the Somme area from 21 to 23 March 1918.

Herbert's children were Stan (Stanley Henry Verdon Nye, born 5 March 1916), Kathleen and Herbert, known as Bert. Kathleen Nye lived in a cottage in Southborough and taught at St Mark's in Tunbridge Wells, when the headmistress was Miss Acton. Bert sang in the choir at St Thomas's. After their father's death, Stan and Bert were brought up by Kathleen, and they all lived at 17 London Road. The house has since been pulled down – it was behind the garage, near Windy Edge.

Stan married Daisy, in 1952, and they lived in Grove Hill Road, where she had lived with her mother before the wedding. Daisy was a Corporal in the WAAF at RAF Tangmere, and Stan also served as a Corporal in the RAF in the Second World War. He was out in Malta as Wireless Operator, and also served in South Africa.

Reginald Nye

Able Seaman C/SSX 15852, HMS Firedrake, Royal Navy. Died Thursday 17 December 1942, age 26. Commemorated on the Chatham Naval Memorial, Kent: Panel 55.2. Son of Harry and Faith Nye, of 28 Great Brooms Road, High Brooms.

Reginald Nye was known to the family as Ginger, or Ginge. He attended High Brooms School, and left at 14, as did his siblings.

The excellent website www.hmsfiredrake.co.uk compiled by John Masters gives extensive information on HMS Firedrake and the HMS Firedrake Association, including the following account: *Firedrake, an 'F' class Destroyer, was the escort leader to convoy ON153, with 43 ships bound for Canada. They sailed in a force 12 storm, the worst the Atlantic had seen for a very long time.*

At about 1700 hrs, the ASDIC operator picked up a contact. HMS Firedrake tracked the contact to about 5 miles south of the convoy, when at 2010 hrs she was hit by a torpedo fired by U-boat U211. The ship broke in two. The bow section sank immediately, with the stern just managing to stay afloat.

Lieutenant DJ Dampier RN had a tally up and found there were 35 still on board. He quickly got the men to work shoring up the bulkheads of No. 3 boiler room, and making safe and jettisoning the depth charges and torpedoes. The gun crew were ordered to fire star shells to attract the attention of the other escorts, because all the radio and signaling equipment had gone with the bow part of the ship.

At about 2200 hrs, one of the other escorts - HMS Sunflower, a Flower class Corvette - was attracted by the star shells so she made towards them, firing star shells herself. The skipper first thought that the stern section of Firedrake was a U-boat and was about to fire HE at it, but then suddenly realised what it was.

He tried to get his ship as close as possible to HMS Firedrake in order to get the survivors off, but the weather was so bad and the sea too rough. There were 60 foot waves breaking over the two ships, which were bobbing about like corks, so he decided to stand by and hope the weather would get better. At about 0040 hrs on the 17th December, the weather worsened and the bulkheads started to give way under the tremendous battering. The stern of HMS Firedrake started to sink, so the men had no option but to take to the water, and at 0045hrs the stern sank. The Sunflower moved in quickly to pick up the men in the water; a Newfoundland rating, G J Furey, had a rope tied around his waist and was lowered down the side of Sunflower. He would swim out to a man and grab hold of him, then his mates on board would heave them back to the ship and get him onboard. He and his mates managed to get 27 on board but one died later. There were 168 of the Firedrake's crew lost and three others that had been picked up earlier that had survived an earlier sinking that night.

It is hard to imagine what the experience of swimming in these seas must have been like for George Furey (left). Surely his Newfoundland upbringing must have had something to do with the incredible powers of endurance he displayed. His son Bill and daughter Helen contacted the Firedrake Association and recalled that their father was a very strong man. He died at the age of 87, in April 1996, a very humble man from a small outpost community. He had lived a full life and raised ten children. Though his children knew that he had helped save 26 men during the war, they didn't know all the details until shortly before he died. He was not one to talk about himself. He didn't see himself as a hero, and was sorry that he couldn't have saved more.

On Sunday 14 December 2003, members of the HMS Firedrake association meet again to pay tribute and lay wreaths at the Cenotaph, (pictured left) for those of the ship's crew who lost their lives when the ship was sunk in the Atlantic on the night of the 16th-17th December 1942.

Reginald Henry Oliver

Private 5681766, 7th Bn, Somerset Light Infantry. Died Tuesday 1 August 1944, age 27. Buried in Hottot-les-Bagues War Cemetery, Calvados, France: Grave ref. XII.C.12. Son of Henry Boaz Oliver and Henrietta Oliver, of Southborough.

Reginald Oliver was the only son of Mrs Oliver, and joined up on 31 March 1941. At the time of joining he lived at 35, Vale Road, Southborough, and was employed at the Dowgate Works in Tonbridge, at the end of Douglas Road, but he had formerly been an apprentice and compositor at Messrs Dee Brothers, Southborough. He was a Sidesman at St Peter's Church, Southborough, and a member of the Young People's Fellowship and the Young Life Campaign. His fiancee LACW Nellie Vinall also lived in Southborough.

The CWGC website includes the following information: *The Allied offensive in north-western Europe began with the Normandy landings of 6 June 1944. Most of the burials in Hottot-les-Bagues War Cemetery were brought in from the surrounding district, where there was much heavy fighting through June and July 1944 as Commonwealth forces tried to press on from Bayeux in an encircling movement to the south of Caen. The cemetery contains 1,005 Commonwealth burials of the Second World War, 56 of them unidentified, and 132 German graves.*

Private Oliver was killed in action in the Advance to Caen. The Battalion had been sent up to the front line near Caen on being landed at

Courcelles-sur-Mer on the morning of 22 June 1944 (on Juno beach, the furthest beach to the east), and thereafter suffered regular casualties as a result of enemy mortar and sniper fire. Private Oliver was one of five men killed by enemy tank fire during a Battalion assault on the village of St Pierre du Fresne.

Charles Henry Pankhurst

Lance Corporal L/8518, 2nd Bn, Royal Sussex Regiment. Died 10 September 1914. Buried at Montreuil-Aux-Lions British Cemetery, Aisne, France: Grave ref. II.C.7.

Charles Pankhurst enlisted at Chichester on 22 August 1906. He was employed as a Regimental Scout for two years and as a Gymnasium Instructor for three years. He was in India from October 1907 until December 1913, and drafted on 12 August 1914.

From a newspaper report of October 1914 : ... *was killed in action on September 10th, at Priez. He was the son of Mr and Mrs (T) Pankhurst, 33, Speldhurst-road, and was in his 27th year. He had seen eight years' service in the Army, six of which had been spent in India ... was called up from the Reserve, and had only left the colours six or seven months. He was a fine athlete, excelling at running and hockey, receiving three medals for the former; while he also had the honour of being the gymnastic leader of the Battalion.*

Charles' mother has also been listed as resident at 30 Speldhurst Road.

Charles Pankhurst was in the same Battalion, died on the same day, and is buried in the same cemetery as **Stephen Alfred Funnell**.

Alfred Barnsdale Parker

Sergeant 331, 2nd Battalion Australian Infantry. Died 5 November 1916, age 26. Buried in Bernafay Wood British Cemetery, Somme, Grave ref. H32. Son of Mrs H Jarvis of 14 Forge Road, Southborough.

Rank is given as Corporal on Southborough War Memorial.

Clive Maier's research reveals that Alfred Barnsdale Parker emigrated to Australia at the age of 17. He worked as a blacksmith at Condobolin, New South Wales. He embarked from Sydney on HMAT A23 Suffolk on 18 October 1914.

From the Courier, 17 November 1916 (named as AB Baker, but named correctly the following week as AB Parker): *Mrs Jarvis, 11 Forge-road, has received the following letter from the Reverend George Carter, Chaplain to the Australian Infantry Contingent: "... was killed in action yesterday near our field ambulance by the explosion of a shell near him, causing instant death. I have buried his body this morning in the Military Cemetery close by with Christian rites." Sgt Baker joined the Transport Section 1st Australians early in 1915, and after training was sent to Egypt, where he remained until he was sent to France in June, 1916. He was home in June for a short leave, and was very pleased that he had been able to see his mother before he was sent to France.*

Henry William Parker

Private, RASC (MT). Died in World War One.

From the Courier, 20 October 1916: *An inquest was held on Saturday at the Bull Inn, East Farleigh, by Mr Thomas Buss, on the body of Henry William Parker, Barrack labourer. Mary Parker, of London-road, Southborough, sister of the deceased, stated that her brother had lived with her, and was 52 years of age. Harry Selves said that he spoke to deceased on the evening of the 11th of October in Barming, about a mile from where the body was found. They talked about different places about which they knew, and deceased appeared very erratic in his statements. The Hon Arthur Henry Hannon, of The Hall, West Farleigh, said he was boating on the Medway when he noticed a body floating near the bank. He got assistance and the body was brought out. PC Overall stated that he was called, and saw deceased lying on the bank of the river. Dr Herbert Watson Southey said death was due to suffocation from drowning, and the Jury recorded a verdict in accordance therewith. Deceased has been missing from Well Marsh, Sheerness, since 1.30pm on the 8th October last.*

From the Courier, 27 October 1916: DEATH OF SOUTHBOROUGH MAN *In our report last week of the inquest on Henry Parker, it should have been stated that he was a transport driver, having been an old soldier. Miss Parker has received a letter from the NCOs and men of the ASC, to which deceased was attached.*

Wilfred James Parrott

Sapper KF 796, 1st/3rd Kent Field Company, Royal Engineers. Died 28 October 1915 in the Hythe disaster. Commemorated on the Helles Memorial, which stands on the tip of the Gallipoli Peninsula in Turkey: Panel 23 to 25 or 325 to 328.

The CWGC website lists a Sapper William Parrott, 796, who died on this date. The author believes this must be Wilfred James Parrott, and there has been some confusion over the name.

Age 21 years, Wilfred was the son of Mr and Mrs A Parrott, of 30 Forge Road, Southborough. He was born in Luton, Bedfordshire, before the family moved to Southborough. Wilfred was an early enlistment into the Company, probably having been a Cadet.

His twin brother, Sapper Charles Arthur Parrott, KF 2022, KF 541163, was also on the Hythe, but was one of the fortunate survivors. Their parents received news that he was safe, but that he had lost all his belongings. It is believed that Edith Ticehurst was his fiancée and that he wrote her an account of his experiences. He is known to have moved to Folkestone later in life and was there in the 1960s.

Ronald Herbert Peacock

Private 6348881, 4th Bn, Queen's Own (Royal West Kent Regiment). Died Sunday 19 March 1944, age 27. Buried in Taukkyan War Cemetery, outside Yangon (formerly Rangoon), Myanmar (formerly Burma): Grave ref. 5.G.24. Son of Albert and May Peacock of Birling Cottage, Powder Mill Lane, High Brooms; husband of Mrs Peacock of 69 Powder Mill Lane.

High Brooms resident Mr Jerry Jones recalls: *Ron and Leslie Peacock lived with their parents Mr and Mrs Albert Peacock in a cottage on Old Forge Farm, Powder Mill Lane, the far side of the Colebrook Viaduct. Ron worked for Adams Nursery in Sandhurst Road, Tunbridge Wells, prior to going into the Forces. Leslie worked for Mr Thomas Darch at Old*

Forge Farm, then went to a farming college, and afterwards worked as a farm manager. When I came home from my service in Assam and Burma my mother told me that they were both killed within a short time of each other, and she thought it was the Battle of Kohima.

From the Courier, 21 April 1944: *News has been received by Mrs RH Peacock, of 10, Highfield-road, High Brooms, that her husband, Pte RH Peacock, died of wounds while serving with the Royal West Kent Regiment in Burma. Pte Peacock, who was a stretcher bearer, was called up in 1940, and had been serving overseas since 1942. He was well known in Southborough, where he was a popular Scout-master. He was educated at High Brooms Council School.*

Lance Sergeant Leslie Charles Peacock, 6350183, 4th Battalion Queen's Own (Royal West Kent Regiment) is not remembered on the Southborough War Memorial, but is commemorated on the Rangoon Memorial: Face 16. He died 11 April 1944, aged 24.

Caleb Pearson

Private 33128, 10th Bn, Yorkshire Regiment (formerly 12661, Royal West Kent Regiment). Died 24 November 1916, age 35. Buried at Vermelles British Cemetery, Pas de Calais, France: Grave ref. V. G. 36. Son of Caleb and Mary Jane Pearson of 42 Holden Park Road, Southborough. Born in Croydon, Surrey.

From the Courier, 8 December 1916: *Mr and Mrs Pearson of Holden Park-road, have received intimation that their eldest son, Caleb Pearson, was killed on the morning of November 24th in France by the bursting of an enemy shell while on sentry duty. In a letter to the bereaved parents Sergt Barlow states that during the short time the deceased had been in his Platoon he had found him one of the best of men.*

Edward John Pearson

Corporal 5073, 8th Bn, Queen's Own (Royal West Kent Regiment). Died 13 April 1917, age 33. Buried at Maroc British Cemetery, Nord, France: Grave ref. III.C.12.

Edward was the younger brother of **Caleb Pearson**.

From the Tunbridge Wells Advertiser of 4 May 1917: *Mr and Mrs Pearson, 42 Holden Park-road (late 120, London-road) have received the sad news that their son, Corporal EJ Pearson was killed in action on April 15th. Corpl Pearson joined the Army soon after the commencement of the war. Before joining he will be remembered by all while he worked in his father's shop. The following letter has been received from a Second-Lieutenant of his Company: "I should like to take this opportunity of offering you the deepest sympathy of all officers of "D" Company in your sad loss of your son, Corpl. Pearson. I have always found him strictly conscientious in all his duties, a ready volunteer for any duty which required courage and endurance, and an absolutely reliable NCO. He won the greatest respect from all the officers and men by his perpetual cheerfulness and his sterling qualities. During the last week or two he accompanied me in some dangerous patrols, and he never showed any signs of fear, and was always ready to help me in any way. He was shot through the head while on a dangerous patrol, and never recovered consciousness. In his death the Battalion has lost one of the finest soldiers and gentlemen it has ever seen." A letter has also been received from the Chaplain of the Company, of which the following is a part: "I felt I must write you a letter of most sincere sympathy in the death of your son, which took place on the 15th. We buried his body reverently quite close to where he fell, side by side with others of his Regiment, and the grave will be properly marked with a cross and the site.*

Not many months ago Mr and Mrs Pearson lost another son who was killed in France. They have two other sons also serving; one is in France and the other, who has been wounded, is now at Crowborough.

George Henry Penfold

Chief Petty Officer 164841, HMS Hawke, Royal Navy. Died 15 October 1914, age 37. Commemorated on the Chatham Naval Memorial, Kent: Panel 1. Husband of Kathleen Agate Penfold of Station House, Bearsted, Maidstone.

The 1881 Census records that George Henry Penfold was christened on 11 March 1877 at St Peter's Church, Southborough. The family, resident then at 7, Holden Corner, included his father George, a labourer (53 when son George was born), and brother John Penfold, also a labourer (older by 17 years than George Henry), born in Penshurst and married to Fanny. Dee's Directory 1915 listed, under Men Serving, J Penfold, of Modest Corner, with the Royal Field Artillery.

From the Tunbridge Wells Advertiser, 23 October 1914: *Chief Petty Officer George Henry Penfold, whose brother lives at Hawkhurst Villas, Woodlands-road, and who has a sister at 12, Southview-road, was on the ill-fated HMS Hawke, which was torpedoed by a German submarine. His name has not so far appeared amongst the saved. Chief Petty Officer Penfold was an acting gunner, and had seen 22 years' service in the Navy, having joined when he was 15 years of age. A tragic coincidence is that he sailed his first voyage, after joining the Navy, and his last voyage on HMS Hawke. He had served two or three years in the Mediterranean and three years in China, only returning from the latter station last Christmas. In addition to the Hawke he had served on HMS Illustrious, HMS Irresistible and HMS London. His wife is staying with her sister-in-law, Mrs Hickmott, at 12, Southview-road.*

HMS Hawke (left) was an old armoured cruiser operating as part of the 10th Cruiser Squadron assigned to the Northern Patrol. Originally launched at Chatham in 1891, and one of the oldest ships still in service, she was being used as a training ship and had many young cadets on board. She had been recommissioned in February 1913 with a nucleus crew and had come up to her full complement on the outbreak of war in August 1914. During September 1914, she had visited Lerwick.

On the fateful day she was in the northern waters of the North Sea with a similar ship, HMS Theseus, when they were attacked. They were operating on October 15th 1914 without a destroyer screen. Unfortunately they were slower than the submarine U9 (below), which was tracking them. Their position was some 60 miles off Aberdeen. At the time, HMS Hawke had just turned to intercept a neutral Norwegian collier.

The U-Boat Commander was Lieutenant Otto Weddigen (below). He missed the Theseus with his first torpedo but unfortunately hit HMS Hawke amidships near a magazine. The detonation was followed by a second terrific explosion, in which a large number of the crew was killed. The ship sank within 5 minutes and was only able to launch one ship's boat. Five hundred and twenty five perished. Only the 49 men in the long boat were saved. They were picked up three hours later by a Norwegian steamer. HMS Theseus was under strict Admiralty orders not to attempt to pick up survivors, as only several weeks earlier there had been a disaster.

On that occasion, on the 22nd September, both HMS Hogue and HMS Cressy had also been torpedoed when going to pick up survivors from HMS Aboukir (see **Alfred Assiter**). The submarine that had sunk these three ships had again been commanded by Weddigen. However, had they had sufficient time to launch other lifeboats from HMS Hawke, then undoubtedly more would have been saved by the Norwegians. Lieutenant Weddigen was commander of U29, the following year, when he was caught in Pentland Firth on March 18th. HMS Dreadnought managed to ram the submarine and sink her with the loss of all her crew.

Another Southborough resident, Private George William Walton, CH/8670 (RMR/B/155), Royal Marine Light Infantry, died on the Hawke that day, and is also commemorated on the Chatham Naval Memorial, Kent (Panel 7), but not on the Southborough War Memorial. Marine Private Walton was age 40, the son of Benjamin Walton of Whittlesea, Cambridgeshire and husband of Alice Walton of 9 Bedford Road, Southborough. (See **Samuel Tilley** re HMS Hawke survivor Pte JE Corke).

George Pierson

Able Seaman J/7047, HMS Jason, Royal Navy. Died 3 April 1917, age 23. Commemorated on the Chatham Naval Memorial, Kent: Panel 22. Son of the late Albert and Mary Jane Pierson, of Tunbridge Wells, Kent.

The Tunbridge Wells Advertiser of 21 August 1914 listed G Pierson, of 94 High Brooms-road (HMS Hibernia), under Local Men On Service.

HMS Jason was the sister ship to HMS Niger, a Torpedo Gun Boat, Alarm Class, which was laid down on 17 September 1891 and launched on 17 December 1892, having been built by the Naval Construction and Armament Co Ltd at Barrow. She was converted to Minesweeper in 1908/09. She was lost at around 56 35N 06 30W between Coll & Mull (Inner Hebrides) on 7 April 1917 with 85 crew lost (all hands), sunk by a mine laid by U-78 (captained by Otto Droscher).

Harold John Player

Private G/17950, 7th Bn, The Buffs (East Kent Regiment). Died on Thursday 3 May 1917, age 19. Commemorated on the Arras Memorial, Pas de Calais, France: Bay 2. Son of Mrs Martha Ann Player, of 15 Speldhurst Road, Southborough & Samuel Player. Born Walton-on-Thames, Surrey.

Michael Mills writes: *Harold Player joined the Buffs in August 1916. On 3 May 1917 the Battalion attacked the village of Cherisy as part of the second phase of the Battle of Arras. The attack commenced in the dark at 0345 hrs. Captain Black's A Company got through the village and crossed the river only to find themselves cut off. D Company in support got held up by German resistance in Cable Trench. B and C Companies fought their way to the river but by 1100 hrs a general retirement was taking place. The Battalion was back in its original position by the evening with the loss of 27 killed, 173 wounded and 178 missing.*

G H Pointer

Private 98193, 46th Coy, Machine Gun Corps (Inf). Died Thursday 3 October 1918, age 31. Buried in Sequehart British Cemetery No. 1, Aisne, France: Grave ref. A.55. Husband of Kate Pointer, The Down, Lamberhurst, Kent.

From the CWGC site: *Sequehart was captured on the 3 October 1918 after three days' fighting, by the 5th/6th Royal Scots and the 15th Highland Light Infantry (32nd Division).*

From the Courier, 22 November 1918: *News has been received by Mrs Pointer, 28, Edward-street, that her husband, Pte GH Pointer, Machine Gun Corps, was killed in France on October 3rd. A letter of sympathy has been received by Mrs Pointer from an officer of her husband's Regiment in which he says that Private Pointer showed great courage in face of danger, and fell with his Section Officer and a comrade. It is gratifying to know that he was spared any pain, death being instantaneous ... Private Pointer was always keen and reliable, and by his loss the Section is deprived of one of its best men. He has been laid to rest with his comrades in a position of honour in an area world-famous for its battles. Before enlisting in January, 1916, Private Pointer was employed by Mr Reeves, Danemore Park, Langton. He was well-known in Speldhurst previously, having lived in Barden-road. He went to France in June 1917.*

Ben Pown

Private 204038, 1st Bn, Northumberland Fusiliers. Died 23 March 1918, age 22. Buried in Doullens Communal Cemetery Extension No 1, Somme, France: Grave ref. V.C.56. Son of Stephen and Selina Pown, of 13 Gordon Road, High Brooms.

Private Pown served in the 1st/4th Northumberland Fusiliers (4/9053); 22nd Northumberland Fusiliers; 19th Northumberland Fusiliers (attached 183rd Tunnelling Company); 9th Northumberland Fusiliers.

www.firstworldwar.com/onthisday for 23 March 1918 for the Western Front: *Germans take Monchy-le-Preux, cross Tortille River (between Bapaume and Peronne), capture Peronne and Ham, and reach line of Somme.*

From a newspaper report of the time: *Official news has been received to the effect that Pte B Pown, of the Northumberland Fusiliers, whose residence was at 13, Gordon-road, High Brooms, has succumbed to his wounds. He had been wounded twice previously, and had been in France since 1916. He was 22 years of age, and an old employee of the High Brooms Brick Company, having been educated at St Barnabas' School. He joined the colours in March, 1915, and general regret will be felt at his death.*

Ben was part of a large family; he had twelve brothers and sisters plus an orphaned first cousin on his father's side that his parents had adopted (listed as the father's niece on a Census return of the time). His mother, Selina Sarah nee Dixon was born in South Hamlet on the outskirts of Gloucester, and his father Stephen Streeter Pown (sometimes written Pound or Pounds in the records) was born in Frant.

Selina Sarah was in service locally so it's more than likely that is how they met, and they married at St George's Church, Sevenoaks Weald on 12th June 1875. Their first child Mary Ann arrived in 1876, followed by Alice Priscilla in 1877, William Albert in 1880, Emily Ellen in 1882 (died in 1884), Stephen George in 1885, and Jesse in 1887 (he worked all his life for the High Brooms Brick and Tile Co). Selina Louisa was born in late 1889 (known as Lena, she later married Robert Arthur Waters, known as Bob), Emma Kate Elizabeth in 1892, Ben in 1894 (according to family member Ella Woolley this is correct despite information on file at the CGWC), Dorothy May came into the world in 1896, May in 1897 and finally Ivy Annie Lawrie in 1900. The adopted niece was Elizabeth Upton, born around 1890 in Brighton, daughter of Stephen's sister Maria. (Pictured above right: sisters Selina, May and Ivy, with baby Geoff).

George Vincent Proctor

Lieutenant, 8th Battalion Lancashire Fusiliers. Died 6 September 1917. Commemorated on the Tyne Cot Memorial, Zonnebeke, West-Vlaanderen: Panel 54 to 60 and Grave 163A.

Lt G Proctor is ranked on Southborough Memorial as 2nd Lieutenant. He is also listed under Lancashire Fusiliers on the War Memorial of Manchester University, which is located in the quadrangle of the John Owens Building, The University of Manchester, Oxford Road, Manchester, inscribed:

TO THE MEMBERS OF THE UNIVERSITY OF MANCHESTER AND OF THE OFFICERS TRAINING CORPS WHO LAID DOWN THEIR LIVES IN THE GREAT WAR.

Arthur Richard Puckett

Guardsman 2616893, 3rd Bn, Grenadier Guards. Died 30 May 1944, age 26. Buried Grave 1.B.8 in Cassino War Cemetery, Italy. Son of Frederick and Catherine Ellen Puckett; husband of Ellen Elfreda Puckett, of High Brooms, Tunbridge Wells, Kent.

A newspaper clipping from the time reported that Arthur died of wounds. His cousin recalls that he was hit by machine-gun fire. The report says further: *His wife, together with her little son, Richard, aged 2½, resides at 18 Bayhall Road. Guardsman Puckett was a keen footballer, having played for the High Brooms Old Boys' Club. He volunteered for service in October 1939, and had been overseas for just a year. On leaving school he was employed by Messrs Newman Clark, the printers, of Tunbridge Wells.*

Arthur Puckett's family home was at 36 High Brooms Road. His brother Harold, known as Harry, was in the RAF in the war, and served in Africa. Cecil, his oldest brother, worked on the railways in the reserved profession of train driver. He died of cancer, reckoned by the family to be brought on by the coal dust in his working environment. Arthur's parents kept a photograph of his grave, with a wooden cross bearing his name, on their wall until they died (pictured right).

The best-known bakery in High Brooms was Puckett's Bakery, situated at the junction of Colebrook Road and High Brooms. The firm was so well-known that the location was given the name Puckett's Corner.

Guardsman Cecil John Wright, 2620721, 6th Battalion Grenadier Guards, who died 7 November 1943, age 30, is also buried in the Cassino War Cemetery, Grave ref. XVIII.E.15. He was the son of William and Lottie Wright; husband of Dorothy Winifred Wright, of Southborough, but is not listed on the Southborough Memorial.

Henry Albert Randall

Private DM2/228248. Died 19 February 1919, age 49. Buried in Southborough Cemetery: Grave ref. 4.342.

The Southborough Memorial gives Private Randall's unit as RASC (MT), while the CWGC gives none. Kelly's Directory 1916 gives a Charles William Randall resident at 110 Springfield-road.

Bernard R Read

Private 82171, 26th Bn (known as the Bankers Battalion), Royal Fusiliers. Formerly 148211, 107 TR (Training Reserve). Died 15 July 1918, age 18. Commemorated on the Tyne Cot Memorial: Panel 28-30 and 162-162a & 163a.

From the Courier, 26 July 1918: *Mrs Read, of 13 Colebrooke-road, High Brooms, has received news that her youngest son, Private Read, was killed in action in France on July 15th, one day before his 19th birthday. Private Read joined the Royal Fusiliers on August 15th, 1917, and his widowed mother had never seen him from the day he left to join up. Mrs Read has received a letter from the Captain of the Regiment, in which he says: "Your son was a true soldier, cheerful, unselfish, and loved by all his comrades, and his death will be mourned by all." Mrs Read has one son still in the Army and one has his discharge with one leg off. Deceased received his education at Grosvenor School, and sang in St Luke's Choir for eight years.*

P Read

Private TR/71572. Died 11 November 1918, age 36. Buried in Southborough Cemetery: Grave ref. 3.368. Son of Edward James and Rose Ellen Read.

The CWGC gives no unit, but the Southborough War Memorial gives P Read's rank as Lance Corporal and his unit as the Royal Fusiliers.

William Albert Read

Gunner 134740, 59th Siege Battery, Royal Garrison Artillery. Died 30 October 1918, age 35. Buried in Etaples Military Cemetery, Pas de Calais, France: Grave ref. LXVI.M.4. Husband of Florence Kate Read, of 26, Windsor Road, Bexhill-on-Sea.

From the CWGC site: *During the First World War, the area around Etaples was the scene of immense concentrations of Commonwealth reinforcement camps and hospitals. It was remote from attack, except from aircraft, and accessible by railway from both the northern and the southern battlefields. In 1917, 100,000 troops were camped among the sand dunes, and the hospitals, which included eleven general, one stationary, four Red Cross hospitals and a convalescent depot, could deal with 22,000 wounded or sick.*

From the Courier, 13 November 1918: *Mrs W Read, of Bexhill (late of Southborough), has received news that her husband, Gunner W Read, has died of wounds received in the last big battle. He was the third son of Mr Read and the late Mrs Read, Holden Park-road, and was an old schoolboy of Mr Fletcher's, Prospect-road, and for many years a member of Christ Church Choir. He left Southborough eight years ago for Bexhill. He joined the RGA in December, 1916, and in May last went to France. He was slightly wounded through being buried in a dugout, but recovered, and was expecting to come home on leave shortly. He leaves a widow and little son of ten years to mourn their loss. Gunner Read has three brothers serving with the Colours.*

William Albert Read's rank is given as Driver on the Southborough War Memorial. He is remembered on his parents' headstone in Southborough Cemetery. His mother Sarah died 8 March 1908 aged 57, and his father Henry died 24 March 1927 aged 76.

Henry Reeve

Private 6343648, 4th Bn, Queen's Own (Royal West Kent Regiment). Died Sunday 26 May 1940, age 20. Buried in Le Grand Hasard Military Cemetery, Morbecque, Nord, France: Sp.Mem. 'A'. Son of Jonathan Thomas Reeve and Lily Reeve, of Southborough.

Henry Reeve was in the same battalion as **Ronald Peacock**. He died on the same day as

Frederick Funnell and two days earlier than **Charles William Barton**, **Frank Hemsley**, **Frank Sutcliffe** and Frederick Scrace, all also in the same battalion. All of them except for Fred Scrace are now commemorated on the Southborough War Memorial, and all of them except for Ron Peacock are commemorated at or buried in the same cemetery.

Henry was the eldest of seven children. Their home, Vulcan Cottage, was situated on the corner of Southborough Common at the junction with Holden Road (now the site of a block of flats). His father, a master blacksmith, worked the forge.

Henry had a love of music; he was a choirboy at St Thomas' Church and played the violin. He was a keen Scouter and at the outbreak of war was the assistant Scout Master. He joined the Royal West Kent Regiment as a Territorial; his close friend was **Clarence Smart** from High Brooms, who, along with his brother **Edward Smart**, also died during the same campaign.

E A Rich

Private, Royal West Kent. Died in World War I.

Kelly's Directory 1915 lists a T Rich at 18 Modest Corner, serving with the KFRE, and the 1917 version lists a Mrs Rich at 21, Springfield-road. There are only three men named Rich on the CWGC, and the only one with these initials is:

Ernest Alfred Rich, Private SR/4886, 1st Bn, Middlesex Regiment. Died on 27 August 1916, age 29. Son of Mr and Mrs Rich, of 10, Brook St, Bruce Grove, Tottenham, London. Commemorated on the Thiepval Memorial, Somme, France, Grave/Memorial Reference: Pier and Face 12 D and 13 B.

Albert Frederick Richardson

Private 35905, 2nd Bn, Essex Regiment (formerly 32599 Suffolk Regiment). Died Wednesday 10 October 1917, age 35. Commemorated on the Tyne Cot Memorial, Zonnebeke, West-Vlaanderen, Belgium: Panel 98 to 99. Born in Marden, Kent. Son of Thomas and Emily Richardson of 38 Taylor Street, Southborough; husband of Emma Richardson, of 6 Taylor Street.

One of four volunteer firemen serving with the Southborough Fire Brigade (left) who died in the First World War and are honoured with a plaque in the Fire Station, and on the Southborough War Memorial.

The Courier of 9 November 1917 reports: *Mrs Richardson, 6 Taylor-street, has received information that her husband Private AF Richardson, Essex Regiment, was killed in action on October 10th. Private Richardson joined the Army in June 1916, and went to France in February 1917. He was invalided back to England in March suffering from pneumonia, and only returned to France in August.*

Henry George Richardson

Warrant Officer 1377980, Air Gunner, 280 Squadron, RAF Volunteer Reserve. Died Saturday 13 November, 1943, age 33. Buried Tunbridge Wells Cemetery, Kent. Grave in Section 19c.

Henry was born in Tonbridge, to Edward and Alice Richardson, and was always known to the family as Harry. At the beginning of the First World War the family moved to 40, Springfield Road, Southborough. Edward Richardson had served in the Boer War and the First World War. Two of Alice's brothers had emigrated to Canada.

Harry's sister Dorothy was born in 1919, and Harry was the youngest of three brothers. All the siblings went to school at St Peter's. Edward (known as Ted), the eldest, was a well-known local footballer; he was given a reserved occupation during the War, building for the Army. Fred was in the Army, and was stationed in Malta when it was awarded the George Cross.

Harry worked for Powells, the electrical firm, and then Wisden's, the cricket-ball factory, and was working there when he signed up for the RAF. He was one of a group of friends who signed up together before they were called up. They had also some years earlier formed a football team, the Invicta Football Team, which won the local Cup Final in Tonbridge on 6 April 1932. In the team photograph above, Harry is in the back row, 2nd from right.

Harry was married to Flora Lilian (pictured together left). He died on Saturday 13 November 1943, aged 33. His plane had been on a mission, had been hit, and had made it back to England. The pilot circled three times, attempting to land, but failed to do so, and hit a hillside and exploded, killing all of the crew.

The motto of 280 Squadron is "We shall be there". No 280 Squadron was formed on 10 December 1941 at Thorney Island for air-sea rescue duties. Originally intended to have Hudsons, the squadron moved to Detling with

Ansons in February 1942 as the Hudsons were required for other units. In June it began taking part in searches along the coasts of south-east England and East Anglia. In October 1943, No 280 Squadron was re-equipped with Warwicks, which could undertake longer patrols over the North Sea and also carry airborne lifeboats.

Raymond Christopher Rigg

Flight Lieutenant 131, 103 RAF (VR) 281 Squadron, Royal Air Force Volunteer Reserve. Died Wednesday 11 April 1945, age 21. Buried in Southborough Cemetery, Sec 11. Grave 388.

Raymond Christopher Pietroni Rigg was known as Chris to the family. His paternal grandfather worked in South America, and died suddenly before the turn of the 20th century, leaving his wife, Isabella (née Pietroni) and children, who were repatriated by the company he worked for to England. Sadly, Isabella was struck down with yellow fever en route at Rio de Janeiro and died. Their three sons, Henry, Arthur and Julius, were taken into the care of a Miss Searle, a member of the South American Missionary Society, and sent to boarding school in Bath.

Henry Charles Pietroni Rigg, the eldest son, went into medicine, trained at Charing Cross Hospital and qualified in 1913. He secured work as Doctor to St John del Rei goldmine in Brazil, at one time the deepest mine in the world, and thus returned to South America, where he stayed until 1936, returning to the UK and eventually setting up as a General Practitioner, taking over Dr Paine's practice at 4 Park Road, Southborough. He had met Chris's mother, Doris Willoughby, when a student, and in 1917 she went out to Brazil where they were married.

There were four children in the family: Alan (born 1918), Eileen (1920), Chris (7 June 1923), and David (1935). Eileen died at nine months old, on the boat returning to the UK. She had been bitten by a mosquito in Rio, which led to septicaemia, and was buried at sea, at Cape St Vincent. During the years in Brazil, Alan and Chris were sent home to schools in Somerset, firstly to a prep school in Bath, then to senior school in Taunton. Their father was allowed leave to come home every

2½ years with their mother, and in the interim the boys spent holidays at a hotel in Ilfracombe. In 1933 Alan and Chris had an extended summer holiday when they went out to Brazil, (pictured L to R: Chris, Doris Rigg and Alan) including a memorable journey by sea and train and the unforgettable experience of going down the deepest mine in the world. In 1934 the family enjoyed a six weeks' holiday together in Newquay, Cornwall, and were reunited finally when the Riggs set up home in 1938 in Southborough.

Chris was, according to Alan, quite an adventurous character at School, on one occasion climbing over the walls with some friends for a swim in a nearby pool. One day at home in Southborough he decided to go on a 100 mile cycle ride. He left at 9am and arrived home at 7pm. When he got home the mileometer on his bike showed 99 miles, so he did another mile round Southborough!

Chris left school at 17, in 1941. He had joined the School Air Training Corps, and was accepted by the RAF. He spent a year studying required sciences at Durham University, then went to Canada for initial training, and thence to Air Force training in Pensacola, near Key West, Florida. Having qualified as a pilot he had several postings in the UK, finally to Limavady, near Londonderry, Northern Ireland, with 281 Squadron.

The 281 Squadron (motto Volamus servaturi - We fly to save) was formed on 29 March 1942 at Ouston for air-sea rescue duties, initially with Defiants. In February 1943, it added Walrus amphibians and by June had replaced its Defiants with Ansons. On 22 November 1943, the squadron was absorbed by 282 Squadron. No 281 reformed at Thornaby on the same day equipped with Warwicks for ASR missions and from February 1944 based detachments around the British Isles, moving its base to Tiree at the same time. Sea Otters were added in April 1944. In February 1945, the squadron moved to Northern Ireland but a detachment remained at Tiree until September.

In April 1945 Chris and four others went on leave, flying to an airfield in South Wales and going their separate ways before meeting up there again to fly back to Limavady on 11 April. There was no navigational guidance from the ground, and on the flight back, mist had settled in the area around the base, and the plane flew straight into a hillside, killing all the crew. Chris's body was brought back to Southborough for burial.

As the war was reaching its final stage in Europe, Chris and an Australian colleague had talked of their futures, agreeing initially to see the world and write about their travels. Chris was killed less than four weeks before the end of the War in Europe on 8 May 1945.

John Richard Rogers

Sapper 742, 1st/3rd Kent Field Coy, Royal Engineers. Died 28 October 1915 in the Hythe disaster, age 22. Commemorated on the Helles Memorial, which stands on the tip of the Gallipoli Peninsula in Turkey: Panel 23 to 25 or 325 to 328.

Frank Stevens' book *Southborough Sappers of the Kent (Fortress) Royal Engineers* includes the following: John was the 27th man to join No 3 Company. He lived with his parents Richard and Sarah Rogers at 19 Speldhurst Road, Southborough, which is very close to the drill hall. He received schooling at St Peter's School, was employed by Mr Parker as a decorator, and was a member of the Ancient Order of Foresters.

William Rollins

Private G/7268, 1st Bn, Queen's Own (Royal West Kent Regiment). Died 26 October 1917. Commemorated on the Tyne Cot Memorial, Zonnebeke, West-Vlaanderen, Belgium: Panel 106 to 108.

Information from www.firstworldwar.com/onthisday gives the following campaign detail for 26 October 1917 for the Western Front: *Franco-British attack east, north-east and north of Ypres. British positions improved from Passchendaele to Poelcapelle.*

Southborough War Memorial

Ronald Edward Russell

Sergeant 1809231, 77 Sqdn, Royal Air Force Volunteer Reserve. Died Thursday 15 February 1945, age 20. Buried in Svino Churchyard, Denmark: Grave 91. Son of Albert Edward and Caroline May Russell.

The CWGC Website gives the following information: *Svino is a small village in Southern Zealand, overlooking Dybso Fjord, some 90 kilometres south-south-west of Copenhagen. Commonwealth forces fought no land campaign in Denmark during the Second World War, but from the German occupation on 9 April 1940, the air forces were active in Danish skies with special operations and raids on strategic targets, supplying the Danish resistance, anti-submarine patrols and bombing missions over northern Germany. Many airmen were killed in these operations and lie buried in churchyards and cemeteries all over Denmark. Svino Churchyard contains a Commonwealth plot of 62 burials, all airmen, eight of them unidentified.*

Miss Megan Davies of Southborough, who played with Ronald when they were children, recalls that his father was the Manager of Young & Manton (the shop on the corner of Holden Park Road and London Road), and that Ronald was his parents' only son. Their address was given in 1940 Kelly's Directory as 120 London Road, Southborough.

Clive Maier's research reveals that Sergeant Russell took off at 1805 hrs from Full Sutton in Halifax III bomber MZ924 KN-D. The mission was Operation Gardening. The aircraft headed for the Kadet Channel and came down in the Smalandsfarvandet, south of Zealand. The crew of seven were all killed but were recovered from the sea and interred in various Danish cemeteries.

From the Courier, 14 December 1945: *Sergeant Ronald E Russell, previously reported missing on sea mining operations over the Baltic Sea on February 14th, is now officially presumed to have lost his life. Sergeant Russell had made many previous operational flights over Germany. Prior to joining the RAF in October 1942, he was employed by Messrs Gilbert and Stamper of Tonbridge, and was also a member of the 129 Squadron, RTC.*

William Ellingham Rye

Private 60701, "D" Coy, 8th Bn, Royal Fusiliers. Died 9 April 1917, age 22. Commemorated on the Arras Memorial, Pas de Calais, France: Bay 3. Son of George and Alice Mary Rye, 33 Vale Road, Southborough.

www.firstworldwar.com/onthisday for 9 April 1917: *Battle of Arras (on 12-mile front from Henin-sur-Cojeul, south-east of Arras, to Givenchy-en-Gohelle, north of Arras). British (Canadians) take Vimy Ridge (northern end excepted), five villages and 6,000 prisoners. North of St. Quentin and towards Cambrai British take six villages and enter Havrincourt Wood.*

From a newspaper account of May 1917: *Great sympathy will be felt for Mr and Mrs Rye, 33 Vale-road, in the loss of their youngest son, Lance-Corporal Rye, 8th Royal Fusiliers, at the age of 22. A letter was received on the 20th April from a Corporal of Lance-Corporal Rye's Company, in which he said he was sorry to say that Lance-Corporal Rye had been missing since April 9th. The writer had promised Lance-Corporal Rye that should anything happen to him he would let his parents know. Another letter was received on the 21st April from an officer of the Royal Fusiliers, saying: "It is with the deepest sorrow that I have to inform you of the death of Lce-Corporal Rye. He was in my platoon for a long time. I cannot speak too highly of him. I always found him a very reliable and good soldier, and one to be trusted. I can only say that I and all who knew him will feel the loss of such a splendid fellow."*

Lance-Corporal Rye enlisted soon after the outbreak of war from Etherington's, Brighton, where he had been for about two years. He originally joined the Royal Sussex, but when he reached France in October, 1916, he was transferred to the Royal Fusiliers. Mr and Mrs Rye have another son serving in the Royal Engineers (Kent Fortress), who has been in France for some months.

Dee's Directory 1915 lists, under Men Serving, WE Rye, 3rd Royal Sussex, and FG Rye, KFRE at 33 Vale-road. WE Rye's Rank on the Southborough War Memorial is given as Lance-Corporal.

Philip Sale

Sapper 540620, 58th Div, Signal Coy, Royal Engineers (originally a member of KFRE, No 1390, transferred to Signal Service). Wounded 25 October 1917 at Poelcapelle and died of wounds on 2 November 1917 in 13 General Hospital, age 25. Buried in Boulogne Eastern Cemetery, Pas de Calais, France: Grave ref. VIII.I.99. Son of William and Frances Sale, of 10, Holden Corner, Southborough.

Employed by Mr Rye of Vale Road (possibly making cricket balls). Philip's mother was a widow, and his brother was serving in Egypt with Armoured Car Coy.

David Reginald Hermon Philip Goldsmith Stern Salomons

Captain, Kent Field Company, Royal Engineers. Died 28 October 1915. age 30. Commemorated on the Helles Memorial, which stands on the tip of the Gallipoli Peninsula in Turkey. Panel 23 to 25 or 325 to 328.

Frank Stevens' book *Southborough Sappers of the Kent (Fortress) Royal Engineers* includes the following: *Born 13th October 1885, the son of Sir David Lionel Salomons of Southborough, Kent and Laura Julia. Educated at Eton College and Gonville and Caius College, he graduated 1st Class, 2nd in merit in History.*

Upon graduation he returned home to Broomhill and then undertook a tour to Far East countries. His father was Honorary Colonel of the Kent (Fortress) RE and David (more commonly known as Reggie) took an interest in this unit. He first became a Captain in the Kent (Fortress) Cadets which he helped to raise in Southborough, Tonbridge and Ashford; his commission for the rank is dated 16 February 1912.

Attempts to raise an adult unit in Tonbridge were not approved until 1913 when a "detachment" of No 1 Tonbridge Company took place; the unit was almost as big as the parent company and in 1914 permission was given to raise No 3 Company in Southborough.

His promotions were 2nd Lieutenant 11th October 1911, Lieutenant 15th August 1913 and Captain 31st October 1914; the officer commanding the unit was Captain Ruston, before the conversion to a Field Company; as Captain Ruston became a Major so Reggie Salomons became a Captain. A very popular officer with his men and of help to the families when they wanted for something. He put on various forms of entertainment for the men at his own expense and did whatever he could to make life a little easier for them.

When HMS Hythe was in collision and sinking he is said to have had the chance to save himself but chose to do whatever he could for those on board and it is said gave away his life-jacket to one of the soldiers and thus died. He is commemorated by his college, the Book of British Jewry, the Southborough War Memorial, St Matthews Church High Brooms and others including a private memorial erected by his father.

The *Warwick Notebook* page by Frank Warwick in the Courier of 10 September 1993 quotes from the work done by Fred Howe, editor of the Sir David Salomons Society journal, in researching the life of Captain Salomons: *The Company met first in Sheffield Hall, Draper Street, then in the former gasworks in Speldhurst Road, later converted by Sir David Salomons at his personal expense into a well-equipped drill hall.*

The 1/3 Kent Field Company left their depot at Gillingham on October 11, 1915, and sailed from Devonport the following day in the converted liner Scotian, not knowing that the government was already preparing to abandon the Gallipoli operation as a lost cause. During the voyage, Salomons wrote of his pride in the men, though fearing few appreciated the dangers into which they were sailing. At the last minute instructions to transfer the REs to another ship for landing at Suvla Bay were cancelled and the Hythe sailed on. Driver Fred Mills, from Speldhurst, was one of those who watched the disaster unfold. He saw the Sarnia bearing down on the Hythe just seconds before the collision. The Hythe's crew had just time to give a warning blast on the siren before the heavier ship hit them forward of the bridge, cutting deep into the little vessel's side, almost cutting her in two…

After relating the story of the collision thereafter, it goes on: *The Hythe's commander, sensing that the ship was about to go down, called to Salomons, "Come on, jump. This is your last chance. I am going now." But Salomons stood firm, saying, "No, I will see my men safe first". He was seen with Company Sergeant Major John Carter, trying to launch a lifeboat. They stood on the bridge, Salomons exhorting his men to keep cool and try to save themselves. They went down with the ship as it slid under the waves.*

The article concludes: *In reply to a message from the chairman of Tonbridge Urban District Council, Cllr Isard, Sir David Salomons said: I have the satisfaction to know that my son was very conscientious and did his duty without coveting favour or popularity. He took an interest in his men and cadets as if they had been his children. An additional grief is present in the knowledge that nearly all his company were drowned, which throws all our district into mourning.*

Driver Fred Mills, a Hythe survivor and member of the 1st/3rd (Kent) Field Company, witnessed as follows: *"I think I can sacredly say that he died trying for others as he was with the other officers who were saved. Our Major had to take to the water only but for remaining almost to the last, and I am told he wanted the Captain to follow. One of the Sappers who was late himself in leaving the ship as she was sinking said the last he saw of him was trying to lower a boat. If he was not thinking of others one would imagine he would have gone straight for his own Life Belt of which he had a beauty and would be impossible for him to sink in that time. It is my own opinion if he had of thought of himself first he would have been saved, and if I am right he died a Hero's death and we honour him."*

William Henry Salter

2nd Corporal 916, 1st/3rd Kent Field Coy. Died 28 November 1915 in the Hythe disaster, age 20. He is commemorated on the Helles Memorial, Gallipoli Peninsula, Turkey. Panel 23 to 25 or 325 to 328. Son of William Gillard Salter and Eliza Salter, of 9 Stewart Road, High Brooms.

Frank Stevens' book *Southborough Sappers of the Kent (Fortress) Royal Engineers* includes the following: *Known as "Harry", he worked as an engine cleaner on the London Brighton & South Coast Railway but was employed in the unit as Orderly Room clerk ... he had been a Sapper for two years when he drowned on 28 October 1915.*

Frederick William Saunders

Private 55513, 24th Bn, Manchester Regiment Died Tuesday 23 April 1918, age 38. Buried in Montecchio Precalcino Communal Cemetery Extension, Italy: Plot 1. Row C. Grave 7.

Frederick Saunders had originally been numbered as KFRE 1959. He is recorded as Lance Corporal, Kent Field Coy, RE on Southborough War Memorial. From newspaper reports at the time: *Official news has been received by Mrs Saunders, of 23, Edward-street, informing her that her husband, Sapper FW Saunders, (better known as "Nimy"), KFRE, attached to the Manchester Pioneers, stationed in Italy, was severely wounded by the bursting of a shell on April 23rd, and died on the 24th. He joined up soon after the outbreak of war, and went to France in September, 1917, and from there to Italy.*

Before enlisting he was a member of the Southborough Fire Brigade for close on 20 years. Mrs Saunders is left with 10 young children, and much sympathy will be felt for her in her loss. The eldest of the children was a little more than fourteen.

The following letter has been received from the Captain: Dear Mrs Saunders, I have the sad news to convey to you that your husband, Sapper FW Saunders, of my Company, died yesterday of wounds received on the 23rd. As his platoon were marching to work a shell burst amongst them, and your husband sustained severe injuries, from which he has since succumbed. He lies together with his Platoon Officer and Sergeant, who were killed at the same time, in a grave at the foot of the hills, where we have set up a cross. My officers wish to convey to you their sympathy in our loss, which is so overwhelming. As his Company Commander I miss him, for he was a good soldier and willing worker and very well liked by both his officers and his comrades in the ranks. Yet our loss is as nothing to yours, and I can only extend to you my sincere sympathy.

Frederick's brother FJ Saunders, with the Royal West Kents, was also killed in the war. Their mother, father, brothers and sisters attended the official opening ceremony for the Southborough War Memorial in 1921.

Thomas Henry Saunders

Sapper 820, 3rd Kent Fortress Coy, Royal Engineers. Died 28 July 1915, age 23. Buried in Southborough Cemetery: Grave ref. 6.328. Son of William and Mary Saunders.

A newspaper of the time gave the following report: *The funeral of Sapper Thomas Henry Saunders, of the Kent (Fortress) Royal Engineers, took place on Saturday at High Brooms, military honours being accorded the remains.*

Sapper Saunders was a popular young fellow in High Brooms, where he had lived all his life, attending the Council School as a lad. He was only 23 years of age, and was the son of Mr William Saunders, of 35, Wolseley-road, High Brooms. He had been a Territorial for over four years, serving in the Southborough Company of the Kent (Fortress) Royal Engineers, and was called up on the outbreak of war last August. For some months past he had been on duty at Chatham.

A short time ago he had the misfortune to fall on a kerb and injure his spine, and he succumbed to an ensuing illness at the Fort Pitt Hospital, Chatham, on Wednesday of last week. Much sympathy is felt for his relatives, and it was greatly in evidence when the funeral took place on Saturday.

The remains were brought to Southborough Station by a special train from Tonbridge, connecting with the train from Chatham, and were accompanied by an officer, NCOs and men of his Company. On arrival at Southborough Station, the coffin was placed in a hearse and covered with the Union Jack. The cortege, to which the deceased soldier's comrades formed a guard of honour, proceeded to St Matthew's Church, where the first part of the service was conducted by the Curate, the Rev MGS Harrison, the Vicar, the Rev P Orme, being away from home.

The cortege afterwards re-formed and proceeded slowly to the Southborough Cemetery, Chopin's "Marche Funebre" and the "Dead March" in "Saul" being played en route by the Band. Following the commital, the firing party discharged three volleys into the air, and the "Last Post" was sounded by the buglers, the scene at the graveside being a very impressive one.

The chief mourners were Mr William Saunders (father), Sapper Robert Saunders and Mrs R Saunders (brother and sister-in-law), Miss Alice Bacon (the deceased's fiancee), Mrs Simmonds, Miss Daisy Simmons, Mrs Fermor (sister), Miss Rose Saunders (sister), Mr Thomas Tester, Mr Jack Saunders (brother), Mrs F Saunders (aunt), and Mrs Jenner (sister).

In the Second World War, the following soldier, pictured on left, who was most likely the son of Thomas Henry Saunders' brother Robert, mentioned above, was reported missing in the Courier, 20 June 1941: MISSING IN THE MIDDLE EAST Among the first contingents to go to France in the war, and one of the last to leave Dunkirk during the evacuation, Driver RA (Bob) Saunders, of the RASC, only son of Mrs Saunders and the late Mr R Saunders, of 35, Wolseley-road, High Brooms, has been reported missing in the Middle East as from April 28. News to this effect was received by his mother this week.

Before the war Driver Saunders had been employed for some 15 years on the local bus services, first with the Redcar and later with the Maidstone and District Motor Services, Ltd. He was called up on the outbreak of war, and within twelve days was in France, where he saw continuous service until the evacuation. He was 35 years of age.

William Saunders

There is only one Sapper W Saunders, Kent Field Company, Royal Engineers, recorded on the Southborough War Memorial, but there were two men of this name and company, who perished when the Hythe went down off Gallipoli on 28 October 1915. They are commemorated on the Helles Memorial, Gallipoli Peninsula, Turkey: Panel 23 to 25 or 325 to 328.

Sapper 2092 William Saunders, age 28. The son of Mrs Selina Saunders, 1 Denbigh Road, High Brooms (later 2, Haywards Cottages, St. John's Road, Tunbridge Wells); husband of Lucy Alice Saunders (later remarried as Howard) of 96 Ealing Park Gardens, South Ealing. He was employed as a printer by FL Saunders Bros. He had been a member of the Mount Pleasant Football Club and of the Sons of Temperance.

Sapper 2361 William Saunders. Age 25 or 28, according to two different accounts. He was married and had two children, and lived at 16, Forge Road. Previously employed by Mr Turley, of Speldhurst, as a brick maker, he had married and moved to Southborough from his mother's home at 13, Albion Square, St John's Road, Tunbridge Wells. He was an old St John's schoolboy. He had only six months' service when he died.

Southborough War Memorial

Charles James Scott

Private O/14654. Died 12 October 1916, age 29. Buried in Southborough Cemetery, England: Grave ref. 3.260. Husband of Mrs F. Jones (formerly Scott), 33 Wolseley Road, High Brooms. Southborough Memorial records unit as AOC (Army Ordnance Corps).

Jerry Jones, of High Brooms, the son of Mrs Jones by her next marriage, (pictured right, below, Reginald and Florence Jones, née Bridger, previously Mrs Scott) recalls her telling him that Private Scott, known as Jim, worked for the High Brooms Brick and Tile Co as a blacksmith, and that he was a farrier in the Forces. He was run over by a gun carriage and injured, either in France or Belgium. From the Courier, 20 October 1916: *The military funeral took place in Southborough Cemetery of the late Private Charles James Scott of the AOC, of Wolseley-road, High Brooms. He passed away the previous Thursday at the Stockport Military Hospital, after a somewhat lengthy illness, at the age of 29 years. He leaves a widow and three children.*

The Tunbridge Wells Advertiser, the same week: ... *has died of wounds received at the Front ... for some years a popular member of the Southborough Fire Brigade. He was also a member of the High Brooms Invicta Football Club and the High Brooms Good Templars.*

James H Scrace

Private 22630, 1st Bn Border Regiment. Died 13 August 1917. Commemorated on Panel 35 of the Ypres (Menin Gate) Memorial, Ypres, Belgium.

From the Tunbridge Wells Advertiser, 2 November 1917: *Mr & Mrs J Scrace, of 15 Stewart-road, have received news that their son, Pte JH Scrace, of the Border Regiment, 22 years of age, has been missing* since August. Pte Scrace joined the West Kent Regiment in 1912. He was stationed in Dublin when the war broke out, and went out with the First Expeditionary Force to France, and has been wounded three times in the hand, elbow and back. He was transferred to the Border Regiment in 1916, and is an old High Brooms School boy.

Albert Victor Seale

Sapper 14616123, 980 IWT (Inland Water Transport) Workshop Company, Royal Engineers. Died Monday 30 July 1945, age 43. Buried in Imphal War Cemetery, India. Grave ref. 4.C.16. Husband of Minnie Seale of High Brooms.

Named as Seal on Southborough War Memorial. There is an Albert Seale, Holden Corner, Royal West Kent Territorials, listed in the Tunbridge Wells Advertiser, 21 August 1914, and H Seale, WK Transport, in Dee's Directory 1915, amongst Southborough Men in the Forces, perhaps relatives of Albert Victor?

Pete Simmons of High Brooms recalls that the family understood that Albert was killed by a sniper while putting up a pontoon bridge. Mr Simmons worked with Albert's son Dennis after the war; they were both bricklayers. Dennis, who also served in WW2, was wounded in the stomach in Malta. He was home on sick-leave when he saw his father off at High Brooms station for the last time.

Walter Sellins

Private 33099, 2nd Bn, Border Regiment (formerly 6490 Middlesex Regiment). Died Thursday 29 March, 1917, age 39. Commemorated on the Arras Memorial, Pas de Calais, France: Bay 6. Son of Robert and Clara Sellins, 13 Norman Road, Tunbridge Wells; husband of Julia Huntley (formerly Sellins), 11 Silverdale Road, High Brooms.

Information from the website www.firstworldwar.com/onthisday gives the following details for 29 March 1917 for the Western Front: *British take Neuville-Bourjonval (seven miles east of Bapaume) after sharp fighting.*

From the Courier, 4 May 1917: *Much sympathy will be felt for Mrs Sellins, who has received notice that her husband was killed in action on March 29th.*

Private Sellins joined the 2nd Border Regiment in July, 1916 and went to France in December. Almost all the time he has been in France he has been in the thick of fighting. Mrs Sellins has received a letter of sympathy from the King. Private Sellins leaves two little girls.

A J Sharp

Private William James Sharp, 6641, 1st/20th Bn, London Regiment. Died 1 October 1916. Commemorated on the Thiepval Memorial, Pier and Face 9D, 9C, 13C and 12C.

Listed on the Southborough War Memorial as AJ Sharp, under London Regiment.

From the Courier, 16 April 1915, with photograph above: *Mrs Sharp, of High Brooms, is to be congratulated on being the mother of four soldier sons, viz. 1. Driver JA Sharp, RFA, who has seen five years' service in South Africa and four years in India. He was besieged in Ladysmith, and has a medal and five clasps. 2. Driver VJ Sharp, ASC has served in the RFA eleven years (eight years in India and three in South Africa). He was also besieged in Ladysmith, and like his brother, has a medal and five clasps. 3. Private C Sharp, "D" Co, East Surrey Regiment 4. Private WJ Sharp, RW Kent Regiment.*

From a 1916 issue of the Courier, accompanied by the picture on left: *Private WJ Sharp, aged 31, the youngest son of Mrs Sharp, of Wolseley-road, High Brooms, who was reported missing, is now reported killed in action. He came home from Canada at the beginning of the War and joined the West Kents. He was an old High Brooms schoolboy, and has four other brothers serving.*

As in so many cases of reporting at the time, the author surmises that initials have been confused here, and that it is WJ, not AJ, who is commemorated on Southborough War Memorial. As the following photographic record shows, EE Sharp was also reported in error in 1916 as being Private C Sharp, since the individual photograph printed in the Roll of Honour, Courier 18 January 1918, shows EE Sharp to be the same man as pictured above in the Sharp family group.

E E Sharp

Private 3576, "C" Coy, 2nd Bn, East Surrey Regiment. Died 25 December 1917, age 39. Buried in Lahana Military Cemetery, Greece: Grave ref. III.A.16.

From the Courier 18 January 1918: *Mrs Sharp of 8, Wolseley-road, has learnt that her husband, Private E Sharp of the East Surrey Regiment, has died in Salonika from meningitis. He was 31 years of age and joined up in September 1914, going to France in the following March, and from thence to Salonika, where he had been for over two years. Before joining up, he was employed by the High Brooms Brick Company for a number of years. He has had three brothers serving, one of whom has been killed and another wounded.*

Cecil William Shoesmith

Private 201262 2nd/4th Bn, Queen's Own (Royal West Kent Regiment). Died 4 November 1917, age 28. Buried in Beersheba War Cemetery, Israel: Grave ref. G31. Born Hartfield, Sussex.

Cecil Shoesmith was in the same company, died on the same day, and is buried in the same cemetery, as **Harry Goodsell**, who is also commemorated on the Southborough War Memorial.

From the Tunbridge Wells Advertiser of 30 November 1917: *Mr and Mrs Shoesmith, of 63 Edward-street, have received news of the death of their eldest son, Pte CW Shoesmith, RWKR, who was killed in action on the 3rd or 4th of November, in Egypt. Pte Shoesmith joined up in*

November, 1915, and went to Egypt in March, 1916. Before enlisting he was employed by Mr Ferguson as gardener, and was also a member of the Christ Church choir. Mr and Mrs Shoesmith have two other sons serving in France.

Frederick Shorter

Lance Corporal 22517, 6th Bn Border Regiment, formerly 4026 Queen's Own (Royal West Kent Regiment). Died Wednesday 27 September 1916 Commemorated on the Thiepval Memorial, Somme, France: Pier and Face 6A and 7C.

From a newspaper report of the time: *Mr James Shorter, Modest Corner, has received information from the War Office that his youngest son, Lance-Corporal Frederick Shorter, 5th Borderers, was killed in action on September 28th. Lance-Corporal Shorter joined the Royal West Kent Regiment on September 28th, 1914, and was transferred to the Borderers in November, 1915. It is a coincidence that he should have been killed on the second anniversary of his joining the Army. Mr Shorter had lost two nephews, who have been killed in action, another was wrecked off a patrol boat, and he has another who is a prisoner of war at Michlanburg.*

Information from the website www.firstworldwar.com/onthis day gives the following campaign detail for 27 & 28 September 1916 for the Western Front: *27: British storm Stuff Redoubt and advance north of Flers to the east of Eaucourt l'Abbaye. 28: British attack Schwaben Redoubt on crest of Thiepval Plateau; most of it taken. They advance north and north-east of Courcelette, and between Martinpuich and Gueudecourt.*

Arthur Smallcombe

Private TF/203977, 1/7th Battalion Middlesex Regiment (formerly G/28693 6th Battalion Royal Fusiliers). Commemorated on the Thiepval Memorial, Somme, Pier and Face 12D and 13B. Died 16 September 1916.

One of two Arthur Smallcombes commemorated on the Southborough War Memorial.

The Courier, 3 November 1916, records: *Information has been received from the War Office by Mr and Mrs Smallcombe, 9 Meadow-road, that their son Private Arthur Smallcombe, Middlesex Regiment, is reported missing since September 16th. Before enlisting he was employed by Paine, Smith & Co as an army baker. He was sent to France on his 20th birthday, July 3rd.*

Arthur Smallcombe

Corporal Arthur Smallcomb, KF903, 1st/3rd Kent Field Company Royal Engineers. Died 28 October 1915 in the Hythe disaster. Commemorated on the Helles Memorial, Turkey: Panel 23 to 25 or 325 to 328.

Recorded on the CWGC Site as Smallcomb, the second man of this name recorded on Southborough War Memorial. From a newspaper report of the time: *Corporal Arthur Smallcombe is the son of Mrs Longhurst, of 27, Edward Street, Southborough. He was 24 years of age, and was an old St Peter's School boy. He joined the Southborough Company of Engineers for a considerable time, transferring to them from the Territorials in Tunbridge Wells. His death is the more pathetic from the fact that only the day previous to hearing that he had been drowned Mrs Longhurst had heard that her younger son, Pte A Smallcombe, of the 2nd Buffs, who had been missing since February last, must be given up as dead. Mrs Longhurst had been in communication with the War Office, and on Thursday received a letter to the effect that as no further information had been received with respect to Pte Smallcombe, and he had not been traced as a prisoner of war in Germany, and in view of the lapse of time, it was feared he could no longer be alive. Pte Smallcombe had been four years in the Army, two of these being spent in India. He came home at Christmas, and went to the Front in January.*

Frank Stevens, local author, records that Arthur was known to his friends as 'Smoke' because he always had a cigarette. Mrs Elliott, 52 Taylor-street, received a postcard, dated October 29th from her son, Corporal Charles Elliott, saying: *Dear Mother, I expect you have heard of our mishap in the sea, but don't worry. I was saved after some time in the water. Harold (2nd Corporal Hever) and Arthur (**Lance-Corporal Jenner**) are safe, but have heard nothing of 'Smoke'. Yours affectionately, Charley.*

Arthur's brother **Albert** was also commemorated – see overleaf.

Albert Smallcombe

Private Albert Smallcomb, L/9523, 2nd Battalion The Buffs (East Kent Regiment) Died 16 February 1915. Commemorated on the Ypres (Menin Gate) Memorial, Belgium: Panel 12 & 14.

Recorded on the CWGC site as Smallcomb, the son of Mrs Longhurst, 27 Edward-street, and brother of **Arthur Smallcombe**, also commemorated on the Southborough War Memorial – see above.

Clarence Kitchener Smart

Private 6342570, 4th Bn, Queen's Own (Royal West Kent Regiment). Died Friday 31 May 1940, age 24. Commemorated on the Dunkirk Memorial, Nord, France: Column 114.

Clary Smart, as he was known in High Brooms, was in the same unit as six other men commemorated on the Southborough War Memorial, and died in the same week as them, and eleven days after his older brother **Edward Frederick Walter Smart**. They were two of the sons of Edward John Smart, formerly of the Queen's Own Royal West Kent Regiment, who had been awarded the DCM and MM for his valour while fighting in the First World War, and of Fanny Smart.

From the Courier, 26 January 1945: *Mr and Mrs E Smart, of 63, Nursery-road, High Brooms, are the parents of one of the largest local serving families. Two sons, L-Cpl Walter, and Gunner John, are in the Army, and one, Donald, is a Flight Sergeant in the RAF. Two other members, Edward and Clarence, were killed during the Dunkirk evacuation, and another, Kenneth, was taken prisoner at the same time and is now in a camp at Marienburg, East Prussia ... Donald, who is a wireless operator in a Middle East squadron, has completed 40 operations. He is now on instructional duties in Palestine. Of all his many experiences, he particularly remembers the eruption of Vesuvius, which he witnessed whilst in Italy, and the air attack on Marseilles, when Frenchmen could be seen celebrating the Normandy landings. On two occasions his plane crash-landed with a bomb-load, but he was lucky enough to escape with minor injuries. During his service in the Mediterranean zone, he* met two other local men, Corpl R Green and G Heath. Walter is soon expected home from Holland, which, he writes, is one of the cleanest and most hospitable countries he has seen. To complete the family record, six Canadian nephews are at present serving in England.

Edward Frederick Walter Smart

Corporal 6341138, 6th Bn, Queen's Own (Royal West Kent Regiment). Died Monday 20 May 1940, age 29. Buried in the Doullens Communal Cemetery Extension No 1, Somme, France: Grave ref. Plot 7. Row B. Grave 6.

From the Courier, 25 July 1941: *It has now been established that Cpl Edward Smart, son of Mr and Mrs Smart, of 63, Nursery-road, High Brooms, who was reported missing, was killed in action on May 20, 1940. Two of his brothers are prisoners of war, and another is with the Forces in England. Cpl Smart was 29, and was formerly in the employ of Nightingale Farm Dairy for seven years.*

From the Courier, 26 July 1940, a reference to another brother: *News has been received that Private Kenneth Norman Smart of the Royal West Kent Regiment, who was reported missing on June 16th, is now a prisoner of war at Stalag Camp, Germany. Private Smart was a member of the High Brooms Old Boys' Football Club.*

Their father (pictured below) was mentioned in the Courier, 13 October 1916: *Private EJ Smart, of Colebrook-road, High Brooms, was wounded by shrapnel on September 25th, and is now in Hospital at Broadstairs. Before joining up, Private Smart was in the auctioneers' office of Messrs. Wenbrook.*

The Courier in 1918 published the following account: *Private EJ Smart, DCM, MM, 7th Royal West Kent Regiment, is understood to be the first and only of our gallant Tunbridge Wells men to receive these two decorations, which he earned by his fearless conduct and bravery under conditions in which he showed no regard whatever for his own personal safety. His home is at*

63, Nursery-road, and he, with his wife and family, is enjoying a well-earned two months' furlough, after having undergone severe trials as a prisoner of war in the hands of the Huns since March last.

He joined the Colours in September, 1914, and went to France in July of the following year. In May, 1916, he was wounded, but remained in Hospital in France until he had sufficiently recovered to return to the fighting line. Then in September of the same year he was wounded a second time, and was sent to England and cared for in a Hospital at Broadstairs, returning once again to the scene of hostilities in the following February. In the November he was sent to Italy, where he remained until the beginning of March last, when he went back to France, and it was at Vaux St Quentin on the 23rd of that month that he was taken prisoner. It was on the 7th June, 1917, that he won his first decoration, the Military Medal, in the Messines offensive, and in his recommendation Major-General Sydney Lawford, KCB, wrote: "I wish to place on record my appreciation of your conspicuous courage and gallantry on the 17th June, 1917, during the attack on the Somme, in doing splendid work in tending wounded under shell-fire. You went forward into your own barrage and fetched a seriously wounded man into a position of safety, thereby undoubtedly saving his life."

Later the same officer recommended Pte Smart for the DCM for gallantry at Tower Hamlets, and he wrote: "I wish to record my appreciation of your gallantry and devotion to duty on the 21st September, 1917. When the enemy were going to counter-attack and our troops began to retire you helped your Commanding Officer by rallying the men, and, going across a shell-swept area, brought back men who had retired still further. Your fearless example inspired confidence in the men."

In addition to receiving these well-earned decorations, he has on several occasions refused offers of promotion, preferring to remain as a Private. It was on the evening of 23rd March that he fell into the hands of the Germans, and he early experienced privations through want of food.

"I first went to a place called Denain," he told our representative, "and stopped there for a day, having to exist on a piece of black bread and one basin of substitute coffee. We were then taken away in cattle-trucks, and all I had in twenty-four hours was a basin of so-called soup made of barley and water, and during that time there was no chance of a wash or any accommodation for sleeping. We arrived at Munster camp on the 29th, when there was a roll-call, and we were served out again with one basin of the substitute coffee. For dinner we had some soup which was like brine, and too salty to eat, and for tea another basin of prepared barley with very little rice in it, and a piece of black bread, which appeared to have been made with sawdust. We stayed there until April 19th, when we were sent on to a place called Heissen, about one-and-a-half kilometres this side of Essen, and were put to work in the coal mines. The next morning I started work at four o'clock in the morning on a basin of cabbage water with stuff like bran in it. We rarely saw a potato. At 5.30 we descended the pit and started work down there an hour later up till 2 o'clock. That was the order on Mondays, Wednesdays, Thursdays and Saturdays. On Tuesdays and Fridays we worked from six in the morning until six in the evening. Meat was a great rarity and we did get it. I should say it was nothing but dog's flesh. When I was first captured my boots were taken away from me, and I was served out with clogs, and have the marks from them on my feet to this day, for they fairly crippled me. We were lucky, however, later to receive parcels of clothes, boots, etc from the Red Cross.

"I was in charge of twelve prisoners," continued Private Smart, "and one day one of the men was killed by one of the machines in the mine. It was a very suspicious case, and I made inquiries into it, but could get no satisfaction, and later I was made to sign a paper in respect to the matter, but never knew what was in it. I was by the poor fellow when he died, and his last words were "You are cruel". During the first four months we received from three to four marks a week, but we could only spend it in the camp. Once a month, too, we had from 14 to 30 marks, according to the work we were doing, and this we could only spend in the canteen, and margarine was 25 marks a pound, and a suit of clothes 300 marks, such as you could have bought for £1 in England before the war. The civilian population in Germany were in a dreadful state, and were absolutely starving. Eventually we declined to do any more work, and we were refused food, but after a while they put us on half rations. We left there and went to Munster, where we stayed for two days, during which time we had plenty of food through the Red Cross Society. Then we went on to Enched, two-and-a-half kilometres between Germany and the borders of Holland, and from there to Rotterdam, subsequently being put on board a vessel which landed us at Hull, where the Fleet and the people met us, and gave us a grand reception. Going on to Ripon, we were placed in a Convalescent Camp, where everything possible was provided for our comfort."

Asked how they were received at Holland, he said the people did not appear to be able to do too much for them. All the comforts possible were provided, and concerts were given them in the evening by the civilians. The people expressed their delight at the fact that we had won the war, because they said it looked very black for them at times.

Arthur Smith

Gunner 68, 13th Battery Canadian Field Artillery Died 6 March 1915. Buried in Brantford (Greenwood) Cemetery, Ontario, Canada. Grave ref: 3.Lot 889. F half.

Arthur Smith is named in a Courier report, 26 November 1915, of a memorial service held at St Peter's Church, Southborough for those who lost their lives in the Hythe disaster and in prior incidents. He was a 'pal' of Gunner **Henry Moon**, and is mentioned in the entry for Gunner Moon, which reported that he was the son of Mr & Mrs Jonathan Smith.

George Edward Smith

Aircraftman 1st Class 1270159, 106 Sqdn, Royal Air Force Volunteer Reserve. Died Tuesday 21 July 1942, age 30. Buried in Southborough Cemetery, Kent, England: Grave ref. Sec. 11. Grave 385. Son of George and Beatrice Smith; husband of Marjorie Smith, of Grangetown, Cardiff.

From the Courier, 31 July 1942: *The son of Mrs and the late Mr G Smith of Rusthall, A/C 1 GE Smith of 21, Speldhurst-road, was killed recently on active service. Thirty years of age, he joined the RAF Volunteer Reserve two years ago. He was formerly employed by the Nevill Bakery, and was married five years ago. Mr Smith was also a member of the Auxiliary Fire Service before the war, and had served in the Home Guard. The funeral took place quietly at Southborough Cemetery on Tuesday. Among the floral tributes were three beautiful wreaths from the Commanding Officer, Officers, NCOs and Comrades in the RAF.*

Sidney Smith

Private S/1590, 2nd Bn, Royal Sussex Regiment. Died 20 August 1916, age 19. Commemorated on the Thiepval Memorial, Somme, France: Pier and Face 7C. Son of Philip and Fanny Smith, of 20, North Farm Road, High Brooms.

From the Tunbridge Wells Advertiser of 29 September 1916: *Mr and Mrs Smith have received intimation that their son, Pte Sidney Smith, of the Royal Sussex Regiment, has been killed in action in France. Pte Smith, who is 19 years of age, went to the Front in November, 1914, and was sent to the firing line about a fortnight afterwards. When he was home on leave in December, 1914, recovering from frostbitten feet, after serving eight days in a trench full of mud and water, Pte Smith said, "So deep was the mud that many of the soldiers had occasionally to be dug out, being unable to extricate themselves." They remained on duty for these eight days* because reinforcements could not be got to the trenches. The fighting was not so bad during the first part of his time in the trenches as in the latter.

After being sent back to the front again, Pte Smith was wounded in the hip, and was sent to England for three months. He was again wounded in July, 1916, in the chest and hand by a shell bursting over the dug-out in which he was located. He was sent back to the firing line after recovering from his wounds, and was killed on August 20th. Pte Smith was an old High Brooms School boy, and previous to joining the Army was employed by Mr G Farrant, of High Brooms.

Frederick Somers

Serjeant KF 722, 1st/3rd Kent Field Company, Royal Engineers. Died 28 October 1915 in the Hythe disaster, aged 37. Commemorated on the Helles Memorial, Panel 23 to 25 or 325 to 328.

Frederick Thomas Somers (named as Summers on his birth certificate) was born on 25 October 1877 at 6 William Street, Tunbridge Wells, to Frederick Summers, brewers' van-man, and Jane Summers (née Byford). He joined up (No. 6938) for the Boer War at the age of 22. His friend **Clement Hawkins** (who also died on the *Hythe* and is commemorated on the Southborough War Memorial), had also been on the South African campaign with him; they were both in the 1st or 2nd Volunteer Active Service Company (100 men) of the West Kents. Frederick received a Queen's South Africa Medal with bars: Wittebergen, Cape Colony, at a ceremony on 22 June 1902 at Tonbridge Castle from the hands of Lord Stanhope.

Fred married Annie Lawrence (known as Nance) and they had three children: Nancy (whose son died in the RAF in the 1930s), Frederick and Edie. They lived at 65, Springfield Road, where Fred used to grow grapes on the back wall. He worked as a plumber for J Carrick Builders, of Southborough, and was also a volunteer fireman with the Southborough Fire Brigade, (see overleaf, of the two men seen standing right at the back, Fred is the one on the right). He used to keep his uniform at the end of his bed so that he could jump into it at short notice.

Fred joined the 1st/3rd Kent Field Co, RE, upon its formation, was the eighth person on the company roll, rising to Sergeant in preparation for overseas. Annie Somers married a Mr Gaston after Fred died in 1918 and moved to Brenchley, to the Halfway House. Mr Gaston worked for Kelsey Brewers, and they had a son, John Gaston.

Reginald Thomas Sotherden

Private 1194, 2nd Bn, Seaforth Highlanders. Died Friday 4 September 1914, age 23. Buried in Porte-de-Paris Cemetery, Cambrai, Nord, France: Grave ref. II.A.24. Son of Thomas William and Grace Sotherden, of 77, Springfield Road, Southborough.

Dee's Directory 1915 lists, under Men Serving, R Sotherden, Seaforth Highlanders, and F Sotherden, KFRE.

From the Kent & Sussex Courier of 1 January 1915: *News of the death of the eldest and beloved son of Mr T Sotherden, the Common, Southborough, and a nephew of Mr & Mrs Daughtrey, of Southborough, was received by his friends on Boxing Day morning.*

The last news coming from himself was on the 22nd August last, saying "We are crossing the Channel tonight". Nothing further was heard of him until the 23rd September, when he was reported wounded at Viesley on the 25th August, which caused a great deal of anxiety amongst his friends, who wrote in all directions for information, and a lady of Tunbridge Wells was kind enough to make personal inquiries in France, but to no avail. Then, as a last resource, it was left in the hands of the Geneva Red Cross Society, who have done splendid work in obtaining news of missing and wounded soldiers, and from them the following message was received: "Dear Sir, We have the sad duty to communicate to you the following information we received just now from Germany: Sotherden, Reginald Thomas William, Soldier No. 1194, of the Highland Regiment died on the 4th September last in the Military Hospital of Cambrai. He was buried in Cambrai."

Private Sotherden was a promising young soldier, with only 2 years' service, he was full of ambition to succeed, and was servant to the Captain of his company. He was granted leave, arriving at his home, on Wednesday 29th July last, but was recalled by telegram next morning. In saying "Good-bye" his last words to his uncle were, "Look out for my name in the list for the VC, Uncle," but he was only destined to have the little wooden cross on his grave at Cambrai.

David Ephraim Standing

Private 13021407, 1st Bn, North Staffordshire Regiment. Died Saturday 28 November 1942, age 27. Buried in Colombo (Kanatte) General Cemetery, Sri Lanka: Grave ref. 6D.D.12. Son of Ephraim Richard and Emily Standing.

From the CWGC site: *The cemetery, at Borella contains War Graves, and a War Cross is erected. The Military Hospital at Colombo received cases of sickness from the troops on the land, or from passing transports.*

From the Courier, 18 December 1942: *Many friends will regret to hear that Private David Ephraim Standing, of the North Staffordshire Regiment, youngest son of Mr and Mrs ER Standing of 12, Castle-street, Southborough, has been drowned while serving with his unit in the Indian theatre of war. Official intimation has been received by his parents. On the last occasion that Mr and Mrs Standing heard from their son he was at Colombo. Pte Standing, who was 27 years of age, joined the Forces about three years ago. He was a plasterer by trade.*

Southborough War Memorial

Edwin Percy Standing

Private G/24415, 32nd Bn, Royal Fusiliers. Died 9 July 1916, age 22. Buried in Berks Cemetery Extension, Comines-Warneton, Hainaut, Belgium: Grave ref. I.E.7. Youngest son of Amos and Ellen Standing, of 34, Holden Corner, Southborough.

From the Courier, 21 July 1916, *Private EP Standing was killed in action in France on July 10th. He was the first Derby recruit from Southborough to give his life for his country. He was called up with his group on January 24th, and joined the Royal Fusiliers, going to the Front early in March. Mrs Standing has three other sons in the Army. The following letter has been received from the Chaplain, the Rev Mowbray Smith: "I feel that I must send to you a line of heartfelt sympathy on the loss of your son. It will be a comfort to you to know that he suffered no pain at all. The funeral was on Tuesday morning last. Several of his mates were present. His body lies in a very beautiful little Cemetery, and the Battalion are putting up a cross over his grave with his name thereon, and you can be certain that this spot will always be kept with all loving and reverent care. You can be proud of your boy, who has given his life for his country."*

The Derby Scheme was a British system of voluntary recruitment instituted by Lord Derby just before conscription was introduced in 1916.

From the Tunbridge Wells Advertiser, 8 June 1917, news of Arthur Standing, pictured left, a possible relative of Edwin's: *Mrs Standing, of 128, London-road, has received a letter from the Captain of her husband's regiment to the effect that Pte Arthur Standing, East Surrey Regiment, has been missing since May 8th. Joining the Army on June 6th, 1916, he proceeded to France in October. Pte Standing was well known as a comedian, and was a prominent goalkeeper for the Southborough Football Club. He also has two brothers serving, and his father is in the Fencibles. Pte Standing is the youngest son of Mr G Standing, plasterer, 55, Edward-street.*

And from the Courier, 1919, included here for interest: *DIARY OF A PRISONER OF WAR Private A Standing, 128 London-road, Southborough, the well-known local comedian, who has been a prisoner of war since May, 1916, has now returned from Germany. He is looking rather thin and is not feeling very well. Below is a very interesting diary, which he managed to keep during his imprisonment, and was able to smuggle past the German frontier:*

"May 6th – We carry German wounded off to the dressing-station. Raining hard. Back to a small village; stood there two hours. March to Douai. On the way inspected by General and escorted by Uhlans to a large Bank. Searched. Given a piece of black bread in a large room at rear of Bank. If we look out of the windows will be shot. Terrible explosion in the night. Our shells had blown the front of the building down. We clear it next day. Soup, coffee and a piece of black bread. Just getting hungry. Some of us go to sink a well. Saw large cage where early prisoners were put. German officers ask us all sorts of questions. They know more than we do.

May 12th - They tell us we go to Germany to work. From Douai by train to Lille; 50 men in a cattle truck. Met by strong guard and taken through town to Fort Macdonald (hidden from the ground). Shall I ever forget the sight? Small windows with iron bars; Englishmen inside, pale faces and starved. They soon told us our fate. German General on horse said we should work behind the lines or be shot in the Fort as reprisal. One hundred and fifty men in a small tunnel-shaped room. All bricks. Tub for sanitary purposes. Lay and sweat; very hot; no fresh air, no exercise. Head swims. Very weak. Cabbage water, coffee and slice of bread; no bowl or spoon; in hat or boot. Several taken out ill. Men fall when getting on their feet.

May 21st – Taken out two hours in the fresh air to Lille Station. What a procession! We eat grass! Many fell to the ground. Women try to give us bread or a cap, but the Postern knock them away. Entrain at 2.30 Friday; 50 men in cattle truck. No water. They always refused us water. Travel all night. Early next morning we go out for a plate of thin barley; back again, and travel day and night. Next morning same. Arrive at Haltern Sunday afternoon (Whit-Sunday). We are marched through the town to give the people a show of English. Five kilometres brought up to Dulmen Camp. It was a terrible walk; hungry and thirsty. Searched again. Soup at night (hogwash). Taken to a barbed wire enclosure; sleep in the open. Next morning 14 to a loaf, first since last Friday. No soap, no shave; we look terrible. We have plenty of lice. From here we get fumigated; taken to another compound, next to French and Russians. Vaccinated, etc, five times. We are now very weak; many ill; many die. I write home, but letter is returned after 10 days. Soup, coffee, and piece of bread each day. Taken to bath. Shirts taken from us; thin cotton ones in exchange. Socks taken and rags given. Large clogs, but could not walk in them. Hats taken, given little round caps. Do camp work. Our men exchange gold rings, watches, etc for three or four biscuits with the French; they give nothing away. Men part with their boots for an old pair and biscuits. They were sorry for this afterwards. Still no soap and no shave.

Wet through. Entrain at Dulmen, June 23rd, in trucks. arrive at Gustrow 24th. Good camp. Many old prisoners here. Soup better. Small issue of smokes and tin goods. Too good to last. Away again July 2nd, and get to Kiel. Few stations away get to Gettorf. Our guards are sailors now. Women shake their fists and children spit at us. Half an hour's walk. Small lager. There are 500 of us. We receive bowl, spoon, and two small, thin blankets; far from being new. We are numbered, and they are painted on our tunics. Start work July 5th, making railway. Very hot; bad boots; no socks; many men no boots. Hard work. Plenty of knocking about with sticks, etc. Coffee at 5.30. Soup at 1 o'clock. Bread at night. One-and-a-half-hour's walk to the work. Many fall down going and at their work. We are very weak. Our guard have it all their own way. How we look for our soup, but it's awful stuff. We ask for more to eat, and strike, but the Germans come in lager with sticks, revolvers, swords, etc and clear us out to work. One day fish soup, and makes us all ill. Very bad camp; small window in roof. We are hungry, miserable and dirty. We are all waiting for help from the Red Cross. My first packet arrives in October; it's bread, but it's rotten, been so long finding one. Several came like that. At last biscuits came. About this time received my first letter from my wife. Things look brighter now. Packets arrive, but they opened all the tins and wasted half of contents. Our packets were opened by the Germans; soap and tobacco, as well as food, were stolen. More than once the packet wagon had been broken into on the railway. Our packets do not arrive regular. My clothes arrive from my Regiment; boots; only one pair of socks (ought to have been three pairs); lots of articles missing. We are told the winter is severe. Jack _____ escapes; back after a few days. Thrashed and 14 days dark cell, bread and water.

 Sunday mornings we are searched. Do our washing in the afternoon. Sometimes we have worked on Sundays. Plenty of snow and ice; very cold. Christmas comes. Only German food. In February I get rheumatics (muscular); get nine weeks in Revier. They have nothing to do one good; paper bandages, aspirins and a pair of scissors. Men get punished for going sick; put on half bread rations, etc. Our packets are robbed again at station. Seventy-five men go away on farms.

 March 15th – Second lot of clothes come through. Much better than first. We get no light in our barrack; all in darkness. We ask for some light. The Commandant says: "Tell your people to take the blockade off. Then will get some." We have to buy our stoves and firewood, pails, etc. The barrack is covered with ice. At times searched at gate when coming in; wood taken away, then made to buy it. Soap is sent in all our packets, but we get little. Sergt-Major struck a chap named _____ behind the ear; knocked him out for several days. It makes me sick. Why should we have to suffer this? We parade to see the Commandant about this cruelty, but the guard is turned out, and we retire. Win for the Germans. Out to work early morning. We sing in our misery. Bread, 16 to a loaf (black). Hard work. Carrying rails, loading wagons etc.

 July 7th – News of exchange; 60 men go away on farms. Rainy season has commenced. We get wet through day after day.

July 12th – Fever breaks out in barrack. I get it bad. Next day 60 men come back ill; then more; 327 men down in three days. Looks serious. Men lay and sweat. Doctor doesn't come near. We must take our chance. We get better and soon go out to work. One hundred and sixty Russians come to our barrack; work with us. I have some farm work.

August 12th – Guns going all night. Twenty men sent to Flensburg in a zinc factory. Sixty Japs arrive at our camp; captured off ship by 'SS Wolf'. We get no war news. I've been three weeks without good food. Impossible to eat German soup now. Russians refuse to work on account of rations. Their rations are cut off. No work, no food is the German motto. They strafe us 10 days with no packets, so we cannot feed the Russians. They still refuse to work. Get one soup in three days. On parade from 5.30 till 4 each day for punishment. After one month of this (I don't know how they lived) they are thrashed unmercifully. Posterns thrash them with sticks, rifles and clogs; quite a battlefield. They are got to work. Another victory for the Germans. One parcel in seven weeks. I have a few potatoes, brought from farm. Cannot take their rotten soup; smell is enough.

September 4th – Neutral comes; first I've seen. We get nothing from him.

October 29th – Sixteen men fill 20 small and 12 large wagons with beach. I'm tired. Dried cabbage for dinner. We hear the end may come before Christmas. I get three packets. All is good now. Something to eat.

November 3rd – Bread arrives.

November 4th – We hear of serious trouble in Kiel; nine officers and several others killed; 500 arrests.

November 5th – No work. Matrosens have the red ribbon up. I saw officers that had been wounded. Looks serious. We are near Kiel and in barbed wire. We hear all trains are stopped. Food is the question of the day.

November 14th – We may be shifted any day. This is the first real news of the end.

November 20th – Still waiting in our dirty little barrack for transport.

November 21st – Get away. Cattle trucks again to Gustrow. Arrive at 3 in the morning. Everything is upside down. Too cold to sleep. Next day we get blankets; sleep on the floor, as usual. All we talk about is Blighty. Days pass; no news of going away. Russian Generals arrive; line up for their soup; thin. Five hundred men go away (1914 men). I was here over a month expecting every day to get away. Left Gustrow December 23rd for Rostock. On boat for Copenhagen. Full up there. Sent on to Sweden. Very cold. Band played to us while we landed. Snowing hard. Train to camp.

It's now Christmas Day. We are getting bully beef and biscuits each day, as there is nothing else in the country. Leave Sweden 30th December for Copenhagen. Leave Denmark December 31st in the 'Porto' for Blighty. Several mines in the North

Sea. Three days on the water. Rough at times. Landed at Leith, Scotland. All's well now. Train to Ripon; clothes, etc; to London and dear old Southborough.

A E Stevens

Private 13437, 2nd Bn, Grenadier Guards. Died 1 November 1914, age 26. Commemorated on the Ypres (Menin Gate) Memorial, Belgium: Panel 9 and 11. Son of Joseph and Emma Stevens, of 104, Clifton Road, Wells; husband of Rose E. Black (formerly Stevens) of 58, Nursery Road, High Brooms.

The website www.firstworldwar.com/onthisday gives the following campaign detail for 1 November 1914: *Western Front: Battle of Ypres continued with great violence: Germans capture Messines, Hollebeke and Wytschaete.*

An account from the Courier, 7 June 1918, refers to another Stevens, for some reason not included on the Memorial: *Mrs Stevens of South View-road has received news that her son, Private John Stevens, was killed in action in France on April 29th. He only reached his 19th birthday on May 11th. Before joining he was a member of Mr Sibthorpe's Brotherhood. Mrs Stevens has two other sons serving.*

Nelson John Still

Private (Rifleman on Southborough War Memorial) 614233, 1st/19th Bn, London Regiment. Died on Tuesday 26 March 1918, age 26. Commemorated on Arras Memorial, Pas de Calais, France: Bay 9 and 10. Son of Mrs Ada Still; husband of Mabel Still, of 31 Shipbourne Road, Tonbridge.

The website www.firstworldwar.com/onthisday gives the following campaign detail for 26 March 1918: *Western Front: British make stand north of Somme on line Roeux-Ayette-Beaumont Hamel-Albert-Bray, but lose Albert and Bray. Very heavy fighting south of Somme; Germans capture Lihons, Chaulnes, Roye and Noyon. Momentous Franco-British conference at Doullens on unity of command.*

Frank Sutcliffe

Lance Serjeant 6343912, 4th Bn, Queen's Own (Royal West Kent Regiment). Died Tuesday 28 May 1940, age 20. Buried at Le Grand Hasard Military Cemetery, Morbecque, Nord, France, grave reference 6.A.16.

Frank Sutcliffe was born in 1919, at 25, Speldhurst Road, Southborough, to Edmund Walter and Marjorie Louisa Sutcliffe (named on the CWGC site as Walter and Mary Sutcliffe). He had two brothers: William Edmund and **Tom** (died in 1942, and also commemorated on the Southborough War Memorial) and two sisters: Kate Mildred, known as Kitty (born 1912) and Dorothy (born 1921). As a boy Frank used to play cricket for his school, St Peter's.

Before the war he worked at Constables, the lily-growing specialists in Kibbles Lane. They used to show at the Chelsea Flower Show, and Frank used to go on the stand. He met the actor Charles Laughton and several other notable people. Frank used to say that after the war, he hoped to have a piece of land in Jersey, to grow tomatoes, and eventually lilies.

Frank was in the Territorial Army, as was his older brother Bill, before the war, and so was called up as soon as war broke out in 1939. He married Lilian Violet Brinkhurst, of Rusthall, not long after this at the Tunbridge Wells Registry office. (After Frank's death, Lilian married Walter Wood, the Sutcliffes' next door neighbour in Speldhurst Road who later became a prisoner of war himself).

Frank and Bill were both among the soldiers on the beaches during the evacuation from Dunkirk, and Bill, who had been shot through the shoulder and was bleeding badly, was told to get on a boat. He said that he wanted to go and see where Frank was, but was ordered onto the boat. Frank died on the beach on 28 May 1940 at the age of 20, and was posted missing, presumed killed.

Pictured above is Frank's sister Dorothy, visiting his grave for the first time in 1979.

Southborough War Memorial

Thomas George Sutcliffe

Petty Officer C/JX 135241, HMS Arethusa, Royal Navy. Died Wednesday 18 November 1942, age 25. Commemorated on the Chatham Naval Memorial in Kent, panel 52.1.

Thomas George Sutcliffe was born on 29 January 1915, the son of Edmund Walter Sutcliffe and Marjorie Louisa Sutcliffe. His parents had originated from the north of England, and his father Edmund, a Quaker, died of cancer when Tom, as he was known to his family, was 8 or 9. Mr Sutcliffe senior had been a very good pianist and worked for the post office in Southborough. At the time of Tom's birth the family (see **Frank Sutcliffe**) lived at 25, Speldhurst Road, Southborough.

Tom used to sing rather nicely, and the Woods next door (Susie Wood later married Eric Tilley, son of **Samuel Tilley**, also commemorated on the War Memorial) used to hear Tom singing in bed in the evenings and would knock on the wall and ask him to sing "Wings of a Dove", which he obligingly did!

Tom's mother later married again, to Bert Andrews, carpenter on the Bentham Hill estate for the Flemings, and a widower who had 5 children of his own. Until then, she had taken in lodgers to eke out her living as a widow. After their marriage, they lived at South Lodge, Bentham Hill, and a child of their own, Roy, was born in 1931. (Pictured on opposite page: the family at Bentham Hill – Tom is in back row far left, Frank far right of middle row next to Dorothy.)

Tom attended St Peter's, the Church of England School on Southborough Common, and left school at 14. At age 16, in December 1930, he volunteered for the Royal Navy. His chest was not big enough, as he suffered from asthma, so he was given exercises and a set of dumb-bells to develop his chest-size, and eventually got into the Boys' Service, with the rating Boy. He served on numerous ships including *HMS Ganges*, *HMS York*, *HMS Pembroke*, *HMS Ramillies*, *HMS Kellett*, *HMS Franklin*, *HMS Vernon*, *HMS Kipling*, *HMS Woolwich*, and *HMS Cleopatra*, and had worked his way up to the rank of Petty Officer on the *HMS Arethusa* by the time he was killed.

Tom rode a motorcycle, and when he came home on leave he would more often than not bring a friend with him who couldn't get home to his own family and who would be put up on a camp bed at the family home. Once, when his sister Dorothy had been ill with 'flu, Tom treated her by taking her to a football match in Tunbridge Wells - Dorothy was not impressed!

The *HMS Arethusa* was en route from Crete to Alexandria when it was bombed from the air, and Tom died on 18 November 1942 at the age of 25, with no grave but the sea.

The website www.hms-arethusa.co.uk gives a lot of detailed information including the following: *In November 1942 HMS Arethusa left Alexandria to form a part of the escort for a convoy to Malta. On the 18th, 450 miles from port, she was torpedoed by low flying enemy aircraft, the explosion and resulting fire took the lives of 156 men from the ship's complement of approximately 500. Arethusa was the only casualty of Operation Stoneage and the arrival of the four merchant ships of convoy MW-13 effectively marked the end of the siege of Malta. The ship was badly damaged but managed, after a gallant struggle by her crew, to get back to Alexandria. Experts who examined her later in dry dock stated that it was a miracle she didn't sink ...*

An extract from the book "The Last Destroyer", the story of HMS Aldenham 1942-1944, first published 1988, describes the burial at sea of the fallen crew members: *... two padres came in board followed by a funeral firing party from HMS Orion, and lastly a very young marine bugler. With a signal from the bridge wires were cast off, and Aldenham slowly moved away, to commence her journey to the open sea. At the same time the cruiser had cleared lower deck, the men standing quietly facing outboard, caps removed in a last farewell gesture to their fallen comrades. Suddenly the peace of the afternoon was shattered by the shrill blast of a bosun's call from high up on the cruisers bridge. The 'still'. Everybody at attention, and not a sound except the Aldenham's screws churning up the water. Then* the 'carry on', as the ship turned away crossing the harbour to the open sea, ensign at half mast. Slowly we cleared the boom and out into the blue calm of the Mediterranean, the sun settling away in the western sky throwing long rays across the placid water.

The ship's engines shut down and slowly we came to a standstill, and with that the C of E Padre stood up on the torpedo tubes platform and commenced this solemn service for burial at sea, his voice sadly droning on, the ships company gathered around with heads bent, and sea breezes playing little tricks on hair and collars. Then it was the RC service. Emotionally and bravely, the Padre carried on this sad service until at the conclusion he closed his prayer book with a definite movement. This was the cue for the funeral firing party. At a command from their officer they raised their rifles to the firing position. Then one volley, another and another until the end, and with that the order 'present arms'. A pause and the marine bugler sprang to attention, his bugle ready at his lips. Loud and clear across that still blue water - the 'Last Post'. Slowly the notes died away and the one minute's silence. Everybody and everything dead quiet, even the sea breezes and birds seemed to pause in stillness at this very heart rending moment ...

As the setting sun disappeared below the distant watery horizon, proclaiming the end of another day, so the last body was committed to the deep. All over, the ships engine room was given the order 'slow ahead' and we turned for Alexandria harbour, a wistful look back at a solitary poppy wreath bobbing lightly on the waves ...

Not long before he died, Tom married Doris Pentecost, who lived in one of the houses next to the Victoria Hall, and they had a daughter, Rosemary. After Tom died they went to live in Burton-on-Trent, and Doris remarried twice. Tom's two grandchildren, Rosemary's son and daughter with her husband Mick Canner, are named Timothy and Sarah.

Nelson Colin Taylor

Corporal 30393, 17th Div Signal Coy, Royal Engineers. Died 12 April 1917, age 25. Buried in Cabaret-Rouge British Cemetery, Souchez, Pas de Calais, France: Grave ref. XVII.G.38. Born at Redhill, Surrey. Youngest son of Edward and Sarah Taylor, of 56, Edward Street, Southborough.

From the Courier, 27 April 1917: *On Wednesday Mr Taylor received the following letter from a*

Captain of his son's Company: *"With feelings of sincere regret, I have to inform you that your son, of this Company, was accidentally mortally burnt at about 7.15 am on the 12th inst. I have a record of the place of burial, and will communicate it to you later. Corpl Taylor was most popular amongst the men and officers of the Company".* Before enlisting in January 1915, he was employed by Mr P Wickenden, of Tunbridge Wells, where he was a clerk for ten years ... a letter of sympathy from Mr Wickenden ... *"It is unnecessary for me to inform you that you and your family have my sincerest sympathy in the great loss you have suffered. You will remember that your boy came to me when I first started in business just over ten years ago. He always received and merited my complete confidence and respect. I hoped that he would for many years remain associated with the business he had helped to build up, and I cannot express how keenly I feel his loss."* Corporal Taylor is one of Mr Fletcher's old boys, and for some years he was closely connected with the "Higher Grade Old Boys' Association". He arranged several cricket matches and socials, etc. He was always very popular with all who knew him. Almost all of the time that he has been in France has been spent in the thick of the fighting. He has had many wonderful escapes, he being one who volunteered for Brigade work. He was in the 17th Signal Company of the RE and went to France in July, 1915. He was home on leave at Christmas, 1916, that being the only leave since going to France.

Sidney Victor Taylor

Private 267040, transferred from the Kent Cyclists to (395691) Labour Corps. Died 28 October 1918, age 23. Buried in Southborough Cemetery, England: Grave ref. 4.379. Son of Mr S Taylor.

Sidney Taylor died in St Mark's, 167 Military Hospital, Broadwater Down, Tunbridge Wells, the cause of death being given as 1. Influenza and 2. Broncho-pneumonia. Present at his death was Nurse Mary Riddle. His residence was given as 7 Nursery Road, High Brooms, and occupation, after his rank and number, as a shell presser in 699th Agricultural Company.

From the Courier, 8 November 1918: THE INFLUENZA – *This epidemic is now subsiding at High Brooms. The Schools re-opened on Wednesday with an attendance of about fifty per cent of the boys and girls, but the number of infants attending was so small that this department was closed till Monday. FUNERALS On Tuesday at Southborough Cemetery, Private Taylor, his wife and their son were laid to rest. Pte Taylor was given a military funeral, the coffin being conveyed on a gun carriage, while a hearse followed with the coffins of wife and son.*

Southborough War Memorial

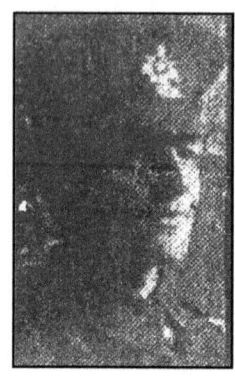

Walter W Teale

Private G/16252, 12th Bn, Royal Sussex Regiment. Died 12 October 1916, age 30. Buried in Euston Road Cemetery, Colincamps, Somme, France: Grave ref. III.O.9.

Private Teale died on the same day as **JF Gilks** and **CJ Scott**, also commemorated on the Southborough War Memorial. The CWGC states that WW Teale was the son of Mr and Mrs FW Teale of 66 Upper Grosvenor Road, Tunbridge Wells. It may be either that his parents moved from Prospect Road in the years following his death, or that there is some confusion here with Walter Teale's cousins, who also died in the War.

From the Courier, 27 October 1916: *Great sympathy will be felt for Mr and Mrs Teale, Prospect-road, in the death of their son, Private W Teale (pictured left), Royal Sussex Regiment, who was killed in action on October 12th. In a letter to his sister, Pte GE Mitchell says: "We were in the advance line for two days, and last night we were relieved by another Platoon, and we had only got away five minutes when a shell burst, killing three men and wounding several others, and, what is worse, is that they were all my old Company boys. One of the boys killed was Walter Teale, of Southborough, who often came home with me." Private Teale joined the Royal Sussex Cyclists early in 1916, and went to France only last month. Before enlisting, he was employed by Mr J Barrow, grocer, at Heathfield, where Mr and Mrs Teale lived before moving to Southborough some years ago. Mrs Teale has heard quite recently that two of her nephews have been killed and one wounded rather badly. These were brothers and only sons.*

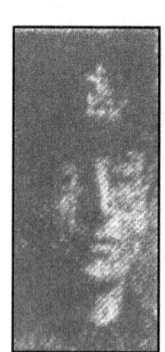

The following extract from the Courier, 27 April 1917, must refer to Walter's brother, pictured on left: *Mr and Mrs Teale, 46 Prospect-road, have heard that their son is in the 1st London General Hospital, Camberwell, suffering from trench fever and rheumatism. Private F Teale joined the Kent Cyclists, and was sent to France early this year, where he was attached to the Royal West Kents. He has been in the front line trenches, and has seen a good bit of fighting. He has also had to undergo a slight operation, the result of the hard life in the trenches. Before joining the Army Private Teale was in the tailoring business in London. Mr and Mrs Teale have another son serving in the Army, who is also in Hospital at the present time. They lost one son some months ago in France ... previous to taking up residence in Southborough Mr and Mrs Teale lived for some years at Heathfield.*

Southborough War Memorial

John Thorpe

Private 41487, 9th Bn, Staffordshire Regiment (a Pioneer unit). Formerly 183786, Royal Engineers. Died 11 December 1917, age 39. Buried in Giavera British Cemetery, Arcade, Italy: Grave ref. Plot 4. Row A. Grave 3. Son of Mr and Mrs R Thorpe, of Speldhurst, Kent; husband of Lily Agnes Thorpe, of 23 Western Road, Southborough.

From the Courier, 28 December 1917: *Private J Thorpe, C Co, Pioneer Battalion, South Staffordshire Regiment was killed in Italy on December 12th. The information was received by Mrs Thorpe in a letter from the Chaplain, in which he tenders his most sincere sympathy, and relates how Pte J Thorpe was billeted in a two-storey house, when a shell came through the roof and killed him instantaneously, and also wounded four others. He was buried in a British Cemetery about a quarter-of-a-mile away from the house where he was billeted. "Jack" Thorpe will be remembered by all football-lovers as having played for Speldhurst, Southborough Rangers, and finally for Southborough, and he was greatly respected by all his fellow-players. Before enlisting in January 1915, he was employed for a great many years by Strange and Sons, Tunbridge Wells, as a bricklayer. He was drafted to France five months ago, and from there he was sent to Italy.*

The CWGC site gives the following information: *Commonwealth forces were at the Italian front between November 1917 and November 1918. On 4 December 1917, the XIth and XIVth Corps relieved the Italians on the Montello sector of the Piave front, with the French on their left. The Montello sector acted as a hinge to the whole Italian line, joining that portion facing north from Mount Tomba to Lake Garda with the defensive line of the River Piave covering Venice, held by the Italian Third Army. The Commonwealth troops on the sector were not involved in any large operations, but they carried out continuous patrol work across the River Piave, as well as much successful counter battery work. Men who died in defending the Piave from December 1917 to March 1918, and those who fell on the west of the river during the Passage of the Piave, are buried in Giavera British Cemetery.*

Fred Thrower

Private 8354, 2nd Bn, Hampshire Regiment. Died 6 August 1915, age 29. Commemorated on the Helles Memorial, Turkey: Panel 125-134 or 223-226 228-229 & 328. Son of George and Mary Ann Thrower, of Speldhurst Road, Southborough.

The website www.firstworldwar.com/onthisday gives the following Gallipoli campaign detail for 6 August 1915: *Southern Front: Two divisions effect surprise landing at Suvla Bay and attack with Anzacs on right, and southern force on Achi Baba.*

From the Courier of 3 September 1915: Mr George Thrower, of Speldhurst-road, Southborough, has received an official communication from the War Office that his son, Private F Thrower, was killed in action on the 6th August with the Mediterranean Force. Private Thrower would have completed seven years in the Army next November, and has seen most of his service abroad. He was home last Christmas, and went to the Front in March.

Samuel John Curd Tilley

Private G/1845, D Coy, 7th Battalion Queen's Own (Royal West Kent Regiment). Died 8 July 1917, age 33. Buried in Dickebusch New Military Cemetery, Ypres, Belgium, Grave ref: II.C.21. Husband of EE Webster (formerly Tilley), of 13 Sheffield Road, Southborough.

From the Courier, undated, but the reference to Trones Wood indicates July 1916: *SOUTHBOROUGH MAN IN TRONES WOOD* The following extracts from a letter dated 15th July, from Private SJC Tilley to his wife, who is living at Sheffield-road, Southborough, will be read with interest: "We have been in another scrap, which, no doubt, you have heard by the time you get this, and thank God I am out of it safe and sound, with only a scratch or two, and you can't see them now. Young "Nip" Tipping was wounded, I think in the leg, but he will get over it all right. I couldn't stay with him, as we had orders to push on, and now we are going for a rest. This turn out, although it did not last as long as our other advance, was ten times worse; it seemed as though the whole lot of us must be wiped out, but thank God we are safe. We were surrounded at one time in Trones Wood. It's one more step towards the finish. Some of the German prisoners say the war will end next month; then, Hoorah! for England! I have tons of news I could tell you. The sights I've seen during the last 48 hours have been terrible. There's another big batch of prisoners just going by our camp. I have had a letter from Will Thorne (of Bidborough) by the same post as yours, and he has been wounded again, and is in Hospital at Cambridge."

Re "Nip" Tipping, mentioned above, Dee's Directory 1915 lists, under Men Serving, HA Tipping, Royal Field Artillery, HC Tipping,

RWK Special Reserve, and P Tipping, Royal Engineers, all resident at 8 Sheffield-road.

Samuel's grandson Alan Waters writes: *Samuel was born the sixth and youngest child of Henry and Ann Tilley on 23 December 1883 at 4 Sunny Vale Terrace in Tunbridge Wells (a small road, no longer there, just behind the Central Station); the 'Curd' in his full name was his mother's maiden name. Henry was a greengrocer/porter, but his son joined the Post Office, perhaps inspired by the brand new General Post Office almost next door to Vale Road. At the age of 23 he became Rural Postman No. 485616 and his duties took him as far afield as Bidborough, where he would have met the staff employed at some of the big houses there. Amongst these was a young servant girl, Elizabeth Emma Baldwin, some six years his junior, who he courted. Elizabeth became pregnant, and this almost certainly meant that she lost her job. They set up home in Victoria Road in Tunbridge Wells and were married on 9 December 1909; their first child, Percy, was born on 18 April 1910 at 58 Pennington Road, Southborough, where the family had moved to, Samuel working now out of the Southborough Post Office.*

By the time Alan Waters' mother, Dorothy Olive, was born in 1912 the family had moved to 36 Charles Street, where the next child, Eric, was born on 15 February 1914. (Eric was to become a friend of **Tom Sutcliffe**). By all accounts they were a very happy family. Samuel joined up almost certainly in the first half of 1915, and about this time the family moved to 13 Sheffield Road. Samuel came home on leave around Christmas time. Their daughter Muriel Annie was born on 23 August 1916.

From the Tunbridge Wells Advertiser, 20 July 1917: *Mrs Tilley, 13, Castle-street ... sad news that her husband was killed on July 7th in his sleep by a shell that burst at the side of him. He volunteered for service in the Army a month after the outbreak of war, and had been in France two years last month ... he had served five years as a sailor, and before that was a telegraph boy at Tunbridge Wells. Pte Tilley's only brother is a time-expired sailor (CP Officer HW Tilley), who is still serving in the Navy, and he had a brother-in-law, Pte JE Corke, 11 Elm-road, who was a survivor of the Hawke, which was sunk in the early days of the war in the North Sea.*

After the devastating news of Samuel's death, apart from the grief there was the very practical problem of providing for her young family – the eldest just seven years old – the war widow's pension then was just 15 shillings per week. Elizabeth however was both resourceful and hard-working – she worked and took in washing to eke out the pension. On 12 December 1918 at St Peter's Church she married Alfred Webster, a young private serving with the HQ of the Royal Warwicks based in Southborough; they had several more children and lived to a good age.

Frank Tindall

Lance Corporal G/5007, 1st Bn, Queen's Own (Royal West Kent Regiment). Died 22 July 1916, age 26. Commemorated on the Thiepval Memorial, Somme, France: Pier and Face 11 C. Son of the late William and Rose Tindall, of 3, The Square, East Peckham; husband of Dorothy May Streeter (formerly Tindall), of 9, Dean Street, East Farleigh, Tovil, Maidstone.

From the Courier, 29 September 1916: *Mrs Tindall of High Brooms-road, Tunbridge Wells, and formerly of East Peckham, has been officially informed that her husband, Lance-Corpl F Tindall, No 5007, of the 1st Battalion, RWKR, 24 years of age, has been missing since an engagement in France in the great advance. He joined the Army in December, 1914, and went to the Front in May, 1915. He has one child, and was formerly in the employ of the Medway Conservancy Board.*

William Jubilee Tingley

Corporal 540922, 10th Field Troop, Royal Engineers. (KF 1745). Died Tuesday 2 April 1918, age 31. Buried in Grave O.83 in Jerusalem War Cemetery, Israel.

William Jubilee Tingley was born on 24 March 1887 at Bidborough. He was named for Queen Victoria's Golden Jubilee, in 1887. He had seven siblings: Sam (half-brother, born 1881 in 67 Springfield Road), Mabel May (born 1889), Charles Edward (born 1891), Rosa Annie (born 1894), Elsie Florence (born 1896 at 54 Springfield Road), Clarence Reginald (born 1899 at 54 Springfield Road) and Hubert Ernest (born 1906 at 58 Springfield Road).

William's father Sam Tingley was born 29 June 1852 in Bidborough, Kent. Sam was a gardener for one of the bigger estates in Southborough and only left Bidborough, where most of his children were born, in the latter years of his life. He died of bronchitis and heart failure on 31 January 1923 in 2 Victoria Cottages, Southborough. William's mother Susannah was born 3 May 1862 in Southborough, the daughter of George Hollamby and Ann (Butcher) Hollamby. She married Sam Tingley on 25 December 1885 in St Lawrence Church, Bidborough, and she died 13 years after her husband, of stomach cancer and exhaustion, on 2 February 1936 in 2 Victoria Cottages.

William's half-brother Sam came home from the First World War to find his wife Alice in prison for child neglect, one of their children having died. His mother, Susannah, had walked from Southborough Common to Pembury Workhouse to bring the other children home.

A local paper report, pre-April 1918, included the photograph shown above of the four serving Tingley brothers with the following text: *Mr & Mrs Tingley of 2, Victoria Road, will be congratulated on having four soldier sons serving. Sapper S Tingley joined the RE (Kent Fortress) in January, 1915, and his brother, Corporal W Tingley, joined the same Regiment the same month. He is now in Egypt, where he has been transferred to the 1st Camel Brigade. Private CE Tingley joined the Royal West Kent Regiment in August 1914 and went to India in October, 1914. A few weeks ago a rumour was afloat that he had been killed, but we are glad to say that Mrs Tingley has had a notice from the War Office to the effect that her son is quite all right, and is serving in Mesopotamia with the East Kent Regiment, where he has been since October. Bugler Clarence Tingley joined the R.E. (Kent Fortress) in February 1915 at the early age of 16 years.*

William married Florence Mary Rabbit, and they had four children: Frederick, Grace, Gladys and Winnie. He was a member of the Southborough Fire Brigade, and is commemorated on a plaque, with four others (see **F Somers**, **F Saunders**, and **F Richardson**) in the Fire Station on London Road, Southborough. He was also employed as a lamplighter in the town.

William's great niece believes he may have survived the sinking of the Hythe in 1915, but Frank Stevens, who researched the Kent Royal Engineers for his book on the Hythe tragedy, doubts this; he thinks that after the companies were formed up at Gillingham, William was with the Ashford No 2 Company, who were not involved with the Hythe incident, but went to Gallipoli, and then on to Egypt, where the Company had to provide 50 soldiers to form a mounted troop to work with cavalry. They were mounted on horses, mules and finally camels, and it was while in camp with the Imperial Camel Corps (Palestine) that William was killed by a bomb dropped by enemy aircraft (three other NCOs were killed at the same time, one of them in the Army Veterinary Corps). At the time of William's death, Florence's address was recorded as 39 Springfield Road. After he died, she remarried and emigrated to Australia with all of their children.

Pictured above: Memorial in Embankment Gardens, London, engraved with the following tribute: *"To the Glorious and Immortal Memory of the Officers NCOs and Men Of the Imperial Camel Corps British Australian New Zealand Indian Who Fell In Action or died of Wounds and Disease in Egypt Sinai and Palestine 1916-1917-1918"*

Harry Todman

Sapper 1411, 1st/3rd Kent Field Company, Royal Engineers. Died 28 October 1915 in the Hythe disaster, age 28. Commemorated on the Helles Memorial, Turkey. Panel 23 to 25 or 325 to 328.

Born on 28 October 1886, so died on his birthday, Harry Todman was the second son of George Todman of Ferrers Estate, Tunbridge Wells. Harry and his wife Gertrude Annie had two children aged eight and three years at the time of his death, and they lived at 35 Bedford Road, Southborough. Harry was employed by Messrs Wood & Wallis as a stone mason; his brother was also in the trade and is said to have carved Harry's name on a memorial. Harry joined up when war was declared so had served for over a year when he died. His wife remarried, becoming Mrs Coulstock, and the family moved to 82 Springfield Road, Southborough.

Percy James Musgrave Tomkin

Private G/15791, 1st Bn, The Buffs (East Kent Regiment). Died Friday 30 March 1917. Commemorated on the Loos Memorial, Pas de Calais, France: Panel 15 to 19.

The CWGC website lists Percy's surname as Tompkin. He attended St James's School in Tunbridge Wells, then moved to Southborough. From a newspaper report of the time: *Mrs Tomkin, 5, Charles-street, has received a notice from the War Office saying that her husband was reported missing on the 29th March. Private Tomkin joined the Kent Cyclist Battalion in December, 1915, and was afterwards transferred to the 1st Buffs. He was sent to France in December, and has been in the firing line ever since. He is a son of Mrs Tomkin, London-road, and a brother of Mr Herbert Tomkin, barber, who, until he enlisted a short time ago, carried on business at 102, London-road.*

A later report adds: *Mrs Tomkin, 5, Charles-street, has now received official information that her husband, who was reported missing in France last March, is now reported killed. He joined the Kent Cyclists ... and was sent to France exactly a year after ... before enlisting he was employed by Mr Dunster, dairyman, London-road. Mrs Tomkin has five brothers serving, two of them being in France, one in India, and one who came from Australia to enlist, is daily expecting to be sent to France. The other brother is in the Royal Flying Corps.*

Frederick Turner

Private 202112, 2nd Bn, Suffolk Regiment. Died 28 March 1918, age 35. Buried in the London Cemetery, Neuville-Vitasse, Pas de Calais, France: Grave ref. III.B.17. Husband of Edith Kate Turner, of 40, South View Road, High Brooms.

Information from the website www.firstworldwar.com/onthis day gives the following campaign detail for 28 March 1918 for the Western Front: *Great German attack on wide front north and south of Scarpe River defeated with very heavy loss. Between Somme and Avre rivers Germans advance, reaching Hamel.*

Frederick George Turner

Rifleman R/39038, 18th Bn, King's Royal Rifle Corps. Died Friday 21 September 1917, age 19. Buried in Ypres Reservoir Cemetery, Ypres, Belgium: Grave ref. IX.A.34. Son of Harry James and Mary Turner, of 241, Cricklewood Lane, London. Native of Southborough.

From the Courier of 16 November 1917: *Official news has been received that Rifleman F G Turner, King's Royal Rifles, who made his home at 23 Meadow-road, the residence of his aunt Miss Turner, when his parents left Southborough to reside at Deal, is officially reported wounded and missing since the 18th or 20th of September. He joined the Colours in November, 1916, as a Motor Transport driver, afterwards being transferred to the above regiment. He proceeded to France on August 3rd, 1917.*

Sidney Turner

Sergeant 540570, 497th (Kent) Field Coy, Royal Engineers. Formerly KFRE 1327. 497th Coy was the re-numbered 1st/3rd Kent, serving with the 88th Brigade, 29th Division. Died 10 July 1917, age 41. Buried in the Bard Cottage Cemetery, Ieper, Belgium: Grave ref. II.A.18. Husband of Mrs Gaston (formerly Turner) of Half Way House, Brenchley, Kent. Native of Southborough.

Frederick Somers' widow is also recorded as having married a Mr Gaston at the address mentioned above. It is possible there is some confusion of information here, unless two widows married brothers at the same address, which seems unlikely.

Southborough War Memorial

From the Courier, 20 July 1917: *Very great sympathy will be felt for Mrs Turner, 12 Taylor-street, in the loss she has sustained in the death of her husband, who was killed by shell fire in action on July 10th. Sergt S Turner joined the RE soon after the outbreak of war, and volunteered to go with the Company who were on the ill-fated "Hythe", when so many lives were lost, but owing to his teeth needing attention he was not able to go. He only went to France in May last, but for three weeks Mrs Turner could get no news of him until the day before he was killed she received a field card from him.*

The following letter has been received from Major Ruston: "Sergt Turner had not long joined the Company, but he had been in it long enough for us to know his sterling worth. He had a difficult task to perform when he came out, namely, to take over Section Sergeant's work, amid all the distractions of warfare. But he did this task well, and in losing him the Company suffers a well-nigh irreparable loss. His Section Officers speak very highly of his keenness and energy, and disregard of danger when he had his duty to perform."

Another letter of sympathy has been received from an officer of Sergt Turner's Company, of which the following is a portion: "Your husband was my Section Sergeant, and was to me my right-hand man. I feel his loss tremendously, and every officer, NCO and man in this Company will deeply sympathise with you. He was a gallant soldier, and he died in his country's service".

Frank Leonard Tutchener

Sapper 757, 1st/3rd Kent Field Coy, Royal Engineers. Died 28 October 1915 in the Hythe disaster, age 23. Commemorated on the Helles Memorial, Turkey: Panel 23 to 25 or 325 to 328.

Frank Tutchener was among the first 40 men to join No 3 Company, and probably came up through the Cadet Unit, as he was the Bugler and reports state that he had three years' service. When the Field Company was raised for foreign service he transferred to it. He was an old St James' School boy.

Mr Geoffrey Tutchener, a Tunbridge Wells resident and cousin of Frank's branch of the family, has traced Tutchener descendants back to 1569 in Horsham, Sussex, and says that a Tutchener came from Tudeley in 1864 to work on the railways in Southborough. In the Tonbridge Reference Library there is a book on the Chalybeate Spring of

Southborough with an advertisement for George Tutchener, Fly-Operator, whose brother William was Frank's grandfather.

Frank's father, James Henry Tutchener (known as Henry) was part of a huge family, many of whom emigrated to Australia and Canada. He worked with horses, in the stables at Great Bounds, and as a fly-driver. Frank's sister Edith (born 1913) recalls driving with her father along The Loo (the main road between St John's Church and the Cross Keys pub) one night in thick fog, when her father assured her that, with the reins hanging slack, the horse would find its way safely home, which it did. He had been born in 1867, and died in 1940 at the family home, 3, The Retreat. Frank's mother, née Mary Luck, was born in 1872 and died in 1943 at the same address. Her own mother lived in High Brooms.

Edith, (pictured left in her 90s), recalled Frank coming in to her bedroom, where she stood in her cot, to say goodbye to her before he left on his last journey. She was only two years old at the time, but clearly remembered his uniform.

There were seven brothers and sisters in the family; Henry and Hubert served in the Air Force during World War Two (Henry long service, Hubert wartime only); Arthur entered the Navy at 13 or 14 in the Boys' Service and retired after 33 years with the rank of Lieutenant. Frank also had three sisters – Violet, who died at the age of twelve, Rose (known as Queenie), and Edith.

Edith married in 1936 at St Thomas's, Southborough. At the age of 40, her father had a bad accident at work, when he was kicked in the groin by a horse, and couldn't get work after this. Her mother went out thereafter to work in people's houses, as there was no social security in those days to fall back on. It was very hard going to make ends meet, Edith recalls, but they were a very happy family. She was 27 when her parents died, and moved thereafter to Rusthall. She has herself researched the family tree as far back as the 17th century, when the name was written Touchner, and she thinks possibly may have originated in Austria.

From the Courier, 22 June 1918, a reference no doubt to a relative: *Mrs Donne, of 71, St John's-road, has received news that her brother, Corporal S Tutchener, of the Royal West Kent Regiment, was gassed on 9th June, and is in a Canadian Hospital in France. He has been in France eighteen months, and has been in several of the great battles.*

Mark Thomas Underhill

Sapper 756, 1st/3rd Kent Field Coy, Royal Engineers. Died 28 October 1915 in the Hythe disaster, age 37. Commemorated on the Helles Memorial, Turkey: Panel 23 to 25 or 325 to 328.

Mark Underhill was an early enlistment into the Company; having formerly been with the 1st Company of the local Royal West Kents, both Volunteers and Territorials, and the Royal Engineer Territorials for a likely combined service of 15 years.

His civilian work was ball-maker with Wisdens, making cricket and hockey balls. He lived at 24 Western Road, Southborough, with his wife and seven children.

James Vesey MC

Lieutenant 2nd Bn, Royal Berkshire Regiment. Died Saturday 25 September 1915. Commemorated on the Ploegsteert Memorial, Berks Cemetery Extension, Comines-Warneton, Hainaut, Belgium: Panel 7 & 8.

Dee's Directory for 1915 gives James Vesey's address as 36 Meadow Road, Southborough.

www.firstworldwar.com/onthisday for 25 September 1915: *Western Front: Germans penetrate between Tower Hamlets Ridge and Polygon Wood; repulsed later.*

From the Courier, 19 February 1915: *Among those mentioned in Sir John French's latest despatch is Second Lieutenant J Vesey, 1st Royal Berkshire Regiment. Lieut Vesey was promoted on the field from Sergeant-Major for distinguished conduct, and was severely wounded in one of the battles. He is a son-in-law of Mr Mark Miller, of 36 Meadow-road, Southborough.*

And on 3 September 1915: *Lieutenant J Vesey has been home this week ... had a distinguished career, having been granted a commission from the ranks. When Sergeant-Major, he was in charge of two companies of the Berkshires at Ghulevelt, and though greatly depleted by losses, they stuck to their trench until* *reinforcements arrived. For this Lieut Vesey was awarded the Military Cross, mentioned in despatches, and granted a commission as 2nd Lieutenant.*

He was promoted to Lieutenant on the 10th May, and joined the 2nd Battalion, and returned to the Front on 17th May. Vesey went to the Front at the commencement of the War, and went through all the early battles – Mons, the Marne, the Aisne, Ypres and the severe fighting around Festubert.

He sustained a machine-gun bullet wound in the foot on November 13th, was invalided home and remained in England for some time. He was presented with the Military Cross by His Majesty the King. Lieutenant Vesey speaks with admiration of the daring of the Allies' airmen. He has seen many brave deeds done by them, and on one occasion saw a French airman "loop the loop" after driving off two German aeroplanes.

On 1 October 1915: *We regret to hear that Lieut. J Vesey has been officially reported missing since Saturday. Mrs Vesey is now residing in Southborough.*

And finally on 8 October 1915: ... *was killed in action during the British advance on September 25th. He had been in the Army for 22 years. He leaves a widow and a three year old son.*

Thomas Arthur Vinall

Private 52927, 17th Battalion, The King's (Liverpool) Regiment. Died 2 August 1917. Buried in Lijssenthoek Military Cemetery, Poperinghe, West-Vlaanderen. Grave ref: XVI.J.14.

Initials given as A T on Southborough War Memorial.

From the Tunbridge Wells Advertiser, 17 August 1917: *There are many in Tunbridge Wells who will regret to learn that Pte Thomas Arthur Vinall, son of Mr S Vinall, 179, Vale-road, Tonbridge, died of wounds whilst serving in France on August 2nd. A born soldier, he had a high conception of duty, and one could gather from his conversation that he was convinced of the righteousness of the war we are fighting. Although his knowledge of army life fitted him for stripes, he would never take them, insisting always that his place was with the rank and file. He was an old Grosvenor School boy, and was 37 years of age when he fell.*

Pte Vinall enlisted in the Royal Sussex Regiment just before the outbreak of the South African War, and served in South Africa for the last nine months of the war. In April, 1911, finding it difficult to obtain work, he went to Canada, and at the commencement of the present war he came back to England again, intending to join up in his old regiment, the Royal Sussex. Being stranded in Lancashire, he joined the Lancashire Fusiliers at Salford in October, 1914, going out to France at the beginning of November, 1915.

He was wounded on the 1st of July, 1916, and on being discharged from Boulogne Hospital, he was transferred to the King's (Liverpool) Regiment. He was in the severe fighting on the Somme previous to coming home for ten days' leave in January, 1917 (when he called in at the ADVERTISER Office to have a chat), and saw the blowing up of Hill 60. Severely wounded in the thigh in action on July 31st, he died on August 2nd in the No 1 Canadian Clearing Station, France.

The Courier, 1 January 1943, reports that Mr George Vinall of 30 Holden Corner died on Christmas Day at the age of 56. He would have been 30 at the time of TA Vinall's death and possibly a relative.

Maurice Carter Voile

Gunner 206181, "C" Bn, Tank Corps. Died Monday 9 April 1917, age 24. Son of George S and Ellen Louise Voile, of Cheltenham; husband of Winifred Voile, of "Pendennis", Cleeve Hill, Glos. Buried at Tilloy British Cemetery, Tilloy-les-Mofflaines, Pas de Calais, France: Grave ref. I.A.24.

Tilloy is a village 3km south-east of Arras, on the south side of the main road to Cambrai. Tilloy-les-Mofflaines was taken by British troops on the 9 April 1917 but it was partly in German hands again from March to August 1918.

The MGC (Machine Gun Corps) had I (Infantry), C (Cavalry), M (Motorised) and H (Heavy) branches. H were those in tanks and remained MGC until the new name of Tank Corps was authorised.

From the Tunbridge Wells Advertiser of 27 April 1917: *The wife of Gunner MC Voile, Machine Gun Corps, has received the sad news of the death of her husband. Before enlisting, Gunner Voile was farming at Ivy House Farm, Pennington-road. He joined the Army in May, 1916, and went to France in August.*

From the Courier, 27 April 1917: *Mrs Voile, 126, London-road, has received the following letter from a Corporal of his Company, who writes for all his comrades: "We have buried him quite close to the spot where he fell. A cross has been placed over his grave to show that 'here lies the body of a gallant soldier and a real* man, one whose companionship was a great joy to all who had the privilege of knowing him'. We shall miss him very much." A letter has also been received from the Co Sergeant-Major of the Company, in which he says: "Gunner Voile was very popular amongst his comrades. He was a real good fellow, hard-working and conscientious, and he had been entrusted with the difficult task of driving his 'bus (as we call them) across the German lines. He did exceedingly well, and got right into the enemy's stronghold, when a shell hit the front of his 'bus', and he was killed instantly, and several others were wounded. He was buried the following day.

Maurice's great-grandson Oliver Davey has kindly supplied further information: Maurice was born in Cheltenham on 11 January 1893 to George Stephenson Voile, a coal merchant, and Ellen Louise Carter. George died in 1904 and in 1912 Maurice moved to Canada with his sister and mother to be nearer his older brother, who had married and emigrated two years earlier. In 1914, Maurice sailed back to England to marry his childhood sweetheart, Winifred Olive.

On attaining the age of 21, he had access to his father's inheritance, which he used to purchase Ivy House Farm (see above). Their only child, Joan, was born there in 1915. However, with no end in sight to the Great War, Maurice sold the farm and in May 1916 joined the Machine Gun Corps, heavy branch. Following training in Bisley, Surrey he moved to Elveden, Norfolk, where Lord Iveagh had provided land so that tank crews could be trained in secret.

Maurice left Southampton for Le Havre on 16 August 1916 and moved up to camps on the Somme. The very first use of tanks was during the Battle of Flers-Courcelette on 15 September, part of the Somme offensive in which C Battalion took part. The family can't be sure if Maurice was involved in the first action as the records were destroyed during the Blitz, but if he wasn't directly involved, he would almost certainly have been in the reserves.

On 9 April, in a combined attack by British and Canadian forces near Arras, Maurice and the crew of Tank C39 were charged with advancing towards a particular German stronghold, known as the Harp. Tank C39 was a Mark II tank, designed for training purposes and fitted with only unhardened armour. They were never meant for combat, but with the delay of the Mark IV a number were used in the Battle of Arras.

David Fletcher's book 'Tanks and Trenches' gives a description of the action. Despite the gains of the first day the British were unable to exploit the situation, and eventually the ground that had been gained that day, with the exception of Vimy Ridge, was recaptured by the Germans.

After the war Maurice's body was moved to its final resting place at Tilloy-les-Mofflaines.

Reginald Walker

Driver 243920, Royal Army Service Corps. Died Saturday 18 April 1942, age 36. Buried in Southborough Cemetery, Kent: Grave ref. Sec. 11. Grave 381. Son of Louisa A Walker, and stepson of Israel G Tompsett, of Southborough.

Harry Wallond

Private 928082, 47th Bn, Canadian Infantry (Western Ontario Regt). Died 17 August 1918. Buried at Fouquescourt British Cemetery, Somme, France: Grave ref. III.C.5.

Fouquescourt is a village 35km east of Amiens. It was captured by the 10th Canadian Infantry Brigade on 10 August, 1918.

Clive Maier's research shows that Private Wallond was born on 20 July 1881. He lived in Guelph, Ontario, and enlisted there on 9 December 1915, when he gave his occupation as farmer. His birthplace is given on his attestation paper as Preston, Kent. He lived at 25 Preston Street in Guelph; the birthplace may be a clerical error or it may refer to Preston near Faversham.

Harry may have been related to Mr Wallond, the publican recorded in 1903 as resident at the High Brooms Hotel, opposite the High Brooms Club.

R Whibley

Driver 661631, 70th Battery Royal Field Artillery. Died 22 November 1918. Buried in Caudry British Cemetery, Nord. France. Grave ref: II.C.14.

Driver Whibley's initials are given as ER on Southborough War Memorial and R on the CWGC site.

Ralph's parents Henry and Cordelia Whibley had six children and lived at 67 Springfield Road (1901 and 1911 census), where Cordelia and their daughter Florence Rosina and her husband ran the corner grocery shop. Henry was a plumber and builder. Ralph's other sister was Cordelia Annie, and he also had two older brothers, Harry (who didn't fight in the Great War because he had 'bad lungs') and Albert, who was in the Army Ordnance Corps. His younger brother Tom's own son remembers living above his parents' shop at 65 London Road, Southborough.

Sadly, Driver Whibley died at age 20 eleven days after the Armistice was signed. From the Deaths Column, the Courier, 13 December 1918: *Driver R Whibley, 70th Battery, RFA, third son of Mrs Whibley, Springfield-road, Southborough, died in France November 22nd. From his sorrowing Mum, Dad, Sisters and Brothers.*

Ernest Ralph, or Ralph as he was known, died from influenza. His Commanding Officer's War Diaries, researched by Ralph's great-niece Vivien Gosden, show that two or three soliders from the Brigade were being sent off to the Casualty Clearing Station nearly every day in November 1918 suffering from influenza.

Ralph's cousin Kathleen remembered Ralph as being ' passionate about his horses. As a Driver in the RFA, he was part of a team of three men, each with two horses pulling the big guns into position in battle.

Cyril Wickens

Private 5507327, 2nd Bn Hampshire Regiment. Died Wednesday 21 March 1945, age 25. Buried in Berlin 1939-1945 War Cemetery, Berlin, Germany: Grave ref. 10.D.17. Son of Ernest and Bertha Ellen Wickens; husband of Catherine Florence Wickens, of High Brooms.

Fred Ongley, now resident in Rusthall, was born two years before Cyril, and lived at 78 Taylor Street, next to Cyril at No 80. There was a well at the back of No 80 which served the four nearest houses. He recalls that they used to play a kind of cricket in their back yards with a tiny bat made of a piece of wood and nails, and a marble. Cyril had a white terrier, and he played a fair bit of football as a boy.

Southborough resident Miss Megan Davies knew Cyril, and worked at one time with him at RN Carr on London Road, where the manager was a Mr Lenihan. She recalls Cyril was a nice chap, who liked a laugh and a joke. He was a plumber.

It is possible that Cyril Wickens had been a prisoner of war in a camp East of Berlin, who had died in Germany's retreat from the Eastern Front and the oncoming Russian forces.

Peter Howard Williams

Lieutenant (A), HMS Peewit, Royal Naval Volunteer Reserve. Died Thursday 22 November 1945, age 29. Commemorated on the Lee-on-Solent Memorial, Hampshire: Bay 6, Panel 3. Son of Stanley and Gertrude Williams; husband of Lavinia Elizabeth Williams.

During the Second World War, the Fleet Air Arm needed places to train pilots, and the airfield at Hatton, Angus, between Carnoustie and Arbroath, was commissioned in the third year of the war as HMS Peewit. The base had an aircraft-carrier deck marked out on the runway to give the pilots something to aim for. It was operational for two years in preparation for the invasion of Europe. In 1946 the Navy paid off the station and HMS Peewit became Condor II, a satellite of the Condor military base at Arbroath, and in 2004 the runway was used as hardcore in the making of the A92 dual carriageway, and the airfield returned to arable use for the first time since 1942.

Robert Wilmshurst

Private 52701, 32nd Bn, Royal Fusiliers. Died 27 June 1917. Commemorated on the Ypres (Menin Gate) Memorial, Belgium: Panel 6 & 8.

From the Courier, 20 July 1917: *Mrs Wilmshurst, 38 Meadow-road, has received information that her husband, Private R Wilmshurst, Royal Fusiliers, was killed in action in France on June 27th. He joined in April, 1916, and went to France in February; after being there a short time was invalided home with trench feet, and was in hospital at Huddersfield for six weeks. He had only been back in France six weeks when he met his death. The following letter has been received from his Captain: "Your husband died one of our Empire's heroes, whose memory, conduct and heroism will go down in history as one of the best. As his Company Commander, I mourn his loss deeply, for he did so well on June 7th in the battles of the Messines. These dear boys pay the great price of sacrifice. Accept the sympathy and condolence of all the officers, NCOs and Men of 'D' Company. We lose a gallant comrade."*

Sapper William Wilmshurst, 826, and Sapper Frank Wilmshurst 958, 1st/3rd Kent Field Coy Royal Engineers, were both from Tunbridge Wells. They enlisted at Southborough, and died in the Hythe disaster on 28 October 1915. They may have been related to Robert Wilmshurst. They are not listed on the Southborough War Memorial.

Walter William Richard Winter DSM

Petty Officer Stoker P/K 60847, HMS Somali, Royal Navy. Died Thursday 24 September 1942, age 38. Son of William T Winter and Rose Winter; husband of Ivy Gladys Winter, of Southborough, Kent. Commemorated on Portsmouth Naval Memorial, Hampshire: Panel 67, Column 3.

Bill, as he was known to friends and family, was born in 1905. He came from Mayfield, and ran away to sea with a friend, underage, before the war. They were sent home, and Bill went to work on a farm.

Bill served on many ships, including the *Queen Elizabeth*, the *Revenge*, the *Victory*, the *London*, the *Resolution* and the *Ajax*. His son Phil thinks he may have been on the *Ajax* during the Battle of the River Plate. The *Ajax* came back for repairs, and two officers had been killed, so Bill was made up to Chief Stoker. He and another officer were promoted, the other being posted back to the *Ajax*, and Bill to the *Somali*. He had served earlier on her, from 6 December 1938 to 31 March 1941.

Bill's son Phil was three years old the first time he saw his Dad. The family was living over the Carpenter's Arms in Tunbridge Wells, near Albion Square, at that time, before they moved to Springfield Road in Southborough.

Bill liked gardening when he was on leave, and he used to help his father and his father-in-law. He used to go hay-making too, if it were that time of the year. He had a mah-jong set, and he took it with him the last time he left for sea.

Ivy Winter was hop-picking with their two sons, Phil and George, who was then 4 years old, on Nightingale Farm, when her parents came to tell her that they had heard on the radio that the *Somali* had sunk. She and the children were living then at 29 Springfield Road, Southborough, but had moved across the road to live with Ivy's father, James Bridgland, at No 46, leaving No 29 for the Chalk family, who had been evacuated to lodge with the Winters before that.

James Bridgland had served in the Boer War and the Great War. He refused all his medals, though he was an army man through and through. His commander in the Boer War was a Colonel Murray, and he called one of his daughters Phyllis Minnie Murray, after him, one of his sons Paget (after General Paget) and another daughter was christened Cavell (after Edith Cavell). His oldest daughter, May, had a son called Stanley, and he actually bumped into Bill during the Second World War in a bar in Russia, when they were both on the Arctic Convoys. James Bridgland had an allotment all his life, and was killed in a road accident at the age of 82. He had volunteered for service in the Second World War, but as he was too old even for the Home Guard, he dug trenches on Southborough Common. Bill's own father, Tom Winter, fought in the Great War too.

After Bill died, his widow Ivy Winter got 11 shillings a week each for the two boys, Phil and George, and she had a pension. Grandfather lived with them still, and they stayed at No 29 until Phil got married.

On 8 June 1943, Phil, aged 11, and in his first long trousers, which had been supplied by SAAFA, went to London for the first time with his mother to receive the Distinguished Service Medal on behalf of his father. They walked from Charing Cross through Trafalgar Square and down the Mall to Buckingham Palace to meet King George.

H.M.S. "SOMALI" SIXTH DESTROYER FLOTILLA.

Extract from COMBINED OPERATIONS 1940 - 1942: Somali takes part in LOFOTEN Raid, March 1941: *The Lofoten Islands had with the rest of Norway fallen into German hands in the early summer of 1940. The herring and cod-oil factories situated in the four ports of Stamsund, Henningsvaer, Svolvaer and Brettesnes had been taken over by the enemy and were supplying him with a product of which he stood in great need. It was decided to send a combined force to destroy the factories, capture the quislings and their German masters, and enlist recruits for the Norwegian forces. Any ships found in the ports would be taken or sunk. The naval forces, under the command of Captain C Caslon, RN, consisted of five destroyers: the Somali, the Bedouin, the Tartar, the Eskimo and the Legion. They were escort to two infantry landing ships commanded by Commander J Brunton, RN and Commander CA Kershaw, RN, carrying No 3 and No 4 Commandos and some Royal Engineers. The military force commander was Brigadier (now Major-*

General) JC Haydon, DSO, OBE, commanding the Special Service Brigade into which the Commandos had been formed. A detachment of Norwegian soldiers and naval ratings, under their own officers, took part in this raid, in the planning of which Norwegian officers collaborated. At sea the only opposition came from an armed trawler, the Krebbs, sighted soon after 6am, sailing out of Stamsund. Despite the odds, she showed fight and courageously engaged the headquarter ship, HMS Somali, which soon set her on fire. She ran aground on a small island, drifted off three hours later, and surrendered. Her survivors were taken prisoner and she was sunk by gunfire. Her captain had been killed at the beginning of the engagement. The prisoners were astonished at the treatment they received, for they had expected something very different. It had, they said, been front-page news in Germany that the captain of the Cossack had shot the whole crew of the Altmark.

The following account is taken from *Special Admiralty Handout (For Colonial Press Officer): HMS Somali and HMS Ashanti*, which was sent to Ivy Winter on 11 July 1946 with a letter from the Secretary of the Admiralty, signed by R Powell, "In reply to your letter dated 5th June, 1946, I am commanded by My Lords Commissioners of the Admiralty to forward the accompanying particulars of the war record of HMS Somali, which they trust will prove of interest to you. I am to add for your information that *HMS Somali* sank in position: 069°11'N, 015°32'W on 24th September, 1942".

When HMS Somali, one of the famous Tribal Class destroyers, was torpedoed during the passage of a recent great convoy to North Russia, another "Tribal" came to her rescue, and but for appalling weather would have brought her to safety. This was HMS Ashanti, which distinguished herself in one of the Malta convoys earlier in the year. After HMS Somali was hit, she was taken in tow by HMS Ashanti, and the two destroyers covered a distance of 470 miles towards a friendly harbour through heavy weather. Then a gale whipped up the seas and swell with such violence that the injured ship broke her back. She sank when she was within only two days of safety. In the wardroom of HMS Ashanti, the First Lieutenant, who holds the DSC, told the story when his ship reached a British port. "We were bitterly disappointed we didn't get her in," he said. "Getting her so far and then losing her has upset us all very much."

During the convoy operation, HMS Ashanti was detached from the escort to attack a U-boat. She hunted her prey for some time, and then HMS Somali was ordered to take her place in the destroyer screen, and HMS Ashanti was assigned a new position. "Two hours afterwards", said the First Lieutenant, "the Somali was torpedoed - in the position we should otherwise have been in." Although there was some swell, there was not much wind, and the Ashanti immediately took the damaged ship in tow, and set off at five knots. For a few hours things went well, although by this time the Somali had developed a steep list. An escort trawler, HMS Lord

Middleton, went alongside her while she was under tow, and took off three-quarters of the crew. The remainder stayed behind to get rid of some of the top-weight. It was thought that there would be a better chance of saving her if depth charges, gun shields and heavy gear on deck were jettisoned.

Then suddenly, without warning, the two parted. By this time it was dark. No one knew what U-boats might be lurking near the stricken ship, but work was immediately started to get another tow line across. The job took about an hour and a half to complete. The Somali had no light and no steam, and her crew had to heave in the heavy towing lines by hand. In spite of the cold they sweated in their duffle coats for half an hour of muscle-binding, nerve-wrecking toil before they got their end inboard. Then once more the Ashanti and the Somali started on the homeward journey.

When daylight came they were still making a steady five knots. All night the men on the Somali worked to keep the ship afloat. They organised a bucket chain to bale out the water; they shoved overboard anything on the upper deck which could be dismantled. The Ashanti sent over a party of twenty men armed with axes and spanners to help in the work. The yards were struck, aerials were taken down, and all the time the hand pumps were manned. In the forenoon the engineers managed to get the diesel dynamo going. That meant the Somali could be steered and mechanical pumps used. By the afternoon the list of twenty-four degrees had been halved. Then the diesel broke down again, and the ship once more began to list to an alarming angle.

"We decided to send a power line over," the Ashanti's First Lieutenant said. "All night a party of men worked joining up electric leads and making them watertight. In all 20 joints were made." With daylight came the task of sending the power line over. The Ashanti's motor-cutter was given the task. It meant attaching the electric line by means of shackles to the towing hawser. In the heavy swell, the towing hawser was slatting up and down with enough weight to kill a man, but in three hours the task was done. The current was switched on. Nothing happened - there was an earth somewhere. Rather than give up, the electric line was heaved in again and with some of the Somali's wire and some borrowed from other destroyers another try was made. This time it was successful and the pumps started again. The Somali had been yawing about dangerously. Now she was able to steer again and speed was increased to six and a half knots.

In the meantime the Ashanti's cutter ran backwards and forwards with rum, provisions and bread for the men on the Somali. Their provision room and spirit store were flooded. Electric torches, batteries and bulbs were sent over for use below decks and at night. And all the time the two ships kept plugging slowly on and on. "That night we were all in high spirits, as it looked as though there was nothing to stop us getting in," said the First Lieutenant.

But next day the weather turned. The wind rose and sea and swell followed. Men cursed their luck. By early evening it had become too rough for the Ashanti's motor cutter, and it had to be hoisted in. By dusk a full gale was rising, with blinding snowstorms at frequent intervals. "We tried reducing speed, but that made the Somali unmanageable, so we had to keep going," was the First Lieutenant's comment.

Then at half past two in the morning without a word of warning the Somali broke her back. "She broached to. She swung broadside on to the swell, turned over on her side and folded up like a book. As she cracked she came upright, and the two halves slid vertically below the seas, bow and stern almost touching. "We couldn't see the Somali at the time the tow parted," continued the Ashanti's First Lieutenant. "Our first warning was a blinding blue flash when the electric cable parted. "We guessed what had happened and then the snow cleared and we saw her. We cleared the end of the tow, which was dragging over our stern, and went up wind to drift back and pick up survivors.

"Other destroyers had already started rescue work, but the Lord Middleton picked up most of them. I should say they were just washed aboard. She was rolling gunwales under and they must have come on board with the water.

"The Captain of the Somali on a Carley float reached one of the destroyers. He had just managed to get his arm through a ladder when he was washed away again. He landed up alongside us and we gaffed him with a meat hook. "One of our chaps had fixed a meat hook to a line and managed to dig the sharp end into his clothes and we hauled him up. It wasn't easy because in his sodden clothes he must have weighed 30 stone.

"After towing the Somali for three days and nights and feeling so sure we would get her in, it was a great blow to lose her like that through the weather."

The following is an extract from the NEWS CHRONICLE - 3 October 1942: *TWO SHIPS ALONG TOGETHER: ONE GOT HOME*
We were on the homeward convoy with our sister ship, the Somali, only 100 yards away, when suddenly she was attacked by a U-boat, and two torpedoes knocked a hole in her as big as a bus. Smoke began to pour from her, she listed heavily to starboard, and we thought she was about to sink. The Ashanti immediately swept around dropping depth charges, while a minesweeper went alongside the Somali and took off 160 ratings and 100 merchantmen survivors. Fifty ratings stayed behind with the skipper, Lieutenant-Commander Maud.

But the Somali didn't sink, and we finally took her in tow. Meanwhile the convoy had gone on, leaving the two sister ships alone together. Temperature was 26 Farh, with an icy wind, and soon snow began to fall. We crept along at about four or five knots, easing passage for the Somali by pumping out oil behind us. After an hour the two cables broke, but we managed to rejoin them. We asked her, "How are you feeling now?" and she replied "Quite well, thank you." The quartermaster piped "No hammocks to be slung".

At the speed we were going we were a sitting target. For the next three days and nights we relieved each other at action stations whenever we could, crashing down on the deck for a cat-nap. At dawn we sent over 20 ratings, in a motor cutter to the

Somali, to help her cut loose her deck stuff. She dumped her oil, ammunition and top gear, and her port engine fell out. She was without light or heat, her steering gear was out of control, and her stern water-logged. We started work to run an emergency cable for light and heat to her, and on the second day secured it, and sent over a second working party. Each party returned safely when their job was done. When the lights went up on the *Somali*, she sent us a message, "Many thanks, sister".

On the third day a telephone wire was secured to her and her skipper, Commander Maud, could speak direct to our skipper, Commander Richard Onslow. The day went quietly, and we were full of hope. All we thought of was saving the *Somali*, and getting some sleep. But in the night the weather got very heavy. Waves ran high, with big tops of white water and very deep smooth troughs. At 2am the towing cable snapped with the light, heat and telephone lines. We had a premonition of what was coming, and were not surprised at the *Somali's* message. "Close in. I'm sinking. Goodbye." With our searchlight focussed on her, we saw men jumping off her, and then she broke in halves and sank, bridge first and fo'c's'le after. Our last sight of her was her fo'c's'le sticking up above a white wave. There was a big groan on board the *Ashanti*, and then we all started to work to pick up survivors.

It was icy, with a wind like a knife, and spits of snow as hard as stones. The *Ashanti* tossed about like a toy ship. We threw nets over, and some of us held codlines. Half-a-dozen went over the ship's side, and were about an hour in the water up to their waists. The searchlight picked out the men, and the water was so clear in the troughs that you could see their arms and legs. We flung lifebelts out, but they were too frozen to grasp them. Then a raft came near with three men on it, one of them an officer, Lieutenant Bruce. We hooked Bruce, but he refused to be brought up until the men were saved first. We got one up safely, but by then the raft was sucked under the ship. If ever a man gave his life for his men, it was Lieutenant Bruce.

We kept scanning the water for about two hours, until we could see no more survivors. The last man we hauled up was singing at the top of his voice, and he kept on singing when we laid him in the skipper's sea cabin. "It's the only way I could keep myself from freezing stiff," he told us. He couldn't bend his legs or arms at first and when we spilled some boiling cocoa on him he said "More, please!" Then we found out who he was - the *Somali's* skipper, Commander Maud. Next morning at eight he was on the bridge with Commander Onslow, as right as rain.

But none of us had slept very much, though we were dead beat, because we were haunted by the thought of the men we hadn't been able to save. We couldn't forget they might have been us. Coming into port we heard terrific cheering. Somebody said, "Who's getting the cheers?" Somebody else stuck his head out of a porthole and said, "Blimey, it's us!" Then we all scrambled on deck and, sure enough, they were cheering, waving, throwing their caps in the air, and making the dickens of a dust-up, all for us. It made us feel pretty good, I can tell you."

Harry Woodland

Private Harry Woodland, G/15718, 7th Bn, The Buffs (East Kent Regiment). Died 18 November 1916, age 19. Buried in Grave B62 in Stump Road Cemetery, Grandcourt, Somme, France.

Harry Woodland was born at 3 Kensington Street, Tunbridge Wells on 8 October 1897. His father Harry's profession was given on the birth certificate as Coachman Domestic. His grandparents owned or leased the Calverley Tap, in Tunbridge Wells.

Harry Woodland senior died at the age of 26 (Harry's older brother Alfred was 7 when his father died, Harry 4). The family believe that Alfred was fostered out while their mother Charlotte (née Sands) brought up Harry at their home at 132 London Road, Southborough. She never re-married. Harry attended King Charles School in Tunbridge Wells. His report for Term ending August 1905 (age 7½) stated that *"he has made rapid progress this term"* and gave him 100% for conduct.

Harry was enrolled in the Cadet Battalion Kent (Fortress) Royal Engineers on 26 June 1912 and was discharged on 27 October 1913 (discharge certificate reads: ... *in consequence of : at his own request, unable to attend drills.*) His rank in the cadet unit had been Sapper, No 1076, and the certificate was signed by Capt and Adj DR Salomons. After he left school, Harry worked as a conductor with Autocar (the Tunbridge Wells bus company).

The Infantry Record Office in Hounslow wrote to Harry's mother on 12 April 1917 (on Army Form B104-82) as follows: *Madam, It is my painful duty to inform you that a report has been received from the War Office notifying the death of: N: G/15718 Rank: Private Name: Harry Woodland Regiment: The Buffs, E Kent which occurred: at the BRITISH EXPEDITIONARY FORCE on the: 18th November 1916 The report is to the effect that he: was killed in Action.*

The War Office wrote to her on 7 July 1917 as follows: *Madam, I am directed to acquaint you that the Command Paymaster, Eastern Command, Science Museum, Exhibition Road, S. Kensington, London SW, has been authorised to issue you the sum of two pounds, twelve shillings and six pence, being the amount that is due on the settlement of the accounts of the late No G/15718 Private Harry Woodland, 7th Battalion, East Kent Regiment ... the above amount is issued you as sole legatee in accordance with the deceased's will.*

Harry's brother Alfred believed that Harry's platoon took a direct hit from a shell, and that Harry was more or less blown to bits. His bloodstained identity disc was returned to his family. It bears the legend: H. WOODLAND. KENT. CYC. BTN. 2240. CE. Alfred Henry Woodland, who was three years older, went off to war first. Alfred used to work in Wisdom's the Butchers in Tonbridge, lodging there before the war, and then went on to work with horses before he was called up or volunteered. Alfred was out in France at the same time as Harry, serving with the Royal Field Artillery behind the front line. He rode the lead horse up to the action point among his duties. He relived his war-time experiences towards the end of his life, and told his son that discipline was very harsh. After the war he courted Doris Wisdom, and after they married they had two daughters and a son, Donald (the last born when Alfred was 42), who later became an Engine Driver after his two years National Service in the Royal Navy (entering as a Stoker, leaving at 20 as an Engineer).

H Woodrow

Private G/19104, 10th Bn, Queen's Own (Royal West Kent Regiment). Died 31 July 1917. Commemorated on the Ypres (Menin Gate) Memorial, Ypres, Belgium: Panel 45 & 47.

Private Woodrow died on the first day of the Third Battle of Ypres, (also known as the Battle of Passchendaele: 31 July - 6 November 1917). The offensive was mounted by Commonwealth forces to divert German attention from a weakened French front further south. It began on this date, when the British and French attacked on a 15 mile front in Flanders, took twelve villages and claimed 5,000 prisoners. By the end of the second day, half a mile had been gained and 35,000 killed or wounded. Haig ordered fresh troops in on 9, 13, 16, 24 and 27 August resulting in another 40,000 men lost for another mile gained.

John Worsell

Private L/6342, 2nd Bn, Royal Sussex Regiment. Died 30 October 1914, age 30. Commemorated on the Ypres (Menin Gate) Memorial, Ypres, Belgium: Panel 20. Husband of Frances C Howick (formerly Worsell), of 8, Red Row, Lower Green, Pembury, Kent.

The following account, from the Courier, 11 December 1914, most probably refers to Private Worsell, but the spelling throughout has obviously been taken down wrongly by the reporter, as happened from time to time: *The roll of local men who have given their lives for their country steadily grows. One of the latest additions is the name of Private John Thomas Warsall, of 64 Silverdale-road. Private Warsall, who belonged to the 1st Royal Sussex, was killed in action at Ypres on October 30th. Only three days before, his wife and parents (Mr and Mrs James Warsall, also of 64, Silverdale-road) had had a card from him saying that he was quite fit and well. Private Warsall was a Reservist. In his civilian capacity he was, and had been for four or five years past, an employee of the Tunbridge Wells Gas Company. His father has worked for this undertaking for the past 47 or more years, and is well-known and respected locally.*

Druce Edmund Young

Private 37028, 7th Bn, Norfolk Regiment. Died 9 March 1918, age 19. Buried in Anzac Cemetery, Sailly-sur-la-Lys, Pas de Calais, France: Grave ref. III.A.7. Son of Herbert and Ellen Young, 31, Gordon Road, High Brooms.

There is a memorial plaque in St Matthew's Church, High Brooms, above that of **Charles Malpass**, also commemorated on the Southborough War Memorial, which tells that Druce Edmund Young was the youngest son of Herbert and Ellen Young. On it is written: *He died to make a righteous and just peace.*

From the Courier, 12 April 1918: *Private DE Young, the youngest son of Mr and Mrs H Young of High Brooms, was killed on March 9th by a shell. In a letter to his parents, his CO writes "Your son died like a soldier, and from this you can, if you will, extract no little comfort." Deceased was an old King Charles' School boy, and had been employed on the SE Railway as a clerk at Battle Station. Mrs Young has a daughter in France in the WAAC and also a son-in-law, 2nd Lieut W Oliver.*

Harry Young

Sergeant 23575, 128th Bty, Royal Field Artillery. Died 25 April 1917, age 39. Husband of Esther Goodrum (formerly Young) of 91, Albany Rd, Camberwell, London. Buried in Aubigny Communal Cemetery Extension, Pas de Calais, France: Grave ref. II.G. 1.

Sgt Young was born in Battersea, and enlisted in Maidstone. From the Tunbridge Wells Advertiser, 18 May 1917: *Mr and Mrs B Young, of 31, Great Brooms-road, High Brooms, have received information that their son, Sergt Harry Young, of the Royal Field Artillery, was killed in action on the 26th of April. He was 39 years, of age, and married, and went out with the first Expeditionary Force in August, 1914, going through the retreat from Mons. He had been in France from that time. Sergt Young was attached to the Field Artillery for 16 years, and previous to joining the Army kept a hairdresser's shop in Colebrook-road. He was an old St Peter's (Southborough) School boy, and has two brothers with the colours, one in the Inniskillens (wounded in France) and the other in the Worcesters.*

James Young

Corporal 457378, 60th Bn, Canadian Infantry. Died 18 December 1916, age 36. Buried in Netley Military Cemetery, Southampton, England: Grave ref. CE 1886. Son of Mr and Mrs Thomas Young, of 23, South View Rd, Tunbridge Wells, England; husband of Adelaide Young, of 464, Moreau St., Montreal East, Canada.

From the CWGC website: *Netley Military Cemetery was at the back of the Royal Victoria Military Hospital, and contains 636 First World War burials but only 35 from the Second World War; it includes 69 German graves dating from the First World War.*

Southborough War Memorial

Samuel Young

Private 5492, 7th Bn, Leinster Regiment. Died Wednesday 15 August 1917, age 37. Buried in Etaples Military Cemetery, Pas de Calais, France: Grave ref. XXII. P.17. Son of John and Elizabeth Young, of High Brooms; husband of S Young of 20, High Brooms Road, High Brooms.

From the Tunbridge Wells Advertiser, 17 August 1917: *Mrs S Young of 20, High Brooms-road, has received news that her husband, Pte S Young, of the Leinster Regiment, has been wounded. In a letter from the Chaplain expressing his sympathy, he says that her husband was wounded by a shell, and is in the 7th Canadian Hospital. A later message from Pte Young stated that he is well looked after and comfortable, and was looking forward to coming home. Pte Young joined the Royal Sussex Regiment 16 months ago, and was transferred to the Leinsters when he went to France in November. Previous to joining he worked for the High Brooms Brick Co.*

William Henry Young

Private 13550, 16th Bn, Royal Sussex Regiment. Died 6 November 1917, age 20. Buried in Beersheba War Cemetery, Israel: Grave ref. M. 27.

From the Courier, 7 December 1917: *Official news has been received by Mr and Mrs R Young, 2 Forge-road, that their youngest son, Private WH Young, Royal Sussex, was killed in action on November 6th, while serving with the Egyptian Expeditionary Force. He joined the Army early in 1916, and was sent to Egypt five months ago.*

www.firstworldwar.com/onthisday for 6 November 1917: *Asiatic and Egyptian Theatres: General Allenby captures Khuweilfesh, 11 miles north of Beersheba.*

The CWGC website includes the following background information: *By October 1917, General Allenby's force had been entrenched in front of a strong Turkish position along the Gaza-Beersheba road for some months, but they were now ready to launch an attack with Beersheba as its first objective. On 31 October, the attack was carried out by the XXth Corps (10th, 53rd, 60th and 74th Divisions) on the west, and the Desert Mounted Corps on the east. That evening the 4th Australian Light Horse Brigade charged over the Turkish trenches into the town.*

William Henry Young

Rifleman S/5619, 10th Bn, Rifle Brigade. Died Friday 30 November 1917, age 21. Commemorated on the Cambrai Memorial, Louverval, Nord, France: Panel 10 & 11. Son of Mrs Kate Pratt, of 21 Colebrook Road, High Brooms.

The Cambrai Memorial commemorates more than 7,000 servicemen of the United Kingdom and South Africa who died in the Battle of Cambrai in November and December 1917 and whose graves are not known.

Rifleman Young died on the same day as **Jabez Bridgland**, who is also commemorated on the Southborough War Memorial and the Cambrai Memorial.

From the Courier, 7 June 1918: *Mrs Pratt, of Colebrooke-road, has received notice that the identity disc of her son, Rifleman WH Young, has been received from Switzerland without any details. Rifleman Young has been missing since November, and the notice says: "We fear the above notice probably means he was killed in action, and his disc found and forwarded, or he has died of wounds in a German Hospital. Further enquiries are, however, being made, and it is hoped good news will be forthcoming." Any information will be greatly appreciated, Mrs Pratt, 21 Colebrooke-road.*

And from what must be an earlier edition of the Courier, undated: *Mrs Pratt, of Colebrooke-road, has received a postcard from her son, Lance-Corporal RE Young, that he arrived in England on the 3rd, wounded in the right arm. He, with his brother, joined at the commencement of the war.*

They shall grow not old
As we that are left grow old.
Age shall not weary them
Nor the years condemn.
At the going down of the sun
And in the morning
We will remember them.

Laurence Binyon (1869 - 1943)

Southborough War Memorial

Names Listed Alphabetically

ALCORN Henry (World War One)
ANDERSON Frederick (World War One)
ASSITER Alfred (World War One)
AVARD Herbert William (World War One)
AVIS Alfred T (World War One)
BAILEY Charles Thomas (World War One)
BAILEY George Henry (World War One)
BALL Harry (World War One)
BARDEN Stephen Frederick (World War One)
BARNETT HV (World War One)
BARTHOLOMEW Henry Frederick (World War One)
BARTON Charles William (World War Two)
BASNETT Frederick William (World War One)
BASSETT Robert (World War One)
BATEMAN James George (World War One)
BAXTER CE (World War One)
BEAN Denis Walter (World War Two)
BELLINGHAM Thomas Peter (World War One)
BETTS Sydney Wyborn (World War One)
BIRD H (World War One)
BONE Cecil John (World War One)
BONWICK Henry William (World War One)
BOORMAN Albert (World War One)
BOTTEN George (World War One)
BOTTEN Brian Anthony (World War Two)
BOWDEN Victor (World War One)
BRADY Bernard John Richard (World War Two)
BRIDGER Lewis Walter (World War One)
BRIDGLAND Jabez (World War One)
BRISTOW Richard John (World War One)
BROOMAN Leonard C (World War One)
BROTHERHOOD Arthur Archie (World War One)
BROTHERHOOD Ernest (World War One)
BROWN F (World War One)
BROWN George James (World War One)
BROWN Henry (World War One)
BRYANT Leonard Francis (World War Two)
BULLEN Albert Reginald (World War Two)
BUTLER Garnett Henry (World War One)
CARTER V (World War One)
CASS William Edward (World War One)
CHEESMAN Leonard (World War Two)
CHILTON J (World War One)
CHUTER W (World War One)
CLARKE Gordon Harvey (World War Two)
COLLINS Stephen William John (World War Two)
COOKE Edward Albert (World War One)

COOPER Edna Lily May (World War Two)
COOPER Edwin George (World War Two)
COPPINS P (COX Percy William) (World War One)
CROCKFORD William Alfred (World War One)
DAMPER Arthur George (World War One)
DAVIES William (World War One)
DEAN Joachim Charles (World War Two)
DEAN Thomas Joseph (World War One)
DELVES Charles Henry (World War One)
DIGGENS Alfred John (World War One)
DITON GH (World War One)
DIXON Sydney George (World War Two)
DOWDELL Harold Bernard (World War One)
DUNN John Edgar (World War One)
DUNN T (World War One)
DUVALL Percy (World War One)
EGGLESON Frederick Charles (World War Two)
ELDRIDGE Roland (World War One)
ELLIS Arthur Thomas (World War One)
ELLIS Edward Alexander (World War One)
ELLIS WJ (World War One)
EMERY Arthur (World War One)
EMMER Alan Douglas Mead (World War Two)
EVEREST William Henry (World War One)
EWEN WFM (World War One)
FENNER Harold (World War One)
FISHER Walter Harold (World War Two)
FLETCHER Harold Arthur (World War One)
FOLLINGTON Stanley Nelson (World War One)
FOUNTAIN John Henry (World War Two)
FRANCIS Reginald Albert Edward (World War Two)
FUNNELL Ernest William (World War Two)
FUNNELL Frank (World War One)
FUNNELL Frederick George (World War Two)
FUNNELL Stephen Alfred (World War One)
FURLEY George Frederic (World War One)
FURLEY Robert Basil (World War One)
GAINSFORD Albert Victor (World War One)
GAINSFORD George Arthur (World War Two)
GAMMON F T (World War One)
GIBBS C (World War One)
GILKS John Frederick (World War One)
GODSMARK Thomas (World War One)
GODSMARK William Henry (World War One)
GOLDBAUM Harry (World War One)
GOODSELL Harry Mark (World War One)
GOODWIN James Edward (World War One)
GROOMBRIDGE William (World War One)
GROVE Frederick James (World War Two)

Southborough War Memorial

HACKETT George Henry (World War One)
HANDLEY Thomas Frederick James (World War One)
HARROWING Hubert (World War One)
HARVEY Thomas John (World War One)
HAWKINS Clement (World War One)
HAYFIELD Allan Sydney (World War One)
HAYMON James George (World War One)
HAZELDEN J (World War One)
HEASMAN Jesse (World War One)
HEASMAN William (World War One)
HEMSLEY Frank Bernard (World War Two)
HOBBS Ernest Henry (World War One)
HODGES Albert E (World War One)
HOLLAMBY Edward (World War One)
HOOK George T (World War One)
HOUSER Earl (World War One)
HUGGETT George T (World War One)
HUNTER Albert Leslie (World War Two)
HUNTRODS Joseph Guy (World War Two)
HUTCHINGS Kenneth Lotherington (World War One)
ISTED H H (World War One)
JAMES William Alfred (World War One)
JENNER George Arthur (World War One)
JOHNSON Arthur Charles (World War One)
JOHNSON John Levi (World War One)
JONES Edwin Malcolm (World War One)
JONES George Alfred Prime (World War One)
JOYCE Robert Ernest (World War One)
KATES Frederick James (World War One)
KELLY J (World War One)
KIMBER Stanley Arthur (World War One)
KING Charles James (World War One)
KING Thomas (World War One)
KIRSTEN John Vincent (World War One)
LATTER Percy James (World War One)
LAWFORD Patrick John (World War One)
LEANEY George Thomas (World War One)
LEANEY Jesse (World War One)
LIPSCOMBE Harry Ernest (World War One)
LORNE Albert Edward (World War Two)
LUCK George (World War One)
LUXTON A William (World War One)
MAIER Oscar Frederick (World War One)
MALPASS Charles Edward (World War One)
MARTIN Frank (World War One)
MARTIN Thomas (World War One)
MARTIN Walter Charles (World War One)
McMILLAN William Roy (Korean War)
McPHEE Denis Livingstone (World War Two)

Southborough War Memorial

MILLER Albert (World War One)
MOON Charles (World War One)
MOON Christopher (World War One)
MOON Henry (World War One)
MOON John (World War One)
MOON Ronald William Albert (World War Two)
MOON Walter (World War One)
MOON William Alfred Henry (World War One)
MOORE HE (World War One)
MORLEY Thomas A (World War One)
MORRIS A (Philip Henry?) (World War One)
MUGRIDGE George Thomas (World War One)
MUGGRIDGE Henry (World War One)
NICKELLS George Henry (World War Two)
NISH James Hooper Dawson (World War One)
NYE Albert (World War One)
NYE Herbert William (World War One)
NYE Reginald (World War Two)
OLIVER Reginald Henry (World War Two)
PANKHURST Charles Henry (World War One)
PARKER Alfred Barnsdale (World War One)
PARKER Henry William (World War One)
PARROTT Wilfred James (World War One)
PEACOCK Ronald Herbert (World War Two)
PEARSON Caleb (World War One)
PEARSON Edward John (World War One)
PENFOLD George Henry (World War One)
PIERSON George (World War One)
PLAYER Harold John (World War One)
POINTER GH (World War One)
POWN Ben (World War One)
PROCTOR George Vincent (World War One)
PUCKETT Arthur Richard (World War Two)
RANDALL Henry Albert (World War One)
READ Bernard R (World War One)
READ P (World War One)
READ William Albert (World War One)
REEVE Henry (World War Two)
RICH AE (World War One)
RICHARDSON Albert Frederick (World War One)
RICHARDSON Henry George (World War Two)
RIGG Raymond Christopher (World War Two)
ROGERS John Richard (World War One)
ROLLINS William (World War One)
RUSSELL Ronald Edward (World War Two)
RYE William Ellingham (World War One)
SALE Philip (World War One)
SALOMONS David Reginald Hermon Philip Goldsmith Stern (World War One)
SALTER William Henry (World War One)

233

Southborough War Memorial

SAUNDERS Frederick William (World War One)
SAUNDERS Thomas Henry (World War One)
SAUNDERS William (2) (World War One)
SCOTT Charles James (World War One)
SCRACE James H (World War One)
SEALE Albert Victor (World War Two)
SELLINS Walter (World War One)
SHARP AJ (William James) (World War One)
SHARP EE (World War One)
SHOESMITH Cecil William (World War One)
SHORTER Frederick (World War One)
SMALLCOMBE Arthur (1916) (World War One)
SMALLCOMBE Arthur (1915) (World War One)
SMALLCOMBE Albert (World War One)
SMART Clarence Kitchener (World War Two)
SMART Edward Frederick Walter (World War Two)
SMITH Arthur (World War One)
SMITH George Edward (World War Two)
SMITH Sidney (World War One)
SOMERS Frederick (World War One)
SOTHERDEN Reginald Thomas (World War One)
STANDING David Ephraim (World War Two)
STANDING Edwin Percy (World War One)
STEVENS AE (World War One)
STILL Nelson John (World War One)
SUTCLIFFE Frank (World War Two)
SUTCLIFFE Thomas George (World War Two)
TAYLOR Nelson Colin (World War One)
TAYLOR Sidney Victor (World War One)
TEALE Walter W (World War One)
THORPE John (World War One)
THROWER Fred (World War One)
TILLEY Samuel John Curd (World War One)
TINDALL Frank (World War One)
TINGLEY William Jubilee (World War One)
TODMAN Harry (World War One)
TOMKIN Percy James Musgrave (World War One)
TURNER Frederick (World War One)
TURNER Frederick George (World War One)
TURNER Sidney (World War One)
TUTCHENER Frank Leonard (World War One)
UNDERHILL Mark Thomas (World War One)
VESEY James (World War One)
VINALL TA (World War One)
VOILE Maurice Carter (World War One)
WALKER Reginald (World War Two)
WALLOND Harry (World War One)
WHIBLEY R (World War One)
WICKENS Cyril (World War Two)

WILLIAMS Peter Howard (World War Two)
WILMSHURST Robert (World War One)
WINTER Walter William Richard (World War Two)
WOODLAND Harry (World War One)
WOODROW H (World War One)
WORSELL John (World War One)
YOUNG Druce Edmund (World War One)
YOUNG Harry (World War One)
YOUNG James (World War One)
YOUNG Samuel (World War One)
YOUNG William Henry (1) (World War One)
YOUNG William Henry (2) (World War One)

Southborough War Memorial

Names By Military Unit

ROYAL NAVY
HMS Aboukir ASSITER Alfred
HMS Arethusa SUTCLIFFE Thomas George
HMS Capel FOUNTAIN John Henry
HMS Firedrake NYE Reginald
HMS Hawke PENFOLD George Henry
HMS Jason PIERSON George
HMS Lord Clive FOLLINGTON Stanley Nelson
HMS Peewit WILLIAMS Peter Howard
HMS Rawalpindi BEAN Denis Walter
HMS Sherwood DIXON Sydney George
HMS Somali WINTER Walter William Richard
HM Trawler Cobbers, Royal Navy Patrol Service LORNE Albert Edward
Royal Naval Volunteer Reserve: Naval Division HARROWING Hubert (Howe Battalion), MOON John (Anson Battalion), MOORE HE (Howe Battalion)

MERCHANT NAVY
SS Poljames LUCK George

ARMY
Australian Army McMILLAN William Roy
Australian Infantry BELLINGHAM Thomas Peter, BOTTEN George, ELDRIDGE Roland, PARKER Alfred Barnsdale
Australian Machine Gun Corps BROTHERHOOD Arthur Archie
Bedfordshire Regiment ANDERSON Frederick
Border Regiment SCRACE James H, SELLINS Walter, SHORTER Frederick
Cameronians (Scottish Rifles) DUNN John Edgar
Canadian Field Artillery BAILEY Charles Thomas, MOON Henry, SMITH Arthur
Canadian Infantry FURLEY George Frederic (Alberta Regiment), GOODWIN James Edward (Quebec Regiment), HACKETT George Henry (Alberta Regiment), MOON Christopher (British Columbia Regiment), NISH James Hooper Dawson (Manitoba Regiment, 79th Cameron Highlanders), WALLOND Harry (Western Ontario Regiment), YOUNG James
Cheshire Regiment MARTIN Thomas
Coldstream Guards HAYMON James George
Dorsetshire Regiment McPHEE Denis Livingstone
Dragoon Guards BASNETT Frederick William, LATTER Percy James
Durham Light Infantry DAMPER Arthur George, MOON William Alfred Henry
East Kent Regiment (The Buffs) BIRD Henry, BOWDEN Victor, EVEREST William Henry, HAYFIELD Allan Sydney, JONES George Alfred Prime, PLAYER Harold John, SMALLCOMBE Albert, TOMKIN Percy James Musgrave, WOODLAND Harry
East Lancashire Regiment MARTIN Thomas
East Surrey Regiment SHARP EE

Southborough War Memorial

Essex Regiment BRIDGLAND Jabez, GILKS John Frederick, NYE Herbert William, RICHARDSON Albert Frederick
Gloucestershire Regiment BALL Harry
Grenadier Guards BUTLER Garnett Henry, PUCKETT Arthur Richard, STEVENS AE
Hampshire Regiment CHUTER W, JOHNSON Arthur Charles, THROWER Fred, WICKENS Cyril
Kent Cyclists TAYLOR Sidney Victor, TOMKIN Percy James Musgrave
King's Own Scottish Borderers BAILEY George Henry, DUNN John Edgar
King's Own Yorkshire Light Infantry MOON Walter
King's Royal Rifle Corps COPPINS P (COX Percy William), ISTED H H, LUXTON A William, TURNER Frederick George
Labour Corps TAYLOR Sidney Victor
Lancashire Fusiliers PROCTOR George Vincent
Leicestershire Regiment BROOMAN Leonard C
Leinster Regiment YOUNG Samuel
Liverpool Regiment (The King's) HUTCHINGS Kenneth Lotherington, VINALL TA
London Regiment CHILTON J **(The Rangers)**, MALPASS Charles Edward **(Artists' Rifles)**, MARTIN Walter Charles, SHARP AJ (William James), DOWDELL Harold Bernard **(Prince of Wales' Own Civil Service Rifles)**, FURLEY Robert Basil **(Prince of Wales' Own Civil Service Rifles)**, STILL Nelson John
Loyal North Lancashire Regiment BAXTER CE, BROWN Henry, DELVES Charles Henry, MILLER Albert
Machine Gun Corps EWEN WFM, MORRIS Philip Henry (See MORRIS A), POINTER GH, VOILE Maurice Carter **(Tank Corps)**
Manchester Regiment SAUNDERS Frederick William
Middlesex Regiment BONWICK Henry William, DITON GH, SELLINS Walter, SMALLCOMBE Arthur
Norfolk Regiment ELLIS Arthur Thomas, YOUNG Druce Edmund
North Staffordshire Regiment STANDING David Ephraim
Northumberland Fusiliers POWN Ben
Oxford & Bucks Light Infantry FURLEY Robert Basil
Parachute Regiment, AAC FRANCIS Reginald Albert Edward, FUNNELL Ernest William, MOON Ronald William Albert
Queen's Own (Royal West Kent) AVIS Alfred T, BARTHOLOMEW Henry Frederick, BARTON Charles William, BOTTEN Brian Anthony, BRIDGER Lewis Walter (given on War Memorial), BROTHERHOOD Ernest, BROWN George James, CHEESMAN Leonard, COLLINS Stephen William John, DEAN Thomas Joseph, DIGGENS Alfred John, DUVALL Percy, ELLIS Edward Alexander, ELLIS WJ, FUNNELL Frederick George, GAMMON F T, GOODSELL Harry Mark, GROVE Frederick James, HARVEY Thomas John, HAZELDEN J, HEMSLEY Frank Bernard, HOLLAMBY Edward, JOHNSON John Levi, JONES Edwin Malcolm, KELLY J, LAWFORD Patrick John, LEANEY George Thomas, LEANEY Jesse, MAIER Oscar Frederick, MALPASS Charles Edward, MARTIN Walter Charles, MILLER Albert, MOON Charles, MUGGRIDGE Henry, PEACOCK Ronald Herbert, PEARSON Caleb, PEARSON Edward John, REEVE Henry, ROLLINS William, SCRACE James H, SHARP AJ (William James), SHOESMITH Cecil William, SHORTER Frederick, SMART Clarence Kitchener, SMART Edward Frederick Walter, SUTCLIFFE Frank,

Southborough War Memorial

TILLEY Samuel John Curd, TINDALL Frank, UNDERHILL Mark Thomas, WOODROW H
Rifle Brigade KING Charles James, YOUNG William Henry (2)
Royal Army Service Corps BRIDGER Lewis Walter, CARTER V, CROCKFORD William Alfred, KATES Frederick James, PARKER Henry William, RANDALL Henry Albert, WALKER Reginald
Royal Artillery – see Royal Garrison Artillery
Searchlight Regiment BRYANT Leonard Francis
Royal Berkshire Regiment VESEY James
Royal Canadian Dragoons HOUSER Earl
Royal Dublin Fusiliers LAWFORD Patrick John
Royal Engineers BARDEN Stephen Frederick, BARNETT HV, BETTS Sydney Wyborn, BONE Cecil John, BRISTOW Richard John, DAMPER Arthur George, DAVIES William, FENNER Harold, FUNNELL Frank, GAINSFORD Albert Victor, GAINSFORD George Arthur, GODSMARK Thomas, GOLDBAUM Harry, GROOMBRIDGE William, HANDLEY Thomas Frederick James, HAWKINS Clement, HEASMAN Jesse, HEASMAN William, HOBBS Ernest Henry, HODGES Albert E, JAMES William Alfred, JENNER George Arthur, KIMBER Stanley Arthur, MOON William Alfred Henry, MORLEY Thomas A, NYE Albert, PARROTT Wilfred James, ROGERS John Richard, SALE Philip, SALOMONS David Reginald Hermon Philip Goldsmith Stern, SALTER William Henry, SAUNDERS Frederick William, SAUNDERS Thomas Henry, SAUNDERS William (2), SEALE Albert Victor, SMALLCOMBE Arthur (1915), SOMERS Frederick, TAYLOR Nelson Colin, THORPE John, TINGLEY William Jubilee, TODMAN Harry, TURNER Sidney, TUTCHENER Frank Leonard, UNDERHILL Mark Thomas
Royal Field Artillery BATEMAN James George, GODSMARK William Henry, WHIBLEY R, YOUNG Harry
Royal Fusiliers COOKE Edward Albert, EMERY Arthur, EMMER Alan Douglas Mead, GIBBS C, MARTIN Frank, MUGRIDGE George Thomas, READ Bernard R, READ P, RYE William Ellingham, SMALLCOMBE Arthur, STANDING Edwin Percy, WILMSHURST Robert
Royal Garrison Artillery LIPSCOMBE Harry Ernest, READ William Albert
Royal Irish Regiment DEAN Thomas Joseph
Royal Irish Rifles NYE Herbert William
Royal Ordnance Corps SCOTT Charles James
Royal Scots Fusiliers FLETCHER Harold Arthur, LEANEY Jesse
Royal Sussex Regiment AVARD Herbert William, BASSETT Robert, BOORMAN Albert, BROWN F, DUNN T, FUNNELL Stephen Alfred, HOOK George T, HUGGETT George T, KING Thomas, PANKHURST Charles Henry, RYE William Ellingham, SMITH Sidney, TEALE Walter W, WORSELL John, YOUNG Samuel, YOUNG William Henry (1)
Royal West Surrey Regiment (The Queen's) ALCORN Henry, JOYCE Robert Ernest
Scots Guards KIRSTEN John Vincent
Seaforth Highlanders SOTHERDEN Reginald Thomas
Somerset Light Infantry OLIVER Reginald Henry
South Lancashire Regiment FUNNELL Ernest William
South Staffordshire Regiment FUNNELL Ernest William, THORPE John

Suffolk Regiment NYE Herbert William, RICHARDSON Albert Frederick, TURNER Frederick
Tank Corps (See Machine Gun Corps) VOILE Maurice Carter
Yorkshire Regiment AVIS Alfred T, HUNTRODS Joseph Guy (Green Howards - 6th Yorkshire), PEARSON Caleb

ROYAL AIR FORCE (formerly Royal Flying Corps)
BRADY Bernard John Richard (615 Squadron), BULLEN Albert Reginald, CASS William Edward, CLARKE Gordon Harvey (620 Squadron), COOPER Edna Lily May (WAAF), COOPER Edwin George (35 Squadron), DEAN Joachim Charles (150 Squadron), EGGLESON Frederick Charles (463 Squadron), FISHER Walter Harold (277 Squadron), JONES George Alfred Prime (RFC), NICKELLS George Henry, RICHARDSON Henry George (280 Squadron), RIGG Raymond Christopher (281 Squadron), RUSSELL Ronald Edward (77 Squadron), SMITH George Edward (106 Squadron)

Southborough War Memorial

Names By Cemetery/Memorial
(Listed in order of country)

BELGIUM
Bard Cottage Cemetery, Ypres TURNER Sidney
Bedford House Cemetery, Ypres MARTIN Walter Charles
Berks Cemetery Extension, Comines-Warneton LEANEY Jesse **(Ploegsteert Memorial)**, STANDING Edwin Percy, VESEY James **(Ploegsteert Memorial)**
Brandhoek New Military Cemetery No3, Ypres ALCORN Henry
Dickebusch New Military Cemetery, Ypres TILLEY Samuel John Curd
Essex Farm Cemetery, Ypres KING Thomas
Klein Vierstraat British Cemetery, Heuvelland DITON GH
La Plus Douve Farm Cemetery, Comines-Warneton HOUSER Earl
Lijssenthoek Military Cemetery, Poperinge FURLEY George Frederic, GODSMARK William Henry, MOON Henry, VINALL TA
Menin Gate Memorial, Ypres BROTHERHOOD Arthur Archie, BROWN George James, DIGGENS Alfred John, GOODWIN James Edward, HOLLAMBY Edward, SCRACE James H, SMALLCOMBE Albert, STEVENS AE, WILMSHURST Robert, WOODROW H, WORSELL John
Menin Road South Military Cemetery, Ypres LIPSCOMBE HE
Oosttaverne Wood Cemetery, Heuvelland HACKETT George Henry
Poelcapelle British Cemetery, Langemark-Poelkapelle JONES Edwin Malcolm, MORRIS Philip Henry (see MORRIS A)
Potijze Chateau Wood Cemetery, Ypres CHUTER W, JOHNSON Arthur Charles
Railway Dugouts Burial Ground, Ypres KELLY J (possible)
Ramscappelle Road Military Cemetery, Nieuwpoort LUXTON A William
Tuileries British Cemetery, Ypres LEANEY George Thomas
Tyne Cot Cemetery, Zonnebeke DEAN Thomas Joseph
Tyne Cot Memorial, Zonnebeke BALL Harry, BONWICK Henry William, JOHNSON John Levi, KELLY J (possible), PROCTOR George Vincent, READ Bernard R, RICHARDSON Albert Frederick, ROLLINS William
Voormezeele Enclosures No 1 and No 2 KELLY J (possible)
Ypres Reservoir Cemetery TURNER Frederick George

BURMA
Taukkyan War Cemetery, outside Yangon (formerly Rangoon) PEACOCK Ronald Herbert

CANADA
Brantford (Greenwood) Cemetery, Ontario SMITH Arthur
St John's (Mount Carmel) Roman Catholic Cemetery, Newfoundland DIXON Sydney George

DENMARK
Svino Churchyard, Southern Zealand RUSSELL Ronald Edward

Southborough War Memorial

EGYPT
Alamein Memorial FISHER Walter Harold
Moascar War Cemetery COOPER Edna Lily May

ENGLAND
Chatham Naval Memorial, Kent ASSITER Alfred, NYE Reginald, PENFOLD George Henry, PIERSON George, SUTCLIFFE Thomas George
Haslar Royal Naval Cemetery, Hampshire FOLLINGTON Stanley Nelson
Lee-on-Solent Memorial, Hampshire WILLIAMS Peter Howard
Netley Military Cemetery, Southampton YOUNG James
Plymouth Naval Memorial, Devon BEAN Denis Walter
Portsmouth Naval Memorial, Hampshire FOUNTAIN John Henry, WINTER Walter William Richard
Runnymede Memorial, Surrey EGGLESON Frederick Charles, NICKELLS George Henry
Southborough Cemetery, Kent BAILEY Charles Thomas, BARDEN Stephen Frederick, BARNETT HV, BRADY Bernard John Richard, BROWN F, BROWN Henry, BRYANT Leonard Francis, BULLEN Albert Reginald, CASS William Edward, CHILTON J, CROCKFORD William Alfred, DEAN Joachim Charles, EMERY Arthur, EWEN WFM, GAINSFORD George Arthur, HOOK George T, HUNTER Albert Leslie, HUNTRODS Joseph Guy, JONES George Alfred Prime, LORNE Albert Edward, RANDALL Henry Albert, READ P, RICHARDSON Henry George, RIGG Raymond Christopher, SAUNDERS Thomas Henry, SCOTT Charles James, SMITH George Edward, TAYLOR Sidney Victor, WALKER Reginald
Tower Hill Memorial, London LUCK George
Tunbridge Wells Cemetery, Kent CARTER V

FRANCE
Albert Communal Cemetery Extension, Somme NISH James Hooper Dawson
Ancre British Cemetery, Beaumont-Hamel, Somme ISTED H H, MOORE HE
Anzac Cemetery, Sailly-sur-la-Lys, Pas de Calais YOUNG Druce Edmund
Arras Memorial, Pas de Calais COPPINS P (COX Percy William), MARTIN Frank, MUGRIDGE George Thomas, PLAYER Harold John, RYE William Ellingham, SELLINS
Walter, STILL Nelson John
Aubigny Communal Cemetery Extension, Pas de Calais YOUNG Harry
Bailleul Communal Cemetery (Nord), Nord HOBBS Ernest Henry
Bancourt British Cemetery, Pas de Calais GILKS John Frederick
Becourt Military Cemetery, Becordel-Becourt, Somme KING Charles James
Bernafay Wood British Cemetery, Somme PARKER Alfred Barnsdale
Boulogne Eastern Cemetery, Pas de Calais SALE Philip
Bouzincourt Ridge Cemetery, Albert HUGGETT George T
Cabaret-Rouge British Cemetery, Souchez, Pas de Calais TAYLOR Nelson Colin
Caestre Military Cemetery, Nord FLETCHER Harold Arthur
Cambrai Memorial, Louverval, Nord BRIDGLAND Jabez, YOUNG William Henry (2)
Caterpillar Valley Cemetery, Longueval, Somme HARVEY Thomas John

Southborough War Memorial

Caudry British Cemetery, Nord WHIBLEY R
Combles Communal Cemetery Extension, Somme KIRSTEN John Vincent
Couin New British Cemetery, Pas de Calais DELVES Charles Henry
Croix-du-Bac British Cemetery, Steenwerck, Nord MILLER Albert
Crucifix Corner Cemetery, Villers-Bretonneux, Somme BOTTEN George
Dantzig Alley British Cemetery, Mametz, Somme MAIER Oscar Frederick
Doullens Communal Cemetery Extension No 1, Somme POWN Ben, SMART Edward Frederick Walter
Dunkirk Memorial, Nord SMART Clarence Kitchener
Epehy Wood Cemetery, Epehy, Somme BOORMAN Albert
Etaples Military Cemetery, Pas de Calais READ William Albert, YOUNG Samuel
Euston Road Cemetery, Colincamps, Somme TEALE Walter W
Fouquescourt British Cemetery, Somme WALLOND Harry
Grevillers British Cemetery, Pas de Calais DUNN T
Grove Town Cemetery, Meaulte, Somme MORLEY Thomas A
Guards Grave, Villers Cotterets Forest, Aisne BUTLER Garnett Henry
Hebuterne Military Cemetery, Pas de Calais FURLEY Robert Basil
Heilly Station Cemetery, Mericourt l'Abbe, Somme ELDRIDGE Roland, MOON Walter
Hottot-les-Bagues War Cemetery, Calvados OLIVER Reginald Henry
Laventie Military Cemetery, La Gorgue, Nord BATEMAN James George
La Kreule Military Cemetery, Hazebrouck, Nord BAILEY George Henry
Le Grand Hasard Military Cemetery, Morbecque, Nord BARTON Charles William, FUNNELL Frederick George, HEMSLEY Frank Bernard, REEVE Henry, SUTCLIFFE Frank
Le Touret Memorial, Pas de Calais AVARD Herbert William, BASSETT Robert, HAYMON James George, JAMES William Alfred
Ligny - St Flochel British Cemetery, Averdoingt, Pas de Calais GAINSFORD Albert Victor
London Cemetery, Neuville-Vitasse, Pas de Calais TURNER Frederick
Loos Memorial, Pas de Calais ELLIS Edward Alexander, MUGGRIDGE Henry, TOMKIN Percy James Musgrave
Mailly Wood Cemetery, Somme BOWDEN Victor
Maroc British Cemetery, Nord MOON Christopher, PEARSON Edward John
Merville Communal Cemetery Extension, Nord DUVALL Percy
Montreuil-Aux-Lions British Cemetery, Aisne FUNNELL Stephen Alfred, PANKHURST Charles Henry
Porte-de-Paris Cemetery, Cambrai, Nord SOTHERDEN Reginald Thomas
Pozieres Memorial, Somme BASNETT Frederick William, DAMPER Arthur George, NYE Herbert William
Puchevillers British Cemetery, Somme HAYFIELD Allan Sydney
Putot-en-Auge Churchyard, Calvados FUNNELL Ernest William
Ranville War Cemetery, Calvados FRANCIS Reginald Albert Edward
Rookery British Cemetery, Heninel, Pas de Calais HAZELDEN J
Rumilly-en-Cambresis Communal Cemetery Extension, Nord MALPASS Charles Edward
Sequehart British Cemetery No. 1, Aisne POINTER GH
St Desir War Cemetery, Calvados CLARKE Gordon Harvey

St Patrick's Cemetery, Loos, Pas de Calais EVEREST William Henry (as DUNNINGS W)
St Sever Cemetery Extension, Rouen, Seine-Maritime LATTER Percy James, SCRACE JH
Stump Road Cemetery, Grandcourt, Somme WOODLAND Harry
Sunken Road Cemetery, Boisleux-St. Marc, Pas de Calais ANDERSON Frederick
Tannay British Cemetery, Thiennes, Nord ELLIS WJ
Thiepval Memorial, Somme BARTHOLOMEW Henry Frederick, BROTHERHOOD Ernest, COOKE Edward Albert, DOWDELL Harold Bernard (brother Ernest at Arras Memorial), HUTCHINGS Kenneth Lotherington, JOYCE Robert Ernest, SHARP AJ (William James), SHORTER Frederick, SMALLCOMBE Arthur, SMITH Sidney, TINDALL Frank
Tilloy British Cemetery, Tilloy-Les-Mofflaines, Pas de Calais JENNER George Arthur, VOILE Maurice Carter
Tranchee de Mecknes Cemetery, Aix-Noulette, Pas de Calais MOON John
Varennes Military Cemetery, Somme HARROWING Hubert
Vermelles British Cemetery, Pas de Calais AVIS Alfred T, PEARSON Caleb
Villers-Bretonneux Memorial, Somme BELLINGHAM Thomas Peter
Villers-Faucon Communal Cemetery Extension, Somme BAXTER CE
Villers Hill British Cemetery, Villers-Guislain, Nord DUNN John Edgar
Vis-En-Artois Memorial, Pas de Calais ELLIS Arthur Thomas, MOON William Alfred Henry
Warloy-Baillon Communal Cemetery Extension, Somme MOON Charles
Wavrans-sur-L'Aa Churchyard, Pas de Calais BRIDGER Lewis Walter

GERMANY
Berlin 1939-1945 War Cemetery, Charlottenburg, Berlin COOPER Edwin George, WICKENS Cyril

GREECE
Lahana Military Cemetery LAWFORD Patrick John, SHARP EE

HOLLAND
Groesbeek Memorial, Gelderland MOON Ronald William Albert

INDIA
Imphal War Cemetery SEALE Albert Victor

IRAQ
Baghdad (North Gate) War Cemetery GAMMON F T

Southborough War Memorial

ISRAEL
Beersheba War Cemetery GOODSELL Harry Mark, SHOESMITH Cecil William, YOUNG William Henry (1)
Jerusalem War Cemetery TINGLEY William Jubilee

ITALY
Caserta War Cemetery BOTTEN Brian Anthony
Cassino War Cemetery PUCKETT Arthur Richard
Catania War Cemetery, Sicily McPHEE Denis Livingstone
Faenza War Cemetery GROVE Frederick James
Giavera British Cemetery, Arcade THORPE John
Montecchio Precalcino Communal Cemetery Extension SAUNDERS Frederick William
Salerno War Cemetery EMMER Alan Douglas Mead
Syracuse War Cemetery, Sicily CHEESMAN Leonard
Taranto Town Cemetery Extension KATES Frederick James

SRI LANKA
Colombo (Kanatte) General Cemetery STANDING David Ephraim

TUNISIA
Medjez-El-Bab Memorial COLLINS Stephen William John

TURKEY
Helles Memorial BETTS Sydney Wyborn, BONE Cecil John, BRISTOW Richard John, DAVIES William, FENNER Harold, FUNNELL Frank, GODSMARK Thomas, GOLDBAUM Harry, GROOMBRIDGE William, HANDLEY Thomas Frederick James, HAWKINS Clement, HEASMAN Jesse, HEASMAN William, HODGES Albert E, KIMBER Stanley Arthur, MARTIN Thomas, NYE Albert, PARROTT Wilfred James (as PARROTT William), ROGERS John Richard, SALOMONS David Reginald Hermon Philip Goldsmith Stern, SALTER William Henry, SAUNDERS William (2), SMALLCOMBE Arthur (1915), SOMERS Frederick, THROWER Fred, TODMAN Harry, TUTCHENER Frank Leonard, UNDERHILL Mark Thomas

Southborough War Memorial

Names By Residence
(Living at or associated with)

BEXHILL-ON-SEA
Cambridge Rd 30 CARTER V

LONDON
Amity Grove, West Wimbledon 30 ASSITER Alfred

SOUTHBOROUGH & HIGH BROOMS
Auckland Road, High Brooms 75 GAINSFORD Albert Victor, **96** DAVIES William
Bayhall Road, High Brooms 18 PUCKETT Arthur Richard
Bedford Road BROOMAN Leonard C, **3** ALCORN Henry, **7** MORLEY Thomas A, **8** DUNN John Edgar, **15** MOON William Alfred Henry, **23** CHILTON J, **35** TODMAN Harry, **39** LIPSCOMBE HE, **41** BROWN George James
Bentham Hill - South Lodge SUTCLIFFE Frank & SUTCLIFFE Thomas George
Bounds Park - Gardener's Cottage AVARD Herbert William
Broomhill SALOMONS David Reginald Hermon Philip Goldsmith Stern**, The Gardens** GILKS John Frederick
Broomhill Park Road 12 CHEESMAN Leonard
Burlington Cottage GODSMARK William Henry
Castle Street 8 BRIDGER Lewis Walter, **11** ELLIS Arthur Thomas, **12** STANDING David Ephraim, **13** HAWKINS Clement and BONWICK Henry William
Charles Street BASSETT Robert **2** HAWKINS Clement (possibly) **5** TOMKIN Percy James Musgrave, **14** FRANCIS Reginald Albert Edward (possibly), **15** BARDEN Stephen Frederick, **34** GODSMARK Thomas; GODSMARK William Henry, **36** TILLEY Samuel John Curd, **38** NYE Albert, **42** HOLLAMBY Edward
Chestnut Avenue 24 McPHEE Denis Livingstone
Church Road – Rose Hill McMILLAN William Roy, **14** LAWFORD Patrick John
Colebrook Road HAYMON James George, **13** READ Bernard R, **21** YOUNG William Henry (2), **34** CHEESMAN Leonard, **35** BAXTER CE (likely), **67** HARVEY Thomas John
Crendon Park 5 BEAN Denis Walter
Denbigh Road, High Brooms 1 SAUNDERS William
Edward Street 2 HAZELDEN J (possibly), **12** CARTER V (possibly), **13** GOLDBAUM Harry, **23** SAUNDERS Frederick William, **27** SMALLCOMBE Arthur (1915) and SMALLCOMBE Albert, **28** POINTER GH, **56** TAYLOR Nelson Colin, **61** BRIDGLAND Jabez, **63** SHOESMITH Cecil William, **67** BOTTEN Brian Anthony, **99** BRADY Bernard John Richard
Elm Road 7 KATES Frederick James, **13** FOUNTAIN John Henry, **14** MARTIN Thomas, MARTIN Walter Charles
Forge Road 2 YOUNG William Henry (1), **3** GOODWIN James Edward, **5** ANDERSON Frederick, **6** GROOMBRIDGE William, **11a** ALCORN Henry, **14** PARKER Alfred Barnsdale, **16** EGGLESON Frederick Charles, SAUNDERS William, **21** ELDRIDGE Roland, **30** PARROTT Wilfred James, **31** BONE Cecil John, **51** FRANCIS Reginald Albert Edward (possibly)

Southborough War Memorial

Gordon Road, High Brooms 5 BOORMAN Albert **13** POWN Ben, **25** GODSMARK Thomas, GODSMARK William Henry, **29A** BONE Cecil John, **31** YOUNG Druce Edmund
Great Brooms Road, High Brooms 10 BROTHERHOOD Arthur Archie, BROTHERHOOD Ernest, **26** GOODSELL Harry Mark, **28** NYE Reginald, **29** BIRD Henry,
31 YOUNG Harry, **61** BAILEY Charles Thomas, **63** DIXON Sydney George
Grove House KIRSTEN John Vincent
High Brooms Road, High Brooms TINDALL Frank, **19** BIRD Henry, **20** YOUNG Samuel, **23** FENNER Harold, **36** PUCKETT Arthur Richard, **51** BAXTER CE, **68** HARVEY Thomas John, **80** BALL Harry, **90** BIRD Henry, **94** George Pierson
Highfield Road PEACOCK Ronald Herbert
Holden Corner 7 PENFOLD George Henry, **10** SALE Philip, **30** VINALL TA (possibly), **34** STANDING Edwin Percy
Holden Park Road READ William Albert, **12** BATEMAN James George, **42** PEARSON Caleb, PEARSON Edward John
Holden Place BARDEN Stephen Frederick, **1** GIBBS C (possibly)
Holden Road EVEREST William Henry, REEVE Henry **(Vulcan Cottages)**
London Road HACKETT George Henry, KATES Frederick James, PARKER Henry William, **Flying Dutchman** BASNETT Frederick William, **3 The Retreat** TUTCHENER Frank Leonard, **4 The Retreat** COPPINS P (COX Percy William), **17** NYE Herbert William, **63** DAMPER Arthur George, **65** WHIBLEY R **71** HUTCHINGS Kenneth Lotherington, **114** BUTLER Garnett Henry, DUNN John Edgar, **120** PEARSON Caleb, PEARSON Edward John, RUSSELL Ronald Edward, **121** MAIER Oscar Frederick, **126** VOILE Maurice Carter, **129** DUVALL Percy, **132** WOODLAND Harry, **147** FUNNELL Frank
Manor Road DIXON Sydney George, **25** BRYANT Leonard Francis
Meadow Road BARDEN Stephen Frederick, **4** HUGGETT George T (possibly), **5** CROCKFORD William Alfred, **6** HUGGETT George T, **9** SMALLCOMBE Arthur, **10** BRISTOW Richard John, **11** BETTS Sydney Wyborn, **12** MILLER Albert, **19** HOBBS Ernest Henry, **22** and **46** EMERY Arthur, **23** TURNER Frederick George, **25** GAINSFORD George Arthur, **36** VESEY James, **38** WILMSHURST Robert
Modest Corner FOLLINGTON Stanley Nelson, SHORTER Frederick
Napier Road 11 ELLIS Arthur Thomas
Nightingale Farm Cottages MUGGRIDGE Henry
North Farm Road, High Brooms 3 KING Thomas, **4** BARNETT HV, **20** SMITH Sidney, **35 (Leybourne)** MALPASS Charles Edward
Norton Road 17 DIGGENS Alfred John
Nursery Road, High Brooms 7 TAYLOR Sidney Victor, **19** HANDLEY Thomas Frederick James, **26** DEAN Joachim Charles, **46** BROWN F, **47** BARTHOLOMEW Henry Frederick, **58** HAYMAN George, STEVENS AE, **63** SMART Clarence Kitchener, SMART Edward Frederick Walter, **65** HEMSLEY Frank Bernard
Park Road 4 RIGG Raymond Christopher, **32** FOLLINGTON Stanley Nelson
Pennington Road HUNTRODS Joseph Guy, **8** HOUSER Earl, **44** FURLEY George Frederic, FURLEY Robert Basil, **46 (Ampthill)** JONES George Alfred Prime, **58** TILLEY Samuel John Curd, **Ivy House Farm** VOILE Maurice Carter
Powder Mill Lane: Birling Farm LEANEY Jesse, LUCK George, **Birling Cottage, Old Forge Farm** PEACOCK Ronald Herbert, **17** GROVE Frederick James (possibly)

Prospect Road LUXTON A William, **21** HAYFIELD Allan Sydney, **46** TEALE Walter W, **60** CASS William Edward
Sheffield Road 13 TILLEY Samuel John Curd
Silverdale Road, High Brooms 11 SELLINS Walter, **64** WORSELL John, **81** BETTS Sydney Wyborn
South View Road, High Brooms 2 BELLINGHAM Thomas Peter, **23** YOUNG James, **26** MUGRIDGE George Thomas, **32** KIMBER Stanley Arthur, **40** TURNER Frederick, **51** BELLINGHAM Thomas Peter, **55** BROWN F
Speldhurst Road THROWER Fred, **The Forge** BOTTEN George, **4** JAMES William Alfred (possibly), **7** KING Charles James, **15** PLAYER Harold John, **19** ROGERS John Richard, **21** LATTER Percy James, SMITH George Edward, **25** SUTCLIFFE Frank, SUTCLIFFE Thomas George, **30** and **33** PANKHURST Charles Henry
Springfield Road 11 MOON Christopher, **18** FUNNELL Stephen Alfred, **29** BRIDGLAND Jabez, WINTER Walter William Richard, **39** TINGLEY William Jubilee, **40** RICHARDSON Henry George, **42** BARTON Charles William, **46** WINTER Walter William Richard, **47** ELLIS Edward Alexander, **54** HEASMAN Jesse, HEASMAN William, TINGLEY William Jubilee, **55** DEAN Thomas Joseph, **57** and **62** EWEN WFM, **59** DUVALL Percy, **65** SOMERS Frederick, **67** WHIBLEY R, **73** BROWN Henry, **86** or **88** EVEREST William Henry, **96** HOOK George T
Stewart Road, High Brooms DELVES Charles Henry, **7** DIXON Sydney George, **9** SALTER William Henry, **15** SCRACE James H
Taylor Street 6 RICHARDSON Albert Frederick, **7** BOTTEN George, **11** AVIS Alfred T, JOHNSON Arthur Charles, **12** TURNER Sidney, **17** JOYCE Robert Ernest, **20** HUNTER Albert Leslie, **28** DUVALL Percy, **36** FLETCHER Harold Arthur, **38** RICHARDSON Albert Frederick, **80** WICKENS Cyril, **82** JENNER George Arthur
The Common SOTHERDEN Reginald Thomas
Vale Road 29 HARROWING Hubert, **33** RYE William Ellingham, **35** OLIVER Reginald Henry
Vauxhall Lane - Honnington Cottages GAINSFORD Albert Victor
Victoria Road 2 TINGLEY William Jubilee
Western Road 13 MOON Charles, MOON Henry, MOON John, MOON Walter, **15** COLLINS Stephen William John, **19** HAWKINS Clement, **23** THORPE John, **24** UNDERHILL Mark Thomas
Wolseley Road, High Brooms SHARP AJ (William James), **1** BONE Cecil John, **8** SHARP EE, **19** DUNN T, JOHNSON John Levi, **22** FUNNELL Ernest William, FUNNELL Frederick George, **26** COOPER Edna Lily May, COOPER Edwin George, **33** SCOTT Charles James, **35** SAUNDERS Thomas Henry
Yew Tree Road 21 CLARKE Gordon Harvey **52** BULLEN Albert **71** EMMER Alan Douglas Mead

SPELDHURST
Barden Road POINTER GH
Northfield Road COOKE Edward Albert

TONBRIDGE
High Street 10 FISHER Walter Harold

Southborough War Memorial

TUNBRIDGE WELLS
Albion Road 81 ISTED H H (possibly)
Albion Square 5 KELLY J (poss)
Camden Road 111 JONES Edwin Malcolm
Highams Road 52 LEANEY George Thomas

Names Listed Chronologically By Death Date

4 September 1914 SOTHERDEN Reginald Thomas
10 September 1914 FUNNELL Stephen Alfred, PANKHURST Charles Henry
20 September 1914 BUTLER Garnett Henry
22 September 1914 ASSITER Alfred
15 October 1914 PENFOLD George Henry
30 October 1914 WORSELL John
1 November 1914 STEVENS AE
25 December 1914 BRIDGER Lewis Walter

1 January 1915 BROWN George James
16 February 1915 SMALLCOMBE Albert
22 February 1915 LEANEY George Thomas
6 March 1915 SMITH Arthur
22 March 1915 BARNETT HV
22 April 1915 HOBBS Ernest Henry
5 May 1915 HOLLAMBY Edward
9 May 1915 AVARD Herbert William, BASSETT Robert, JAMES William Alfred
20 May 1915 HAYMON James George
19 July 1915 JONES Edwin Malcolm
28 July 1915 SAUNDERS Thomas Henry
6 August 1915 THROWER Fred
9 August 1915 MARTIN Thomas
23 September 1915 HOUSER Earl
25 September 1915 VESEY James
26 September 1915 ELLIS Edward Alexander, MUGGRIDGE Henry
21 October 1915 GODSMARK William Henry
28 October 1915 BETTS Sydney Wyborn, BONE Cecil John, BRISTOW Richard John, FENNER Harold, FUNNELL Frank, GODSMARK Thomas, GOLDBAUM Harry, GROOMBRIDGE William, HANDLEY Thomas Frederick James, HEASMAN Jesse, HEASMAN William, HODGES Albert E, KIMBER Stanley Arthur, NYE Albert, PARROTT Wilfred James, ROGERS John Richard, SALOMONS David Reginald Hermon Philip Goldsmith Stern, SALTER William Henry, SAUNDERS William (2), SMALLCOMBE Arthur (1915), SOMERS Frederick, TODMAN Harry, TUTCHENER Frank Leonard, UNDERHILL Mark Thomas

25 January 1916 FURLEY Robert Basil
18 April 1916 KING Charles James
28 May 1916 JONES George Alfred Prime
2 June 1916 HACKETT George Henry, MOON Henry
4 July 1916 MOON Walter
9 July 1916 STANDING Edwin Percy
13 July 1916 BARTHOLOMEW Henry Frederick
16 July 1916 BATEMAN James George

Southborough War Memorial

21 July 1916 HARVEY Thomas John
22 July 1916 COOKE Edward Albert, TINDALL Frank
26 July 1916 BELLINGHAM Thomas Peter
9 August 1916 CHUTER W, JOHNSON Arthur Charles
14 August 1916 MOON Charles, MOON John
20 August 1916 SMITH Sidney
31 August 1916 MAIER Oscar Frederick
3 September 1916 HUTCHINGS Kenneth Lotherington, ISTED H H
15 September 1916 DOWDELL Harold Bernard
16 September 1916 NISH James Hooper Dawson, SMALLCOMBE Arthur
27 September 1916 SHORTER Frederick
1 October 1916 SHARP AJ (William James)
6 October 1916 HAYFIELD Allan Sydney, LAWFORD Patrick John
7 October 1916 BROTHERHOOD Ernest
12 October 1916 GILKS John Frederick, SCOTT Charles James, TEALE Walter W
22 October 1916 AVIS Alfred T
5 November 1916 PARKER Alfred Barnsdale
11 November 1916 ELDRIDGE Roland
13 November 1916 MOORE HE
14 November 1916 HARROWING Hubert
18 November 1916 WOODLAND Harry
24 November 1916 PEARSON Caleb
18 December 1916 YOUNG James

14 January 1917 KIRSTEN John Vincent
27 February 1917 JOYCE Robert Ernest
5 March 1917 MORLEY Thomas A
29 March 1917 SELLINS Walter
30 March 1917 TOMKIN Percy James Musgrave
3 April 1917 PIERSON George
9 April 1917 RYE William Ellingham, VOILE Maurice Carter
12 April 1917 TAYLOR Nelson Colin
13 April 1917 PEARSON Edward John
15 April 1917 EVEREST William Henry, JENNER George Arthur
23 April 1917 MARTIN Frank
25 April 1917 YOUNG Harry
3 May 1917 COPPINS P (COX Percy William), PLAYER Harold John
16 May 1917 KELLY J (possible)
27 May 1917 HAZELDEN J
4 June 1917 CASS William Edward
24 June 1917 DIGGENS Alfred John
27 June 1917 WILMSHURST Robert
6 July 1917 MARTIN Walter Charles
7 July 1917 LUXTON A William
8 July 1917 TILLEY Samuel John Curd
10 July 1917 TURNER Sidney
24 July 1917 KING Thomas
31 July 1917 WOODROW H

Southborough War Memorial

2 **August 1917** VINALL TA
4 **August 1917** DEAN Thomas Joseph
11 **August 1917** DITON GH
12 **August 1917** MOON Christopher
13 **August 1917** SCRACE James H
15 **August 1917** YOUNG Samuel
19 **August 1917** ALCORN Henry
6 **September 1917** PROCTOR George Vincent
21 **September 1917** KELLY J (possible), TURNER Frederick George
4 **October 1917** BROTHERHOOD Arthur Archie
9 **October 1917** MORRIS Philip Henry (See MORRIS A)
10 **October 1917** RICHARDSON Albert Frederick
12 **October 1917** JOHNSON John Levi
22 **October 1917** BONWICK Henry William
26 **October 1917** ROLLINS William
31 **October 1917** LIPSCOMBE HE
2 **November 1917** SALE Philip
4 **November 1917** GOODSELL Harry Mark, SHOESMITH Cecil William
6 **November 1917** YOUNG William Henry (1)
8 **November 1917** FURLEY George Frederic
20 **November 1917** BAXTER CE
30 **November 1917** BRIDGLAND Jabez, YOUNG William Henry (2)
11 **December 1917** THORPE John
25 **December 1917** SHARP EE

9 **March 1918** YOUNG Druce Edmund
10 **March 1918** DUVALL Percy
23 **March 1918** NYE Herbert William, POWN Ben
26 **March 1918** STILL Nelson John
27 **March 1918** DAMPER Arthur George
28 **March 1918** TURNER Frederick
30 **March 1918** BASNETT Frederick William
2 **April 1918** TINGLEY William Jubilee
3 **April 1918** MUGRIDGE George Thomas
5 **April 1918** HUGGETT George T
10 **April 1918** MILLER Albert
12 **April 1918** LEANEY Jesse
14 **April 1918** BALL Harry
18 **April 1918** LATTER Percy James
23 **April 1918** SAUNDERS Frederick William
3 **May 1918** BOTTEN George
16 **May 1918** BOWDEN Victor
1 **June 1918** ELLIS WJ
8 **June 1918** DELVES Charles Henry
23 **June 1918** BROWN F
15 **July 1918** READ Bernard R
18 **July 1918** GAINSFORD Albert Victor
19 **July 1918** FLETCHER Harold Arthur

Southborough War Memorial

26 July 1918 BAILEY George Henry
17 August 1918 WALLOND Harry
2 September 1918 MOON William Alfred Henry
8 September 1918 CHILTON J
18 September 1918 BOORMAN Albert
24 September 1918 SCRACE JH
1 October 1918 ANDERSON Frederick
2 October 1918 LUCK George
3 October 1918 DUNN John Edgar, KATES Frederick James, POINTER GH
8 October 1918 ELLIS Arthur Thomas, MALPASS Charles Edward
17 October 1918 FOLLINGTON Stanley Nelson
28 October 1918 TAYLOR Sidney Victor
30 October 1918 READ William Albert
31 October 1918 BAILEY Charles Thomas
1 November 1918 CARTER V
11 November 1918 READ P
14 November 1918 DUNN T
22 November 1918 WHIBLEY R
20 December 1918 GAMMON F T

19 February 1919 RANDALL Henry Albert
22 February 1919 EWEN WFM
4 April 1919 CROCKFORD William Alfred
23 July 1919 BROWN Henry
27 December 1919 HOOK George T

20 May 1920 EMERY Arthur

26 June 1933 GAINSFORD GA

23 November 1939 BEAN Denis Walter

20 May 1940 SMART Edward Frederick Walter
26 May 1940 FUNNELL Frederick George, REEVE Henry
28 May 1940 BARTON Charles William, HEMSLEY Frank Bernard, SUTCLIFFE Frank
31 May 1940 SMART Clarence Kitchener
14 August 1940 BRADY Bernard John Richard
10 December 1940 BRYANT Leonard Francis

3 March 1941 LORNE Albert Edward
5 July 1941 NICKELLS George Henry

18 April 1942 WALKER Reginald
31 May 1942 DEAN Joachim Charles
21 July 1942 SMITH George Edward
24 September 1942 WINTER Walter William Richard
24 October 1942 BULLEN Albert Reginald
17 November 1942 COLLINS Stephen William John
18 November 1942 SUTCLIFFE Thomas George
28 November 1942 STANDING David Ephraim
12 December 1942 DIXON Sydney George
17 December 1942 NYE Reginald

26 April 1943 FISHER Walter Harold
19 July 1943 McPHEE Denis Livingstone
12 August 1943 CHEESMAN Leonard, CLARKE Gordon Harvey
24 August 1943 COOPER Edwin George
22 September 1943 EMMER Alan Douglas Mead
13 November 1943 RICHARDSON Henry George

19 March 1944 PEACOCK Ronald Herbert
30 May 1944 PUCKETT Arthur Richard
6 June 1944 FRANCIS Reginald Albert Edward
1 August 1944 OLIVER Reginald Henry
12 August 1944 BOTTEN Brian Anthony
19 August 1944 FUNNELL Ernest William
29 August 1944 COOPER Edna Lily May
20 September 1944 MOON Ronald William Albert
26 December 1944 FOUNTAIN John Henry

22 January 1945 HUNTRODS Joseph Guy
15 February 1945 RUSSELL Ronald Edward
21 March 1945 WICKENS Cyril
11 April 1945 RIGG Raymond Christopher
13 April 1945 GROVE Frederick James
30 July 1945 SEALE Albert Victor
22 November 1945 WILLIAMS Peter Howard

19 July 1946 HUNTER Albert Leslie

22 June 1953 McMILLAN William Roy

Southborough War Memorial

Locations of Cemeteries/Memorials
(with kind permission of the Commonwealth War Graves Commission, details from their website)

BELGIUM

Bard Cottage Cemetery, Ypres On the Diksmuidseweg road (N369) in the direction of Boezinge. From Ieper station turn left into M.Fochlaan and go to the roundabout, turn right and go to the next roundabout. Here turn left and drive to the next roundabout, where you should turn right into Oude Veurnestraat. Take the second turning on the left, which is the Diksmuidseweg and carry on under the motorway bridge and the cemetery is another 300 metres on the left hand side of the road. NB Bard Cottage Cemetery is the first cemetery on the left, the second being Talana Farm Cemetery.

Bedford House Cemetery, Ypres 2.5 Km south of Ieper town centre; on the Rijselseweg (N336), the road connecting Ieper to Armentieres. From Ieper town centre the Rijselsestraat runs from the market square, through the Lille Gate (Rijselpoort) and directly over the crossroads with the Ieper ring road. The road name then changes to the Rijselseweg. The cemetery itself is located 2 Km after this crossroads on the left hand side of the Rijselseweg.

Berks Cemetery Extension, Comines-Warneton, Hainaut 12.5 kilometres south of Ieper town centre on the N365 leading from Ieper to Mesen, Ploegsteert and on to Armentieres. From Ieper town centre the Rijselsestraat runs from the market square, through the Lille Gate (Rijselpoort) and directly over the crossroads with the Ieper ring road. The road name then changes to the Rijselseweg (N336). 3.5 kilometres along the N336 lies a fork junction with the N365. The N365 which forms the right hand fork leads to the town of Mesen. The cemetery lies 3 kilometres beyond Mesen on the right hand side of the N365 and opposite Hyde Park Corner Royal Berks Cemetery.

Brandhoek New Military Cemetery No3, Ypres 6.5 km west of Ieper town centre, on the Zevekotestraat, a road leading from the N308 connecting Ieper to Poperinge. From Ieper town centre the Poperingseweg (N308), is reached via Elverdingsestraat then directly over two small roundabouts in the J. Capronstraat. The Poperingseweg is a continuation of the J. Capronstraat and begins after a prominent railway level crossing. 6 km along the N308, after passing the village of Vlamertinge and just beyond the church in the hamlet of Brandhoek lies the left hand turning onto the Grote Branderstraat. After crossing the N38 Westhoekweg, the first right hand turning leads onto the Zevekotestraat. The cemetery is located 300 metres along the Zevekotestraat on the left hand side of the road, beyond the N38 dual carriageway, which it is necessary to cross.

Dickebusch New Military Cemetery, Ypres From Ieper town centre the Dikkebusseweg (N375), is reached via Elverdingsestraat, straight over a roundabout onto J.Capronstraat (for 30 metres), then left along M.Fochlaan. Immediately after the train station, the first right hand turning is the Dikkebusseweg. On reaching the village of Dikkebus, the cemetery is located on the Kerkstraat, which is a small street turning left off the Dikkebusseweg. 200 metres along this street, and just beyond the village church, lies the cemetery.

Essex Farm Cemetery, Ypres Boezinge is a village in the province of West Flanders, north of Ieper on the Diksmuidseweg road (N369). From the station turn left into M.Fochlaan and go to the roundabout, then turn right and continue to the next roundabout. Turn left and drive to the next roundabout and then turn right into Oude Veurnestraat. At the roundabout turn left onto the Diksmuidseweg, and follow the road under the motorway bridge; the Cemetery will be found on the right hand side of the road.

Klein Vierstraat British Cemetery, Heuvelland 6 km south west of Ieper town centre, on the Molenstraat, a road branching from the Kemmelseweg (joining Ieper to Kemmel N331). From Ieper town centre the Kemmelseweg is reached via the Rijselsestraat, through the Lille Gate (Rijselpoort), and straight on towards Armentieres (N365). 900 metres after the crossroads is the right hand turning onto the Kemmelseweg (made prominent by a railway level crossing). 5 km along the Kemmelseweg lies the right hand turning onto Poperingestraat. There are four cemeteries located along this road - all well signposted. 1km along the Poperingestraat lies Kemmel No 1 French Cemetery. Immediately to the left of this cemetery is a road called Molenstraat. Klein Vierstraat British Cemetery is located 30 metres along the Molenstraat on the right hand side of the road.

La Plus Douve Farm Cemetery, Comines-Warneton, Hainaut 10.5 Kms south of Ieper town centre on a road leading from the Rijselseweg (N365) which connects Ieper to Wijtschate, and on to Armentieres. From Ieper town centre the Rijselsestraat runs from the market square, through the Lille Gate (Rijselpoort) and directly over the crossroads with the Ieper ring road. The road name then changes to the Rijselseweg. On reaching the town of Mesen the first right hand turning leads onto the Nieuwkerkestraat (N314). 2 Kms along the Nieuwkerkestraat lies the left hand turning onto Plus Douve. The cemetery lies 600 metres along Plus Douve on the right hand side of the track. Visitors should note there is an 80 metre grassed access path which is unsuitable for vehicles.

Lijssenthoek Military Cemetery, Poperinge 12 Kms west of Ieper town centre, on the Boescheepseweg, a road leading from the N308 connecting Ieper to Poperinge. From Ieper town centre the Poperingseweg (N308) is reached via Elverdingsestraat, then over two small roundabouts in the J. Capronstraat. The Poperingseweg is a continuation of the J. Capronstraat and begins after a prominent railway level crossing. On reaching Poperinge, the N308 joins the left hand turning onto the R33, Poperinge ring road. The R33 ring continues to the left hand junction with the N38 Frans-Vlaanderenweg. 800 metres along the N38 lies the left hand turning onto Lenestraat. The next immediate right hand turning leads onto Boescheepseweg. The cemetery itself is located 2 Kms along Boescheepseweg on the right hand side of the road.

Menin Gate Memorial, Ypres Situated at the eastern side of the town on the road to Menin (Menen) and Courtrai (Kortrijk). Each night at 8 pm the traffic is stopped at the Menin Gate while members of the local Fire Brigade sound the Last Post in the roadway under the Memorial's arches.

Menin Road South Military Cemetery, Ypres 2 Kms east of Ieper town centre, on the Meenseweg (N8), connecting Ieper to Menen. From Ieper town centre the Meenseweg is located via Torhoutstraat and right onto Basculestraat. Basculestraat ends at a main crossroads, directly over which begins the Meenseweg. The Cemetery is located 800 metres along the Meenseweg on the right hand side of the road.

Oosttaverne Wood Cemetery, Heuvelland 6 Kms south of Ieper town centre on the Rijselseweg N336 connecting Ieper to Lille. From Ieper town centre the Rijselsestraat runs from the market square, through the Lille Gate (Rijselpoort) and directly over the crossroads with the Ieper ring road. The road name then changes to the Rijselseweg. 3 Kms along the Rijselseweg the road forks with the N365. The N336 is the left hand fork towards Lille. The cemetery is located 2 Kms after this left hand fork on the right hand side of the road.

Poelcapelle British Cemetery, Langemark-Poelkapelle 10 Kms north-east of Ieper town centre on the Brugseweg (N313), a road connecting Ieper to Brugge. Two streets connect Ieper town centre onto the Brugseweg; Torhoutstraat leads from the market square onto the Kalfvaartstraat. At the end of Kalfvaartstraat is a large junction on which Brugseweg is the first right hand turning. The cemetery itself lies 10 Kms along the Brugseweg on the right hand side of the road after passing through the village of Poelkapelle.

Potijze Chateau Wood Cemetery, Ypres North-East of Ieper. From the station turn left and drive along M.Fochlaan to the roundabout, turn right and go to the next roundabout. Here turn left into M.Haiglaan and drive to the next roundabout. Here turn right into Oude Veurnestraat, this then changes into Diksmuidseweg and Brugseweg. Drive along this road and continue straight over the traffic lights to the end of the road. At the T junction turn left (still Brugseweg) and continue along this road (the N313) to the village of Sint Jan. At the crossroads in the village turn right onto the N345 (Potijzestraat), follow along to the next crossroads and turn left into Zonnebeekseweg. The cemetery is located on the left hand side approx 50 metres after the crossroads.

Railway Dugouts Burial Ground, Ypres 2 Kms south-east of Ieper town centre, on the Komenseweg, a road connecting Ieper to Komen (N336). From Ieper town centre the Komenseweg is located via the Rijselsestraat, through the Rijselpoort (Lille Gate) and crossing the Ieper ring road, towards Armentieres and Lille. The road name then changes to Rijselseweg. 1 Km along the Rijselseweg lies the left hand turning onto Komenseweg. The cemetery itself is located 1.2 Kms along the Komenseweg on the right hand side of the road.

Ramscappelle Road Military Cemetery, Nieuwpoort 2 Kms east of Nieuwpoort on the N367, which leads from Nieuwpoort to Sint Joris. From Nieuwpoort town centre the Willem Deroolaan leads for 500 metres onto the N367 Brugsesteenweg. The cemetery lies 1 Km along the N367 on the junction with the N356 Ramskapellestraat.

Tuileries British Cemetery, Ypres 3 Kms east of Ieper town centre, on the Maaldestedestraat, a road leading from the Meenseweg (N8), connecting Ieper to Menen. From Ieper town centre the Meenseweg is located via Torhoutstraat and right onto Basculestraat. Basculestraat ends at a main cross roads, directly over which begins the Meenseweg. 1.5 Kms along the Meenseweg lies the right hand turning onto the Maaldestedestraat. The cemetery itself is located 1.2 Kms along the Maaldestedestraat on the right hand side of the road.

Tyne Cot Cemetery, Zonnebeke 9 Kms north-east of Ieper town centre, on the Tynecotstraat, a road leading from the Zonnebeekseweg (N332).

Tyne Cot Memorial, Zonnebeke Located in Tyne Cot Cemetery, see above.

Ypres Reservoir Cemetery North-West of Ieper. From the station turn left and drive along M.Fochlaan to the roundabout, turn right and go to the next roundabout. Here

Southborough War Memorial

turn left into M.Haiglaan and continue for 300 metres and then turn right into M.Plumerlaan. The cemetery is on the right hand side, approximately 200 metres along the road.

BURMA
Taukkyan War Cemetery, outside **Yangon (formerly Rangoon)** Adjoins the village of Taukkyan which is about 35 kilometres north of Yangon (formerly Rangoon). It is on PY1 road (formerly Prome road), about 15 kilometres from the airport and can be easily seen from the road.

CANADA
Brantford (Greenwood) Cemetery, Ontario This cemetery is bordered by Dundas Street on the north side, Clarence Street on the east side, West Street on the west side and the Canadian National Railway tracks on the south side. The main entrance to the cemetery is from West Street, opposite Buffalo Street, also, there is an entrance off Clarence Street.

St John's (Mount Carmel) Roman Catholic Cemetery, Newfoundland At the foot of Longs Hill.

DENMARK
Svino Churchyard, Southern Zealand Svino is a small village in Southern Zealand, overlooking Dybso Fjord, some 90 kilometres south-south-west of Copenhagen. The Commonwealth Plot is in an extension of the churchyard, to the north of the church.

EGYPT
Alamein Memorial Forms the entrance to the El Alamein War Cemetery. Alamein is a village, bypassed by the main coast road, approximately 130 kilometres west of Alexandria on the road to Mersa Matruh. The first Commission road direction sign is located just beyond the Alamein police checkpoint and all cemetery visitors should turn off from the main road onto the parallel old coast road. The cemetery lies off the road beyond the ridge, and road direction signs are in place approximately 25 metres before the low metal gates and stone wing walls which are situated centrally at the road edge at the head of the access path into the cemetery.

Moascar War Cemetery Just off the main Ismailia-Cairo road, 10 kilometres by road from Ismailia. The cemetery is contained within an army camp, 3 kilometres along Treaty Road, and the cemetery is open from 07.30 to 14.30 Saturday to Thursday, excluding Public Holidays.

ENGLAND
Chatham Naval Memorial From the Brompton Barracks Chatham - At the traffic signals turn right onto Globe Lane - A231 (signposted 'Historic Dockyards'). Keep in left hand lane then turn left onto Dock Road (signposted Gillingham). At roundabout take the 2nd exit onto Wood Street - A231 (signposted Gillingham). Turn Right on Mansion Row (The memorial is signposted from here), then 1st left on Sally Port Gardens and finally 1st right on King's Bastion. Follow road through the housing estate, the car park to the memorial is at the end of this road. The Memorial overlooks the

town of Chatham and is approached by a steep path from the Town Hall Gardens. As a result of constant vandalism at the Memorial, the Commonwealth War Graves Commission has had to arrange for it to be regularly patrolled and public access limited to the period from 08.30 to 17.00. Should for any reason the Memorial be closed during the stated hours, please telephone the Guard Room at Brompton Barracks on 01634 822442 who will arrange for the gates to be opened.

Haslar Royal Naval Cemetery, Hampshire Located in Gosport, a town on the western shore of Portsmouth Harbor.

Lee-on-Solent Memorial, Hampshire This Memorial will be found on the main sea front, sited on Marine Parade West, approximately half a mile west of the town centre.

Netley Military Cemetery, Southampton A permanent military cemetery, the property of the Ministry of Defence. The cemetery was at the back of the Royal Victoria Military Hospital. The cemetery lies within Royal Victoria Country Park, and access is by way of a private road with a lockable security barrier. The Royal Victoria Country Park, by the shores of Southampton Water, contains all that remains of the Royal Victoria hospital, the chapel, which acts as a heritage centre providing history of the hospital.

Plymouth Naval Memorial, Devon Situated centrally on The Hoe which looks directly towards Plymouth Sound. After the First World War, an appropriate way had to be found of commemorating those members of the Royal Navy who had no known grave, the majority of deaths having occurred at sea where no permanent memorial could be provided. An Admiralty committee recommended that the three manning ports in Great Britain - Chatham, Plymouth and Portsmouth - should each have an identical memorial of unmistakable naval form, an obelisk, which would serve as a leading mark for shipping.

Portsmouth Naval Memorial, Hampshire Situated on Southsea Common overlooking the promenade.

Runnymede Memorial, Surrey Overlooks the River Thames on Cooper's Hill at Englefield Green between Windsor and Egham on the A308, 4 miles from Windsor.

Southborough Cemetery, Kent Located on the A26 between Tunbridge Wells and Tonbridge.The entrance is located on the right at the bottom of Victoria Road (leading down off the A26 at Southborough Common), just before it bends left up Bentham Hill.

Tower Hill Memorial, London Commemorates men and women of the Merchant Navy and Fishing Fleets who died in both World Wars and who have no known grave. It stands on the south side of the garden of Trinity Square, London, close to The Tower of London.

Tunbridge Wells Cemetery Contains 72 scattered First World War burials. Second World War burials number 63, more than half of which form a war graves plot in the south-eastern part. Located in Benhall Mill Road, Tunbridge Wells, Kent, TN2 5JH.

FRANCE
Albert Communal Cemetery Extension, Somme Albert is 28 Kms north-east of Amiens. The Communal Cemetery is on the south-east side of Albert and at the junction of the roads to Peronne (D938) and Bray sur Somme (D329), and the

Southborough War Memorial

extension is entirely enclosed by it. The main entrance to the cemetery is on the Peronne road.

Ancre British Cemetery, Beaumont-Hamel, Somme About 2 Kms south of the village of Beaumont-Hamel, on the D50 between Albert and Achiet-le-Grand.

Anzac Cemetery, Sailly-sur-la-Lys, Pas de Calais On the north-west side of the road between Armentieres and Bethune, the D945, just north of the village Sailly-sur-la-Lys.

Arras Memorial, Pas de Calais In the Faubourg-d'Amiens Cemetery, which is in the Boulevard du General de Gaulle in the western part of the town of Arras. The cemetery is near the Citadel, approximately 2 kms due west of the railway station.

Aubigny Communal Cemetery Extension, Pas de Calais Aubigny-en-Artois is approximately 15 Kms north-west of Arras on the road (N39) to St. Pol. From the N39 turn onto the D75 towards the village of Aubigny-en-Artois. The Cemetery lies south on a road leading from the centre of the village, and the Extension is behind it.

Bailleul Communal Cemetery (Nord), Nord Bailleul is near the Belgian border, 14.5 Kms south-west of Ieper and on the main road from St. Omer to Lille. From the Grand place, take the Ieper road and 400 metres along this road is a sign indicating the direction of the cemetery. Turn down the right into a small road and follow for approximately 400 metres, the cemetery is on the right.

Bancourt British Cemetery, Pas de Calais Bancourt lies approximately 4 kms due east of Bapaume on the north side of the D7, Bapaume to Bertincourt road. Bancourt British Cemetery is situated east of Bancourt village, 300 metres off the D7 on the north side. The CWGC direction signs on the D7 indicate the best approach to the cemetery.

Becourt Military Cemetery, Becordel-Becourt, Somme Becourt is 2 kms on the east side of Albert. The Military Cemetery is on the south side of the road from Becourt to Albert.

Bernafay Wood British Cemetery, Montauban, Somme 10 kms east of Albert and 2 kilometres south of Longueval on the D197, in the direction of Maricourt.

Boulogne Eastern Cemetery, Pas de Calais In the district of St Martin Boulogne, just beyond the eastern (Chateau) corner of the Citadel (Haute-Ville). This is a large civil cemetery, split in two by the Rue de Dringhem, just south of the main road (RN42) to St Omer. The CWGC plot is located down the western edge of the southern section of the cemetery, with an entrance in the Rue de Dringhen. Car parking is available along the Rue de Dringhen.

Bouzincourt Ridge Cemetery, Albert, Somme Bouzincourt is 3 kms north-west of Albert on the D938 road to Doullens. The Cemetery is east of the village. In the centre of Bouzincourt take the direction for Aveluy (D20) and the Cemetery is signposted. Approximately 1.5 kms along the D20 road there is a track leading to the cemetery, which is approximately 500 metres along this track and is unsuitable for cars.

Cabaret-Rouge British Cemetery, Souchez, Pas de Calais Souchez is 3.5 kms north of Arras on the main road to Bethune. The cemetery is about 1.5 kilometres south of the village on the west side of the D937 Arras-Bethune Road.

Caestre Military Cemetery, Nord Caestre is in the Department of the Nord, on the main road midway between the towns of Cassel and Bailleul, and about 10 kms from either place. The Military Cemetery is in the middle of pasture land, about 500 metres west of the village on the north side of the road to Hondeghem.

Cambrai Memorial, Louverval, Nord Louverval is on the north side of the N30, Bapaume to Cambrai road, 13 kms north-east of Bapaume and 16 kms south-west of Cambrai. The Memorial stands on a terrace in Louverval Military Cemetery, on the north side of the N30, south of Louverval village. CWGC signposts on the N30 give advance warning of arrival at the Cemetery.

Caterpillar Valley Cemetery, Longueval, Somme Longueval is a village approximately 13 kms east of Albert and 10 kms south of Bapaume. Caterpillar Valley Cemetery lies a short distance west of Longueval on the south side of the road to Contalmaison.

Caudry British Cemetery, Nord Caudry is some 13 kms east of Cambrai on the south side of the main road (N43) to Le Cateau. Caudry British Cemetery is on the eastern outskirts of the town among the 'Nouveaux Cimetieres', which include the German Military Cemetery and the New Communal Cemetery. Visitors should not enter the town, but take the eastern by-pass road (a dual carriageway). At the first set of traffic lights on this road turn left: the British Cemetery is located down the second turning on the right.

Combles Communal Cemetery Extension, Somme Combles is 16 kms east of Albert and 13 kms south of Bapaume. From Bapaume take the N17 towards Peronne. Just after the village of Sailly Saillisel, take the D172 towards Combles. The Communal Cemetery is on the right just before the village, and the Extension is at the back, or north-east, of the Communal Cemetery.

Couin New British Cemetery, Pas de Calais Couin is 15 kms east of Doullens. Visitors should follow the main Doullens to Arras road, N25, as far as the crossroads with the D23. Follow the D23 to Souastre, then the D2 to Couin, as indicated by the CWGC sign. Couin British Cemetery and Couin New British Cemetery are at the side of the road just before entering the village.

Croix-du-Bac British Cemetery, Steenwerck, Nord Steenwerck is approximately 5 kms south-west of Armentieres and a similar distance north-east of Estaires. Croix-du-Bac is a hamlet 3.5 kms south of Steenwerck. Leave Croix-du-Bac on the D10 and head south east. The Cemetery is 1 km from the church on the right hand side of the D10.

Crucifix Corner Cemetery, Villers-Bretonneux, Somme Villers-Bretonneux lies on the N29 road from Amiens to St Quentin. Enter the village of Villers-Bretonneux on the D23 heading south. At the crossroads head in the direction of Demuin and Mozeuil, remaining on the D23. Two CWGC signposts will be seen. On leaving the village, carry on south for 2 kms, still on the D23 Demuin road. After passing over the A29 Motorway (Amiens-St Quentin), the cemetery is signposted down a side road on the right.

Dantzig Alley British Cemetery, Mametz, Somme Mametz is about 8 kms east of the town of Albert. The Cemetery is a little east of the village on the north side of the road (D64) to Montauban.

Doullens Communal Cemetery Extension No 1, Somme Doullens is approximately 30 kms north of Amiens on the N25 road to Arras. The Communal Cemetery and

Southborough War Memorial

Extensions lie on the eastern side of the town, about 270 metres south-east of the road to Arras.

Dunkirk Memorial, Nord Stands at the entrance to the British War Graves Section of Dunkirk Town Cemetery, at the south-eastern corner of Dunkirk, immediately south of the canal and on the road to Veurne (Furnes) in Belgium. On entering the cemetery through the columns of the Dunkirk Memorial, two Commonwealth war graves sections will be seen: Plots IV and V from the First World War and Plots I and II from the Second World War. There is also a further First World War section (Plots I, II and III) in the main part of the cemetery to the right of the main entrance. Dunkirk witnessed the landing of the British Expeditionary Force in September and October 1914.

Epehy Wood Cemetery, Epehy, Somme Epehy is between Cambrai and Peronne about 18 kms north-east of Peronne. Epehy Wood Farm Cemetery is a little west of the village and on the north side of the road to Saulcourt.

Etaples Military Cemetery, Pas de Calais Etaples is about 27 kms south of Boulogne. The Military Cemetery is to the north of the town, on the west side of the road to Boulogne.

Euston Road Cemetery, Colincamps, Somme Colincamps is 11 kms north of Albert. From Arras take the D919 in the direction of Amiens for 28 kms. The cemetery is situated about 1 km from the D919 on the right hand side of the road. Pass Serre Road Cemetery No.2 and continue for 2 kms. Take the first right, and the CWGC direction sign to Euston Road Cemetery will be seen at the next Y junction.

Fouquescourt British Cemetery, Somme Fouquescourt is 35 kms east of Amiens and 8 kms due north of Roye. The British Cemetery is a little north of the village on the east side of the road to Maucourt.

Grevillers British Cemetery, Pas de Calais Grevillers is 3 kms west of Bapaume. From Bapaume take the RD929 in the direction of Amiens, turn immediately right onto the RD7, where a signpost indicates the cemetery. After 500 metres turn left at junction onto RD29, where a signpost indicates the cemetery which is on the right after a further 50 metres.

Grove Town Cemetery, Meaulte, Somme Meaulte is just south of Albert. From Albert head south-east on the D329 in the direction of Bray-sur-Somme. Just before the main buildings for the Aerobus turn right for the centre of Meaulte. Approximately 200 metres west of the church, take the road south "rue de Etinehem" Continue south past Meaulte Military Cemetery, and approximately 2.3 kms further on turn left (eastwards) Grove Town Cemetery is 600 metres along on the right side of this track. For those wishing to approach the cemetery from the south side, take the D1 Bray-sur-Somme / Corbie road, at the junction of the D1 and C2 Etineham / Meaulte minor road is the first back to back Commission roadsign. Head north towards Meaulte, until reaching a fork in the road, where there is a CWGC road sign. Take the right fork in the direction of the airfield perimeter fence. At the Commission road sign and take the left track north, Grove Town Cemetery is ahead and to the left side of the track.

Guards Grave, Villers Cotterets Forest, Aisne Villers-Cotterets is 22 kms south-west of Soissons in the direction of Meaux. From Soissons take the N2 (signposted to Paris, Meaux, Senlis), passing after 3.5 kms the Military Cemetery of Vaubuin and after a further 6 kms a French War Memorial on the right. DO NOT TAKE the left hand turn towards the town of Villers-Cotterets, but continue along the N2 as the Cemetery is north of the town. Take the next right hand slip road and then turn right along the D81 towards Vivieres. After a further 3 kms you will arrive at the Cemetery which is set down in a hollow next to the road to the right.

Hebuterne Military Cemetery, Pas de Calais Hebuterne is 15 kms north of Albert and 20 kms south-west of Arras. Using the D919 from Arras to Amiens you will drive through the villages of Bucquoy, Puisieux then Serre Les Puisieux (approximately 20 kms south of Arras). On leaving Serre Les Puisieux, 3 kms further along the D919, turn right following the signs for Hebuterne. Hebuterne Military Cemetery lies to the west of the village and a CWGC signpost clearly indicates the way from the village green to the cemetery.

Heilly Station Cemetery, Mericourt l'Abbe, Somme Mericourt-l'Abbe is approximately 19 kms north-east of Amiens and 10 kms south-west of Albert. Heilly Station Cemetery is about 2 kms south-west of Mericourt-l'Abbe, on the south side of the road to Corbie.

Hottot-les-Bagues War Cemetery, Calvados Hottot-les-Bagues is 14 kms south-east of Bayeux. This cemetery can be reached from Bayeux by taking the D6 southeastwards. After about 13 kms and after passing through Tilly-sur-Seulles, turn right (westwards) at Juvigny onto the main road (the D9) that runs from Caen towards Caumont l'Evente. The cemetery will be found after a few hundred metres on the right hand side on rising ground.

Laventie Military Cemetery, La Gorgue, Nord Laventie and La Gorgue are adjoining towns. Laventie Military Cemetery is on the north-east outskirts of Laventie. From Laventie, head north out of the town on the D166. Approximately 1 km along this road turn right at the first junction and follow the small road for 400 metres. The Cemetery is on the right hand side.

La Kreule Military Cemetery, Hazebrouck, Nord La Kreule is a small hamlet 2 kms north of Hazebrouck, on the road to St Sylvestre-Cappel and Steenvoorde. Leave Hazebrouck on the D916 heading north. The Cemetery is visible from the roundabout where the D916 crosses the Hazebrouck by-pass. The access road to the cemetery is 100 metres off the roundabout, on the left hand side.

Le Grand Hasard Military Cemetery, Morbecque, Nord Morbecque is 3 kms south-west of Hazebrouck. Leave the church in Morebecque and head north on the D916 towards Hazebrouck. After approximately 1 km there is a Plant Nursery on the left hand side. Take the small road through the nursery and the cemetery will be found on the right hand side in amongst farm land.

Le Touret Memorial, Pas de Calais At the east end of Le Touret Military Cemetery, on the south side of the Bethune-Armentieres main road. From Bethune follow signs for Armentieres until you are on the D171. Continue on this road through Essars and Le Touret village. Approximately 1 km after Le Touret village and about 5 kms before you reach the intersection with the D947, Estaires to La Bassee road, the Cemetery lies on the right hand side of the road.

Ligny-St Flochel British Cemetery, Averdoingt, Pas de Calais Ligny-St.Flochel is about 6.5 kms east of St.Pol off the main road to Arras, approximately 24 kms from Arras. Ligny-St. Flochel British Cemetery is south of the village on the east side of the road to Averdoingt (D81).

London Cemetery, Neuville-Vitasse, Pas de Calais Neuville-Vitasse is 5 kms south-east of Arras on the D5. London Cemetery stands on the west side of the road to Arras in a shallow valley.

Loos Memorial, Pas de Calais Forms the side and back of Dud Corner Cemetery, and commemorates over 20,000 officers and men who have no known grave, who fell in the area from the River Lys to the old southern boundary of the First Army, east and west of Grenay. Loos-en-Gohelle is a village 5 kms north-west of Lens, and Dud Corner Cemetery is located about 1 km west of the village, to the north-east of the N43 the main Lens to Bethune road.

Mailly Wood Cemetery, Somme 9 kms north of Albert on the D919. The Cemetery is situated on the outskirts of the village of Mailly-Maillet on the left hand side of the road to Amiens, where it is signposted from the main road onto a 500 metre mud track.

Maroc British Cemetery, Grenay, Nord Grenay is about 15 kms south-east of Bethune. From Lens take the N43 towards Bethune. After Loos-en-Gohelle turn left (after the petrol station) and continue straight on. The Cemetery is a few kms on the right side of the road, in the village.

Merville Communal Cemetery Extension, Nord Merville is 15 kms north of Bethune and 20 kms south-east of Armentieres. The Communal Cemetery is on the north-east side of the town to the north side of the road to Neuf-Berquin. The Extension is now surrounded by the Communal Cemetery.

Montreuil-Aux-Lions British Cemetery, Aisne Montreuil-aux-Lions is 17 kms west of Chateau Thierry. The British Cemetery is set on the side of a main road, situated to the east of the village. The cemetery can be reached from the direction of Chateau Thierry, following the N3 Chateau Thierry to La Ferte-sous-Jouarre road. On leaving Chateau Thierry via the N3, the road continues through several hamlets. After about 20 kms the road starts to descend into the village of Montreuil-aux-Lions, and at this point the cemetery is visible on the left side of the road. Alternatively, the cemetery can be reached from the A4 motorway at the junction for Meaux and La Ferte-sous-Jouarre by following the N3 road to the centre of the town of La Ferte-sous-Jouarre. The second exit should be taken at the roundabout, with a war memorial on the right side of the road, and then continue over a bridge and out of the town of La Ferte-sous-Jouarre, still following the N3 road to Chateau Thierry. After about 10 kms you will pass through the village of Montreuil-aux-Lions and the cemetery is then visible on the right side of the road.

Morlancourt British Cemetery No2, Somme Morlancourt is 6.5 kms south of Albert. British Cemetery No.2 is on the north-west side of the village, near the road to Ville-sur-Ancre.

Porte-de-Paris Cemetery, Cambrai, Nord Cambrai is 32 kms south-east of Arras on the main straight road to Le Cateau. The Cemetery stands in the south-west outskirts of the town near the old gate on the road to Paris, the N44.

Pozieres Memorial, Somme Pozieres is 6 kms north-east of Albert. The Memorial encloses Pozieres British Cemetery, a little south-west of the village on the north side of the main road, D929, from Albert to Pozieres.

Puchevillers British Cemetery, Somme Puchevillers is on the D11, 19 kms north-east of Amiens. The Cemetery is a little west of the village; the first CWGC signpost is by the church.

Putot-en-Auge Churchyard, Calvados Putot-en-Auge is 22 kms east-north-east of Caen and the same distance north-west of Lisieux. Take the Caen-Pont l'Eveque-Rouen road (RN175) and turn right at Putot-en-Auge. The cemetery stands by the church at the end of the village. There are 32 Commonwealth burials of the 1939-1945 war in the churchyard.

Ranville War Cemetery, Calvados Ranville is best reached by taking the D513 north-eastwards out of Caen, and after about 9 kms turning left at Herouvillette. Go north for one km, then turn left into Ranville village. The War Cemetery is on Rue des Airbornes.

Rookery British Cemetery, Heninel, Pas de Calais Heninel is 10 kms south-east of Arras. The Cemetery is 1.5 kms from Heninel village, 165 metres north-east of the road to Fontaine-les-Croisilles opposite Cuckoo Passage Cemetery.

Rumilly-en-Cambresis Communal Cemetery Extension, Nord Rumilly is on the east side of the main Cambrai to St Quentin road (N44), about 5 kms from Cambrai. The Cemetery is located in the Rue de l'Egalite and the extension is on the east side of the Communal Cemetery, signposted from the centre of the village.

Sequehart British Cemetery No. 1, Aisne Sequehart is 8 kms north-east of St. Quentin, and the Sequehart British Cemeteries No. 1 and No. 2 are just south of the road to Levergies.

St Desir War Cemetery, Calvados St Desir is a village on the N13 to Caen, 4 kms west of Lisieux. The war cemetery is about 1k west of the village and lies on a secondary road, the D159.

St Patrick's Cemetery, Loos, Pas de Calais Loos-en-Gohelle is just north of Lens on the N43, Lens to Bethune road. Turn right off the N43 onto the D165, signposted for Wingles and La Bassee, and continue along this road for 500 metres. Turn left at the village square and left again. Continue along this road and the cemetery is on the right after approximately 200 metres.

St Sever Cemetery Extension, Rouen, Seine-Maritime within a large communal cemetery situated on the eastern edge of the southern Rouen suburbs of Le Grand Quevilly and Le Petit Quevilly. If approaching Rouen from the north, head for the centre of town and cross over the river Seine, following signs for Caen. Follow this route until you get to the 'Rond Point des Bruyeres' roundabout (next to the football stadium), then take the first exit into the Boulevard Stanislas Girardin. The cemetery is 150 metres down this road on the left. If approaching Rouen from the south, follow the N138 (Avenue des Canadiens) towards the centre of town. At the 'Rond Point des Bruyeres' roundabout (next to the football stadium), take the fourth exit into the Boulevard Stanislas Girardin. The cemetery is 150 metres down this road on the left. If arriving on foot, take the metro to St Sever Metro Station, then follow the Avenue de Caen until you get to the Avenue de la Liberation, then take this road and follow this, which will become the Boulevard du 11 Novembre. At the end of this road is the 'Rond Point des Bruyeres' roundabout.

Stump Road Cemetery, Grandcourt, Somme Grandcourt is about 12 kms north-east of Albert. The Cemetery (signposted in the centre of village) lies about one km south of

Grandcourt, some 500 metres along a single track lane (suitable for cars) off the road (D151) Grandcourt-Thiepval.

Sunken Road Cemetery, Boisleux-St. Marc, Pas de Calais Boisleux-St Marc is 8 kms south of Arras. Sunken Road Cemetery is down a 1 km track on the west side of the road running between this village and the adjacent village of Boisleux-au-Mont (D42E).

Tannay British Cemetery, Thiennes, Nord Thiennes is about 8 kms east of Aire-sur-la-Lys, a town on the N43 between Bethune and St. Omer. Leave Thiennes on the D122, heading east towards Haverskerque. Cross over the canal and continue towards Tannay, a hamlet on this road. The Cemetery is on the right hand side of this road and access is gained by passing along a 300 metre track in front of a farm house. The Cemetery is on the left immediately after the farm.

Thiepval Memorial, Somme on the D73, next to the village of Thiepval, off the main Bapaume to Albert road (D929).

Tilloy British Cemetery, Tilloy-Les-Mofflaines, Pas de Calais Tilloy-les-Mofflaines is 3 kms south-east of Arras, on the south side of the main road to Cambrai. Tilloy British Cemetery is south-east of the village on the north-east side of the road to Wancourt, the D37.

Tranchee de Mecknes Cemetery, Aix-Noulette, Pas de Calais Aix-Noulette is 16 kms north of Arras, about 2 kms south-west of Bully-les-Mines on the Arras-Bethune road. Tranchee de Mecknes Cemetery is about 2 kms east of the village.

Varennes Military Cemetery, Somme Varennes is 11 kms from Albert and 18 kms from Amiens. Take the D938 from Albert to Doullens. In Hedauville turn left on the D47E towards Varennes for 2 kms; at the crossroads in the village of Varennes; turn right. About 300 metres further, turn left following CWGC sign; the Cemetery is 500 metres further on the right.

Vermelles British Cemetery, Pas de Calais Vermelles is 10 kms north-west of Lens. From Lens take the N43 towards Bethune, to its junction with the D75 in Mazingarbe. Turn right here and continue for approximately 900 metres; the Cemetery is on the left hand side of the road.

Villers-Bretonneux Memorial, Somme Villers-Bretonneux is 16 kms east of Amiens on the straight main road to St Quentin. The Military Cemetery is about 2 kms north of the village on the east side of the road to Fouilloy.

Villers-Faucon Communal Cemetery Extension, Somme Villers-Faucon is about 17 kms north-east of Peronne. From the centre of the village take the D72 towards Lieramont. Turn right at a CWGC signpost opposite a parking area. The Cemetery is on the left hand side of the road and the Commonwealth War Graves Plot is on the north-west side of the cemetery.

Villers Hill British Cemetery, Villers-Guislain, Nord Villers-Guislain is 16 kms south-south-west of Cambrai and 4 kms east of Gouzeaucourt, a large village on the main road from Cambrai to Peronne. Villers Hill British Cemetery is one km south-east of the village.

Vis-En-Artois Memorial, Pas de Calais Vis-en-Artois and Haucourt are villages on the straight main road from Arras to Cambrai about 10 kms south-east of Arras. The

Memorial is in the grounds of Vis-en-Artois British Cemetery, west of Haucourt on the north side of the main road.

Warloy-Baillon Communal Cemetery Extension, Somme Warloy-Baillon is about 21 kms north-east of Amiens along the D919 to Arras. The Communal Cemetery is on the east side of the village and the extension is on the eastern side of the cemetery.

Wavrans-sur-L'Aa Churchyard, Pas de Calais Wavrans sur l'Aa is some 20 kms south-west of St Omer and 3.5 kms south-south-east of Lumbres on the D192. The Commonwealth war grave is in the south-east of the churchyard (in centre of village) on the right hand of the main entrance.

GERMANY
Berlin 1939-1945 War Cemetery, Charlottenburg From the A2 Hannover to Berlin motorway follow the A10 Berliner Ring, direction Prenzlau/Hamburg. Continue for approx 27kms and take exit 26 (Ausfahrt 26) B5 Berlin/Spandau. Continue for approx 17kms following the signs for Charlottenburg along the Hamburger Chaussee, which then becomes the Heerstrasse. Turn right onto the parallel Heerstrasse road (CWGC sign) and continue for 300m to Heertstrasse 151.

GREECE
Lahana Military Cemetery 1 km west of the village of Lachanas on the old Thessaloniki-Seres road, about 56 kms north-east of Thessaloniki.

HOLLAND
Groesbeek Memorial, Gelderland Groesbeek is in the east of the Netherlands, approximately 10kms south east of Nijmegen. From the A73 motorway Nigmegen to Venlo take exit 3 (Afrit 3) Malden/Groesbeek/Mook/Heumen/Overasselt. Follow signs for N271 Mook. Continue through the village of Molenhoel, and in the village of Mook turn left at the roundabout (CWGC sign for Mook War Cemetery) onto the Groesbeeksweg. Continue for approx 4.5kms and then turn left at the roundabout onto the Pannenstraat. Continue through the town where the road name changes to Dorpstraat. Turn left onto Burgemeester Ottenhoffstraat (CWGC Sign). After approx 100m turn right (CWGC sign) onto Zevenheuvelenweg. The cemetery is approx 2kms along this road on the right.

INDIA
Imphal War Cemetery Imphal, the capital of Manipur State, is in north east India and borders on upper Burma. The cemetery lies 10km from the airport on the Imphal-Dimapur road (Highway 39) in the Deulahland district of the town. The small road leading to the cemetery is 1km along this highway on the right side, opposite the D M College.

IRAQ
Baghdad (North Gate) War Cemetery in a very sensitive area in the Waziriah Area of the Al-Russafa district of Baghdad. The main entrance to the cemetery is located opposite the College of Arts and the Institute of Administration in Baghdad University and adjacent to the Iraqi Cigarette Factory in Waziriah Area and the Press of Ministry of Defence.

ISRAEL

Beersheba War Cemetery Beersheba is on the edge of the Negev Desert, 75 kms south-west of Jerusalem. The Cemetery is on the south-west of the town. On arrival in the town via route 40, continue on until you reach a large junction with a shopping complex on your left. Turn right onto road No. 25, sign-posted Hazerim. Follow this road for 2 kms, turning left at the traffic lights opposite the high rise blocks, sign-posted Hazerim. The cemetery is on the left. Owing to the one way road system, you must do a complete tour to reach the entrance so continue and turn left at the next set of traffic lights. Then take the next left onto Harzfeld Street. At the end of this street, turn left and the cemetery entrance is on your left.

Jerusalem War Cemetery 4.5 kilometres north of the walled city, situated on the neck of land at the north end of the Mount of Olives, to the west of Mount Scopus. The cemetery is on Churchill Blvd, sandwiched between Hadassah Hospital and the Hyatt Hotel.

ITALY

Caserta War Cemetery Take the autostrada A1 (Roma to Napoli), and leave it at the Caserta Nord exit. Proceed to the first set of traffic lights and then turn left and continue along the main street eastward for about 1.8 kms; just prior to an Army barracks and well before the Royal Palace (Palazzo Reale) there is a small left turn. Turn left here and proceed to the T-junction at the end. Here turn right and continue along, under the bridge to the main crossroads. You will see a CWGC signpost; turn left and carry on for a short distance to the large roundabout at the end of the road. The large Communal Cemetery is on the far side; turn right into the obvious car park. The CWGC plot is at the far end of the cemetery.

Cassino War Cemetery, Cassino, Province of Frosinone 139 kms south-east of Rome. Take the autostrada A1 from Rome to Naples and leave it at the Cassino exit. At the junction of this exit and the road into Cassino, is the first of 6 clearly visible signposts to the cemetery and memorial. The cemetery is approximately 1 km from the railway station in Via Sant Angelo and visitors arriving by train are advised to take a taxi from the station.

Catania War Cemetery, Sicily 7 kilometres south-west of Catania. From Catania Airport follow the tangenziale (main road) towards the A19 (in the direction of Palermo). Before reaching the A19 the cemetery is signposted. Cemetery address: Stradale Passo del Fico - 95121 Catania Zona Industriale (CT) Sicily.

Faenza War Cemetery Take the Bologna-Ancona autostrada A14 and exit at Faenza. The War Cemetery lies 1.5 kms south-east of Faenza and is approached by a secondary road which branches off the main road Bologna-Forli (Route No.9) just east of the town.

Giavera British Cemetery, Arcade, Province of Treviso 12 kms east of Montebelluna and 14 kms west of Conegliano on the main road between the two places. Giavera British Cemetery is 500 metres north-west of the town close to the church.

Montecchio Precalcino Communal Cemetery Extension, Province of Vicenza 4 kms north of Dueville and 16.8 kms north of the town of Vicenza. Take autostrada A31, Vicenza Schio; leave it at Dueville. Follow signs for Montecchio Precalcino, on arriving in the village a CWGC sign will be seen.

Salerno War Cemetery Coming from Rome, proceed along the A30 following the signs for Salerno-Reggio Calabria; then take the A3, exiting at Pontecagnano or Battipaglia. Turn back towards Salerno on the SS18 coast road. Signs for the cemetery, which is on the north side of the road, should be seen after passing through Bellizzi.

Syracuse War Cemetery, Sicily is in the Contrada of Canalicchio in the Commune and Province of Syracuse. It lies 3 kms west of Syracuse. Turn left at the end of the Catania to Syracuse autostrada and the cemetery will be found approximately 5 kms along on the left hand side.

Taranto Town Cemetery Extension Proceed along the Highway A14, Bologna-Taranto, and take road 57 into Taranto from the direction of Bari, passing the large industrial complex on the left. Follow the sign to Grottaglia and then the signs to Tamburi Cimitero (Cimitero San Brunone). The CWGC Cemetery is on the road (which is one-way) just past the communal cemetery. The cemetery gates are kept locked, except during the CWGC's gardening staff's working hours. If you wish to visit the cemetery when the gates are locked, the combination to the padlock is 1221. To open the lock you should press a button on the lock after having dialled the combination number.

SRI LANKA
Colombo (Kanatte) General Cemetery At Borella, an important road junction on the Kanatte Road, and is known locally as Borella Cemetery. Graves shown in the cemetery register to be in Plots 6B and 6C are within the War Graves enclosure, while all others are dispersed. To locate any of the dispersed graves, it is advisable to make prior contact with the Cemetery Manager. To reach the Commonwealth War Graves Plot, follow the main avenue from the entrance for 150 metres and turn right at the sign for Plot 5. Continue past the Cross of Sacrifice on the left side, and the plot is found 100 metres further along on the right side, enclosed within a fence and hedge.

TUNISIA
Medjez-El-Bab Memorial Medjez-el-Bab is 60 kms west of Tunis. Medjez-el-Bab War Cemetery, in which the Memorial stands, is situated 3 kms west of Medjez-el-Bab on the road to Le Kef (Route P5).

TURKEY
Helles Memorial, Gallipoli Peninsula The Anzac and Suvla cemeteries are first signposted from the left hand junction of the Eceabat- Bigali Road. From this junction travel into the main Anzac area. Follow the road to Helles, opposite the Kabatepe Museum, at 14.2 kms take a right turn at the 'T' junction and at 14.3 kms take the left fork. After a total of 22.8 kms, take a right turn to the memorial along a rough track 500m long. The Helles Memorial stands on the tip of the Gallipoli Peninsula. It takes the form of an obelisk over 30 metres high that can be seen by ships passing through the Dardanelles.

Acknowledgements

My thanks are due to the following people. If I have left anyone off the list through oversight, I now extend my apologies and appreciation for help and information received:

Mr Bailey, Martin Beevis, David Bews & Stephen Cashmore, Martin & Sheila Birchall, Mrs Berry, Kevin Brand, Roger Brown, Mrs Vera Button, Jim Christmas,The Commonwealth War Graves Commission, Oliver Davey, Miss Megan Davies, Susan Davies, Ms Jill Dowdell, Mrs Dorothy Drawbridge, Peter Eagling, AJ Everest, Dennis Exall, Mrs Beryl Fulker, family of George Furey, Vivien Gosden, Mrs Valerie Green, Eric Hook, Tracey Hook, Guy Huntrods CBE, Clare Jeffrey, Jerry Jones, The Kent & Sussex Courier, Mr H Kershaw, Mrs W Lorne, Lieutenant Colonel Maxwell Macfarlane, Clive Maier, Mrs Ruth Marshall, Mr K I McMillan, Liz & Brian McPhee, Darren Milford, Mrs Dorothy Mills, Michael Mills, Christine Nye-Gibbons, Mrs Daisy M Nye, Fred Ongley, John V Phillips, Miss EM Pook, Miss Lee Reeve, Alan (Henry Alan Pietroni) Rigg, George Rowswell, Tom Rusbridge, Mr Fred Scales, Mr John Scrace, Pete Simmons, Ted Sparrow, Frank Stevens, Colin Stronghill, Ron Styles, Tempus Publishing, Mrs Janice Tomkinson, Tunbridge Wells Reference Library, Geoffrey Tutchener, Frank Warwick, Alan Waters, Mrs Margaret Weller, Mrs Edith Whitmore, Jancis Wilson, Phil Winter, Fiona Woodfield, Donald Woodland, Ella Woolley and, last but not least, to Martin and Thomas Johnson for their patience, encouragement and generous support in the production of this book.

The information on HMS Hawke is from the web pages dedicated to the memory of the Fallen from the two World Wars, who lived in Abberton & Langenhoe, prepared by Saint Andrew's Parochial Church Council. The photo of HMS Hawke was kindly provided by Maritime Photo Library, 8 Jetty Street, Cromer, Norfolk NR27 9HF, who retain copyright. The picture of U-9 is reproduced with permission from the website www.worldwar1.co.uk/cressy.htm thanks to Darren Milford.

The author has sought to gain permission for extracts wherever possible, and if any permission has not been included, makes her apology, and will make every effort to include of these any drawn to her attention in future editions.

Southborough War Memorial

Bibliography
including online sources:

BOOKS:
Soldiers Who Died in the Great War
Dee's Directory of Southborough 1915 and *Kelly's Directories*
Southborough Sappers of the Kent (Fortress) Royal Engineers by Frank Stevens (published by FAST, 34 Ridgewaye Crescent, Tonbridge, Kent TN10 4NR)
The Last Destroyer, The story of HMS Aldenham 1942-1944, first published 1988
Three Before Breakfast by Alan Coles (Kenneth Mason, 1979)
Voices of Southborough and High Brooms by Chris McCooey (Tempus Publishing)

PUBLIC RESOURCES:
Kent & Sussex Courier 1914-1918 and 1939-45 records, Tunbridge Wells Reference Library
Tunbridge Wells Advertiser 1914-1918 records, Tunbridge Wells Reference Library

WEBSITES:
www.hms-arethusa.co.uk
www.cwgc.org - The Commonwealth War Graves Commission
www.hmsfiredrake.co.uk (compiled by John Masters)
www.firstworldwar.com/onthis day
www.worldwar1.co.uk/cressy.htm
www.iprom.co.uk/archives/caithness/rawalpindi.htm - Against All Odds – HMS Rawalpindi www.raafmuseum.com.au
www.raf.mod.uk/history - Royal Air Force website, History section
www.wartimememories.co.uk – Wartime Memories Project
www.uboat.net

www.ingramcontent.com/pod-product-compliance
Lightning Source LLC
Chambersburg PA
CBHW061954180426
43198CB00036B/884